Matthias McDonnell Bodkin

Lord Edward Fitzgerald

An Historical Romance

Matthias McDonnell Bodkin

Lord Edward Fitzgerald
An Historical Romance

ISBN/EAN: 9783744675741

Printed in Europe, USA, Canada, Australia, Japan

Cover: Foto ©Thomas Meinert / pixelio.de

More available books at **www.hansebooks.com**

LORD EDWARD FITZGERALD

An Historical Romance

BY

M. McD. BODKIN, Q.C.

WITH ILLUSTRATIONS BY LEONARD LINSDELL

LONDON: CHAPMAN AND HALL, Ld.

1896

Dedicated

BY PERMISSION TO THE

RIGHT HON.

WILLIAM EWART GLADSTONE

THE BEST ENGLISH FRIEND

IRELAND EVER HAD.

———————

"What a noble fellow was Lord Edward Fitzgerald, and what a romantic and singular history his was! If it were not too near our own time, it would make the finest subject in the world for an historical novel."—*Lord Byron.*

PREFACE

HISTORY supplies the most romantic part of this Historical Romance. The main incidents of Lord Edward Fitzgerald's marvellous career, as herein set down, his stirring adventures in the American War of Independence, even his adoption into the Indian tribe of the "Great Bear," are absolutely true. For the rest, though some liberties have been taken with dates, the pictures of Ireland's condition under the "Penal Laws" are painted from life.

CONTENTS

CHAPTER I.

PAGE

"A very Valiant Rebel of the Name" (*Henry IV.* Part I.) 11

CHAPTER II.

"This most wise Rebellion" (*Coriolanus*) . . . 20

CHAPTER III.

"Who is here so base as will not love his Country?" (*Julius Cæsar*) 33

CHAPTER IV.

"And Maidens call it 'Love in Idleness'" (*Midsummer Night's Dream*). 46

CHAPTER V.

"A Plague on all Cowards say I, and a Vengeance too" (*Henry IV.* Part I.) 58

CHAPTER VI.

"That She should Love this Fellow and refuse Me" (*Cymbeline*) 84

CHAPTER VII.

"The Pangs of despised Love" (*Hamlet*) . . . 95

CHAPTER VIII.

"Daffed the World aside and bid it pass" (*Henry IV.* Part I.) 109

CHAPTER IX.

"The Air bites Shrewdly; it is very Cold" (*Hamlet*). 125

CHAPTER X.

"Are You Content to be our General?" (*Two Gentlemen of Verona*) 144

CONTENTS

CHAPTER XI.

PAGE

"OUT, OUT! BRIEF CANDLE!" (*Macbeth*) . . . 157

CHAPTER XII.

"PERFECT GALLOWES" (*The Tempest*) . . . 182

CHAPTER XIII.

"YOU SHALL NOT LACK A PRIEST" (*Merry Wives of Windsor*) 203

CHAPTER XIV.

"I DO LOVE THAT COUNTRY GIRL" (*Love's Labour Lost*) . 215

CHAPTER XV.

"AN EXCELLENT STRATAGEM" (*Henry IV.* Part II.) . . 23

CHAPTER XVI.

"O LOYAL FATHER OF A TREACHEROUS SON!" (*K. Richard II.*) 265

CHAPTER XVII.

"SAVES THE THIEF" (*Cymbeline*) 289

CHAPTER XVIII.

"LOVE'S LABOUR LOST" 297

CHAPTER XIX.

"TELL THE TRUTH AND SHAME THE DEVIL" (*Henry VI.* Part I.) 314

CHAPTER XX.

"A KEEPER BACK OF DEATH" (*King Richard II.*) . . 337

CHAPTER XXI.

"FLAT BURGLARY AS EVER WAS COMMITTED" (*Much Ado About Nothing*) 360

CHAPTER XXII.

"O HEAVEN, O EARTH, BEAR WITNESS" (*The Tempest*) . 379

CHAPTER XXIII.

"THAT ENDS THIS STRANGE, EVENTFUL HISTORY" (*As You Like It*) 400

LIST OF ILLUSTRATIONS

LORD EDWARD FITZGERALD.   .   .   *Frontispiece*

CHAP.   PAGE

I. "He slung up his heavy sword high over his shoulder"   15

III. "A black man, with his back to him, reading at a small table, on which were bottles and bandages" .   . 34

IV. "We cannot set our hearts to what tune pleases the story-tellers" 52

V. "Jerked it roughly away" 66

VI. "They passed out into the garden, and paced together down the moonlit walk" .   .   . 91

VIII. "Better the noble sorrow than the low delight" .   . 118

IX. "The black quivering shadow of a deer's head was projected flat on the white ground" .   .   . 132

X. "'Lord Edward,' said Pitt, 'an expedition is in preparation against Cadiz; will you accept the command?'" 150

XI. "The lights shone full on the pale faces of the two men that stood waiting there so quietly to kill or be killed" 175

XII. "One end of the rope was drawn tight over his shoulder; from the other end his victim dangled" 197

XIV. Christy Culkin 216

XIV. "The pail of milk tottered and fell right on the head of the falling man" .   .   . 229

XVI. "The prone and pitiful figure, with ghastly face and dishevelled white hair" .   .   . 276

XIX. "With a supreme effort, Sir Valentine hurled him down into the swift, full current of the river" . . 332

XX. "It was his own face that smiled back on him from the picture on the floor" .   .   . 353

XXI. "One hand, thrown wildly out and up, caught the projecting edge of the window-sill" .   . 374

XXII. "'I demand your lordship's direction for the plaintiff,' repeated Curran, sternly" .   .   . 398

XXIII. "They rolled over and over in the long grass" . . 409

XXIII. Pamela 412

LORD EDWARD FITZGERALD

CHAPTER I.

"A VERY VALIANT REBEL OF THE NAME."
Henry IV. Part I.

"Swords out and tilting one at other's breasts
In opposition bloody."—Othello.

THROUGH the long aisles of the great wood he came, riding slowly and cautiously. His chestnut thorough-bred, reined tightly in, and stepping short and high, danced lightly along the smooth sward. The trees stood well apart, and the sod beneath was close and short; but the great pillars of the wood stretched so high that their closing branches made a green sky overhead, through which the wearied eye strove in vain to pierce.

The young horseman rode warily. He had caught up the scabbard close to his side lest its clatter should betray him. But concealment was impossible. A gay parrot might as well try to hide itself behind the wires of its cage. Every bird that fluttered through that high roof of translucent green, every beast that fled through the long arches, or slipped round the great pillars of the wood, saw him as he passed.

The sunbeams that here and there broke through the high roof lay in wait for him and caught him and brightened his scarlet uniform into a blaze, and struck flashes of light from his steel accoutrements.

Let us have a good look at him while we may, for he is worth looking at. He has scarcely crossed the line that parts the boy from the man. The figure, though slight, is agile, and graceful as a leopard's. The brown hair and long silken lashes are like a girl's. But the quick, glancing grey eyes and resolute lips speak the alert courage of a man. It is a face to turn and gaze at. He seems rather a knight of the old days in quest of adventure, than the modern officer whose trade it is to kill or be killed for hire.

A circle of sunshine at the end of the long vista warns the young horseman of an opening in the wood. As a river widens into a lake, the green tunnel through which he rode opened into a clear oval space walled round with high trees.

Just as the bright scarlet uniform flashed into the open sunshine two scouts, who plainly had watched his movements, rode sharply out from the edge of the wood and barred his path in front and rear. They were a strange contrast to the brilliant young officer. They were clad in coarse grey uniform, and armed to the teeth; men meant for use, not show. They drew their swords as they halted. The man behind spoke.

"Surrender!" he shouted. "Resistance is useless, flight impossible. We are two to one, fully armed, and our comrades are close at hand."

The young officer cast one scornful glance behind him. He saw a man a little older than himself, but taller and broader, with an honest, kindly face, fair haired and blue eyed. Then his sword flashed out of its scabbard, he put spurs to the chestnut, and rode straight at the horseman in front. He made a quick, fierce cut at his head as he swept past. But the man ducked as the diver ducks at the gun flash, and the sword swept into empty space, nearly drawing the striker from the saddle by the force of his own blow.

So he escaped the sharp, downright stroke dealt in return. It fell short a couple of inches of his head, and the heavy steel bit deep into the leather and wood of the saddle.

With a wrench of the reins the chestnut was wheeled right round on its hind legs as on a pivot, and the fight renewed. His second blow was parried, the third evaded. The return stroke almost broke through his guard. The foe was plainly not to be despised—a gaunt, grey man, with a hard face and a keen eye, and muscles as pliant as whalebone.

Skilfully and boldly the deadly game was played, of which life was the stake. The blows came thick and fast, and the quiet wood rang with the angry clash of steel. The young soldier was a brilliant swordsman—his blade played like sheet-lightning around the head of his opponent. He assailed him now on the right, now on the left; but the other still turned resolutely to meet him. His quick eye seemed to anticipate each movement, and ever the young soldier's sword cut into empty space or clashed upon opposing steel.

The fiery youth grew reckless at last, and almost paid with his life for his audacity. A sudden cut, that would have shorn his head in two, was parried so closely that the sword's edge sliced his forage cap into the air.

He reined the chestnut back in time to escape a second stroke, threw aside the long hair that fell across his eyes half blinding him; then, with up-lifted sword, he dashed again at his foe. Just as they met, however, he dropped the point, and with a quick, straight thrust ran his enemy through the un-guarded sword arm.

The older man made no sign or sound of pain. His close, set lips never so much as quivered. His great sword dropped from his disabled right hand, but with his left he drew a huge horse pistol from the broad belt he wore, and levelled it steadily at the young officer, who, carried ten paces past him by the impetus of his last charge, was now completely at his mercy. But just as his finger pressed the trigger, a sword blade struck the barrel down, and the bullet ploughed up the green sod at the horse's feet.

"For shame, Christy!" cried the voice of his

"He slung up his heavy sword high over his shoulder."

comrade close beside; "for shame! It was a fair match, sword against sword, and he beat you. The lad must get fair play. Stand aside. It is my turn now."

Without a word, Christy gave place.

The young officer, flushed with his first victory, was nothing loth to engage a second foe. But this time he met his match, and more than his match, with the sword. Strike where he would, high or low, to right or left, his quick blows seemed to fall on a wall of steel, so true and steady was the defence. The new-comer made scarce an effort to return the blows that were showered so fiercely on his ready sword. Once, indeed, he pierced the right sleeve of the scarlet uniform, and just raised the skin by a lunge so quick it was impossible to parry. Twice he almost strained his foe's wrist with a dexterous effort to disarm him.

But his patience gave way at last, or, it may be, his quick ear caught some sound in the wood that counselled haste. He now suddenly changed his tactics. For the first time he slung up his heavy sword high over his shoulder, to give full impetus to the downward stroke. The guard was quick and true. But the great sword flashed down, sheer on the opposing steel, shivering it like an icicle.

Never did blacksmith's sledge strike starker blow on anvil. The young soldier's right arm was jarred to the elbow by the shock. The broken sword hilt dropped from his numbed fingers on the grass. He was at the mercy of his enemy. The "rebels," he had been told, showed no mercy. He bowed his head and murmured a prayer as he waited for the second stroke that was to end him: but no stroke fell.

"Yield!" cried! the conqueror, in a kindly voice, in which there was a touch of frank admiration. "Yield to Maurice Blake, Captain in the Army of the United States. You have made a good fight— it is no shame to yield to such odds. Be sure you will be honourably treated."

The young soldier in his first skirmish would have thought it deadly disgrace to have been beaten by a regiment. Anger made him dumb. He could only bow his head in shame-faced submission. The sudden tramp of horses' feet made him look up, and the blood went surging back to his heart, leaving his face quite pale.

"A rescue! a rescue!" he cried, gleefully. "Just in the nick of time."

From the wood's edge all round there broke a troop of horsemen in the scarlet uniform of England. Rapidly forming, they caught the conqueror and con-quered in a narrow circle.

The disarmed officer seemed half ashamed of the shout of joy into which he was betrayed at the first sight of his comrades. It looked so like an un-generous triumph over a gallant foe. There was a tone almost of apology in his voice as, turning to the American captain, he said—

"It is your turn to yield now. It is fortune of war—a hard fortune for you, I must confess, to lose the stake when you had won the game. Your sword, and I will pledge my life for your honourable treatment."

Not a word the other answered, while the troops closed in slowly to make sure of their prisoners. Not a motion he made, either of surrender or resistance.

The nearest soldier was not twenty yards off.

"Now!" cried the American captain suddenly to his attendant, who watched him closely, "follow me;" and he rode straight at the circle where the line was thinnest. Before a pistol could be plucked from a holster he was upon them. Two sweeping sword strokes to right and left sent two dragoons sprawling down under the horses' feet. Straight through the gap in their line he galloped, followed by Christy, like his shadow, into the thick cover of the woods, where pursuit was useless, and might prove dangerous to strangers.

The troopers were so taken by surprise that he was gone before the quickest-witted amongst them thought of firing. Then there was a harmless splutter of pistol bullets in the direction in which the enemy vanished. But this silly performance was promptly checked by the elderly officer in command.

"Cease firing!" he cried, angrily.

"Do you want to signal our position to the whole

rebel army?" he added, as he rode past a young ensign, who sat like a statue of astonishment, with a smoking pistol in his hand. "There is no sense left in the service."

He was still angry; yet there was a touch of admiration mingled with his anger as he turned to our first acquaintance, who sat quite still where the American captain had left him, ruefully contemplating the fragments of his broken sword on the grass.

"Lord Edward Fitzgerald," the senior officer said, sternly, when he had come so close that he could address him without others hearing, "you must consider yourself under arrest. I should have your sword, but the enemy has been beforehand with me. But I am bound to send you with a file of soldiers back to the camp to report yourself to Lord Moira.

"I admire your pluck," he added more gently, softened in spite of himself by the shamefaced penitence of the young fellow, who sat silent before him, blushing like a schoolgirl caught in some frolic. "I admire your pluck, but pluck is not everything in an officer. Discipline would be impossible if every young fellow with a taste for adventure were allowed to go patrolling on his own account. We waited a good hour for you before we started. Now you have warned the enemy of our coming."

"Lucky for me you did not wait longer," replied Lord Edward. "One minute more would have done for me. The rebel captain had me at his mercy as you arrived. I have to thank you for my life, Major Doyle—for my liberty at least——"

"And for your arrest," replied the Major.

"You will forgive me," pleaded the other earnestly. "Even if you cannot forgive me, do not send me back to the camp like a schoolboy in disgrace. I was bluemoulded with idleness. I could not resist the temptation of a ride through the woods, and I hoped to be forgiven if I brought in a prisoner. As I was to have come with you let me stay with you. I will myself report to Lord Moira when we return."

It was not in human nature to resist the pleading voice and eyes. Major Doyle's stern face melted like ice in the sunshine. There was a twinkle in his grey eye and a smile under his heavy moustache as he replied—

"There is no limit to your audacity. I suppose you will next ask me for a sword, and leave to ride at the head of the column."

"The very two favours I had in my mind," returned Lord Edward, emboldened by the other's smile. "But I had not the courage to mention them."

"Then have them without asking, as a reward for your cowardice," retorted the Major. "It is a virtue I am most anxious to encourage in you."

"Tomkins," he called, to a burly non-commissioned officer, "give your sword to Lord Edward Fitzgerald. Your pistols must serve you for this bout."

The sword was surrendered with a smiling alacrity,

which showed that the high-spirited young lord was a prime favourite with the men.

"Keep a sharp look out in front, Lord Edward," said Major Doyle, assuming the commanding officer as the men approached. "Instantly report to me the first trace of the rebels. Do not charge them," he added, in a lower tone, "as a bulldog charges a bull. Let your caution atone for your rashness, and Lord Moira shall know of it."

But Lord Edward had exhausted his adventures for that day. The scarlet uniform of the troopers flamed like fire in the darkening woods, and was as a beacon seen afar off to warn the enemy. Now and again the young officer at their head thought that he caught sight of moving figures in the distance. But they vanished in an instant, and in the darkening twilight he could not even be sure if they were men or deer.

With an uneasy feeling in his mind that he was not the watcher but the watched, Major Doyle, as the night fell, marched his men back to the camp from their bootless expedition, as ignorant of the enemy's whereabouts as they had marched out in the morning.

CHAPTER II.

"THIS MOST WISE REBELLION."

Coriolanus.

" The dangers of the days but newly gone
Have put us in those ill beseeming arms
Not to break peace or any branch of it,
But to establish here a peace indeed
Concurring both in name and quality."

King Henry IV. Part II.

LORD EDWARD FITZGERALD slept late into the following morning, overcome at once by fatigue and by the reaction that follows excitement. It was the first time he had stricken a blow in anger, and the events of the previous day mingled incoherently in his dreams. He found himself charging the British troops with the American captain by his side. He was struck from his horse amid the trampling hoofs. He lay helpless on the ground. His comrade leaped down and strove to save him, for a dozen weapons were aimed at his life. He saw a man, whose face he did not know, point a pistol straight at his head. He tried to shift himself out of the line of fire, but he seemed glued to the ground. The turmoil of the conflict ceased suddenly. All eyes were turned on the man with the pistol. He waited in an agony of suspense for the flash and the bullet. The strain grew too great to be borne, and he awoke.

He was lying half out of his camp bed, and the morning sun was streaming through an opening in the canvas. Yesterday's adventures came trooping back at once to his memory, and with them the unpleasant thought that he had got to report his breach of duty to Lord Moira, and take his chance of reprimand or punishment.

It was his nature to face trouble and get it over. Lord Moira received him with a kindliness that was only in a very slight degree due to the fact that he was son of a duke, for the gallant young officer was a favourite for his own sake with everyone, from the drummer boy to commanding officer.

Though there was a good-humoured twinkle in the General's eye, as he listened to Lord Edward's penitent recital, he managed to speak seriously.

"My lad," he said, "if you cannot cure yourself of this longing to get killed at any cost you will never be a credit to your profession—the noblest in the world. Rashness is not courage. Is it not quite sufficient that you should be ready to die whenever His Most Gracious Majesty requires the sacrifice? You must not anticipate."

Lord Moira spoke of "His Most Gracious Majesty" in a voice only one tone less reverent than he spoke of the Creator. It was amusing to note how the reverence was reflected on the face of the young soldier who heard him.

" It is impossible I can let you off scot free for your frolic," he added. " It would be a bad example to every young scapegrace in the camp who has got more courage than common sense. We engage the rebels, I trust, within a week. They are encamped under General Steward at Eutaw Springs, and must be driven out. Your punishment shall be that you shall take up your position "——

He spoke slowly, and made a long pause. His listener's countenance fell, for his fears supplied the words " in the rear."

But as Lord Moira repeated, " You shall take up your position in the van," his whole face brightened with delight.

He looked up quickly, and for the first time caught the good-humoured, amused smile on the veteran's face. With voice and eyes and every motion of his body he thanked him.

" Why, this is wages," he cried, " and not punishment. I thank you a thousand times, my lord. Indeed, indeed, you may rely on my zeal."

" And discretion," put in Lord Moira.

" And my discretion, too," he replied, laughing and blushing. " No maiden aunt was ever more discreet than I will be for the future."

" Then," said the General, clapping him kindly on the shoulder, " I will scold you no more. Your worst punishment shall be that you will breakfast with me this morning. I hear you have a keen eye for a map or the lie of a country. There is some nasty ground for ambushes between this and the Springs, and I want your help. Lord Edward," he went on, more kindly than ever, but more seriously, "you will be a great general yet, if you will only lock enthusiasm up in the guard-room and put a sentry at the door. A perfect soldier is a bit of military mechanism that nothing can put out of order."

But a nobler fame than his commander promised was in store for him, though he knew it not—to live in the loving remembrance of a suffering nation as one who died to serve her—to be the one Irish noble-man who proved himself truly noble, who, for wealth, rank, and what the world calls renown, took suffering and glorious shame in the service of a sorely-oppressed people.

The Americans held a strong position at Eutaw Springs, but the English troops, who slightly out-numbered them, advanced to the attack with absolute confidence of victory. There was not a man amongst them, from the commanding officer to the full private, that had the slightest doubt of the result.

It is, indeed, strange how completely experience seemed to have lost her authority during the war of American Independence. No matter how often the British troops were beaten by the "rebels," they always felt quite sure of victory—next time. Their defeat was always the result of some unlucky accident, which could not be repeated. They believed firmly as an article of faith that it was impossible that British troops—the bravest, the best disciplined, and the best-accoutred in the world—could be beaten by the rebel riff-raff—except by accident.

It did not matter in the least that the accident was always happening. They forgot the deadly aim of the long brown rifle, and the fierce stab of the heavy hunting knife the instant the rifle was silent and blade unsheathed.

Least of all had Lord Edward Fitzgerald, as he proudly marched before his men in the front of the battle, the faintest shadow of misgiving of the result. He looked forward eagerly to a gallant fight and a glorious victory. His whole soul was aflame with the fierce war fever, and he longed only to be within striking distance of the foe.

The American leader,—General Steward—had chosen his position with consummate skill. His forces were ranged on a promontory of open prairie jutting back into the great ocean of forest, and so guarded at the rear and side by a line of high close wood. A stream, rapid but shallow, crossed the open ground in front, well within musket shot of his advance guard, and lost itself in the wood to the left.

The English forces, as they advanced, were under a galling flank fire from the woods, which dropped man after man in their lines with a bullet through his head or heart. To reply would be to waste ammunition on the tree trunks, and, what was worse still, to waste time.

"Double quick!" was the word all along the

British line, and they advanced at a run into the stream in front. The deadly patter of the musket bullets grew thicker and thicker as they came on within the closing arms of the wood. The main body of Americans in front stood steadily to their weapons and made no sign.

The attacking party reached the bank and plunged waist deep into the stream ; still not a movement in the American line.

In wild confusion the British scrambled out on to the near bank, which was higher and steeper than the far. All order was lost. Their guns cumbered them in wading and climbing. For a moment they were a mob, not an army. But discipline quickly reasserted itself. They were rapidly forming for a bayonet charge when the word " Fire !" rang out at last like a rifle crack from the American line.

The withering volley at close quarters made lanes through the confused mass of men huddled on the river's bank. The dead and wounded tumbled into the water over their comrades, who were scrambling out. The confusion was changing to panic. Lord Edward Fitzgerald saw the danger. He was in command of the front column, and was amongst the first across the stream. He heard the storm of bullets hiss about his ears. He saw men struck down to his right and left. Yet the thought of danger never touched him for a moment. He was as cool as when breakfasting with Lord Moira—eye and mind equally on the alert.

His quick glance caught a slight hollow on the ground to the left.

"Down, men, and follow me," he cried, and, falling on his hands and knees, he crept rapidly towards the shelter.

His men trailed after him. In a moment they were under cover from the rifles of the Americans in front. Pushing their guns over the ridge that sheltered them, the English were in turn enabled to pour a deliberate and effective fire upon the enemy.

Under cover of this well-directed discharge, the main body of the English crossed the stream, and formed, though not without loss, on the near bank. Meanwhile, however, the riflemen in the wood to the left, had got the range of Lord Edward's little band, whose flank was completely unguarded, and now played upon them with terrible effect.

The crouching English soldiers were shot through the side or head by these terrible marksmen. So deadly was the aim, the victims never moved after they were hit, but lay dead, with their muskets at their shoulders pointing at the enemy in front.

The young officer saw that his whole party would be quietly killed off in a few minutes more. There was but one desperate chance left—a bolt for the woods.

The main bodies on both sides were by this time hotly engaged, and an unintermittent fire flashed from their ranks. The rattle of musket shots never ceased for a moment.

"Steady, my lads," cried Lord Fitzgerald, in a voice that was heard through the din. ".Steady and ready! Watch and follow me. We must drive those skulking rebels out of the shelter of the woods."

He rose to his knees as he spoke. His men's eyes were on him. He leaped suddenly to his feet. "Now!" he shouted, waving his sword over his head, and raced across the belt of land for the wood from which the deadly fire came. In an instant his men were up and after him. It was a race for life or death. Every muscle was strained to the utmost point of tension. Lord Edward kept his lead. The distance was not a hundred yards in all. A dozen seconds would cover it at the pace they went.

The Americans seemed to be taken off their guard by the sudden rush. More than half the ground was passed and not a shot came.

Lord Edward and his men were scarce thirty yards from the edge of the wood—only a few seconds off— when suddenly fifty tongues of fire, with fifty spitting puffs of smoke, darted out from among the tree trunks, followed by a roar of rifle shots, and a hurricane of bullets broke right into the thick of them.

Full half the advancing party were swept off their feet by this terrible fusilade. The men in the rear tripped over the falling corpses of their comrades in front, but the headlong fury of the charge was not checked even for a moment.

The smoke had not cleared when the survivors, with Lord Edward still unhurt, at their head, broke furiously into the wood.

The parties were pretty equally matched. The struggle was desperate and to the death. The passion for blood absorbed them. To strike and kill was all they thought of. They fought like wild beasts—the same fierce instinct of slaughter, the same insensibility to wound or danger.

The Americans had clubbed their guns after their last deadly discharge. It was rifle butt against bayonet point. Cruel stab and crushing blow were interchanged with terrible rapidity.

Lord Edward, active as a deer, dodged the blows aimed at him, and made tremendous play with his sword. Three of the enemy he slew with his own hand. His followers seconded him bravely. But in that hand-to-hand struggle, the advantages of drill and discipline were lost, and man to man they were no match for the stalwart backwoodsmen, whose muscles were of wrought steel. The British were slowly and sullenly beaten back.

Foremost amongst the Americans a tall, strong figure fought, swinging his rifle like a flail.

"Strike, boys!" he shouted, "for America and Freedom! Freedom! Freedom! Freedom!" And he swept down a man at each repetition of the word.

The voice caught Lord Edward's ear. Even in that wild hurley-burley he knew the man. It was the same who had foiled him in single fight a week before.   The sight sent a hot thrill through his blood.

"For England and the King," he shouted back, and made at him through the press. An American soldier barred his way. He passed his sword through his body and leaped over the corpse. But two paces on, a dying man, with a bayonet wound through his breast, caught him by the leg as he passed, and raising his right hand with a long knife in it dealt him a ghastly flesh-wound in the thigh, from which the blood spouted as from a fountain.

He staggered forward and fell on his face. His dying enemy crawled after him : the red knife in his hand was raised for the fatal blow, when it was sent spinning through the air by a stroke from a rifle butt, and he fell on the body of his intended victim, dead. It was Maurice Blake who had leaped forward to answer Lord Edward's challenge, and reached in time to save him.

When their leader fell the few surviving English soldiers fled in all directions, and, crossing the stream, rejoined the main body, which was now sullenly retreating after a desperate hand-to-hand encounter with the Americans.

Blake held his men back from pursuit, and forbade firing on the fugitives.

"There has been slaughter enough and more than enough," he said. "Thank God the victory is ours."

He knelt as he spoke beside the body of Lord Edward, and examined the wound, through which the blood was oozing as a spring through the moss, draining his life away in its red current.

He started as he saw the face of the wounded man, and recognised it at a glance.

"Strange," he muttered. "Twice we have met as enemies, and each time it has been my fortune to save his life. What link has fate fastened between our lives?"

His hands were meantime as busy as his thoughts. He uncovered the wound, and staunched and bound it rapidly and firmly with a practised hand. Lord Edward lay limp, motionless, and senseless as a corpse. His brown hair looked black by contrast with the deadly pallor of his face, whose ghastly hue was made more ghastly by a disfiguring streak of blood.

Blake caught his wrist tightly, and could distinguish a feeble flutter in the pulse.

"There is a chance for him yet," he said softly to himself, "and he must not lose it. A gallant young fellow. How bravely he faced us a fortnight ago, and how fiercely he fought to-day. What a noble face it is, and I doubt not a noble nature to match. Pity such a bright young life should be cut off in an obscure scrimmage, fighting against freedom. It shall not be if I can help it."

"Christy," he called out, and in an instant his inseparable companion stood before him without a word.

"Can you carry him?" Blake asked.

Christy, for answer, took the wounded man in his arms.

"Where?" he said, laconically.

"To Tony's hut," responded the other. "Fortunately it is pretty close at hand. If anyone living can nurse him back to life, Tony is the man."

Christy said never a word in reply, but carrying his burden as tenderly and almost as easily as a mother carries her year-old baby, moved off with long, swift strides, and disappeared. Blake meantime gathered his men together, and carefully tended the wounded before he rejoined the main body of the Americans, who had encamped victoriously on the battle-field, from which the enemy had been driven.

The space between stream and wood was thickly strewn with corpses. The scarlet uniforms sprinkled thickly over the green sward showed how terrible had been the slaughter of the English. The fair blue sky smiled down placidly on the grim battle-field. But the frightened stream which saw this great murder done, rushed away with a red tinge in its clear waters to tell the quiet woods the old, old story of man's inhumanity to man.

CHAPTER III.

*"WHO IS HERE SO BASE AS WILL NOT LOVE HIS
COUNTRY?"*

Julius Cæsar.

" Here I clip
The anvil of my sword, and do contest
As hotly and as nobly with thy love
As ever in ambitious strength I did
Contend against thy valour."—*Coriolanus.*

" But if the cause be not good, the King himself hath a heavy reckoning to make, when all those legs and arms and heads chopped off in battle, shall join together at the latter day."—*Henry V.*

THE scramble through the stream under the pelting shower of bullets, the rush for the woods, the fierce struggle, the sudden blow, all came floating back through the mind of Lord Edward, dimly and vaguely, like the incidents of a story heard long ago, with which he had no personal concern. Was it a dream, he wondered vaguely, or had it all happened? Where, when, and to whom?

He had a faint remembrance that he had been wounded in the wood. What had come to him since? Was he still lying on the ground, under the shadow of those tall trees, alone, deserted.

He opened his eyes in languid curiosity. He

found himself on a bed of beaver skins in a log hut full of fresh air and sunshine. Even then he was not surprised. He had not strength left to wonder strongly. He had a curious feeling of familiarity with the place, as if he had dreamed of it or seen it through his closed eyelids as he lay insensible. His bed faced the door, which looked down towards the woods, from which the soft morning breeze stole up and fanned his face deliciously.

He lay quite still at first, with hardly strength or wish to turn his eyes from where they first chanced to fall. Half unconsciously he began to count the logs from floor to ceiling. Then he counted them from wall to wall. So his eye travelled lazily round till it lit on a black man, with his back to him, reading at a small table, on which were bottles and bandages. It was his first sight of " the faithful Tony," thenceforward to the hour of his death his devoted friend and follower.

With fresh air and sunshine, and simple wholesome food, and Tony's untiring attendance, Lord Edward's recovery surely, if slowly progressed. The pure air and the soft murmur of the wilderness were soothing ministers to his weakness. Through every sense, health visited his frame. His wound was soon completely healed. A little red began to show in his pale cheek, and his bright grey eye grew quicker in its glance. He was still very weak, when he managed to hobble to the door, to sit on the bench at the porch and gaze out over the top of the interminable

" A black man, with his back to him, reading at a small table, on which were
bottles and bandages.'

expanse of forest at his feet, with here and there a stupendous tree shooting up above its companions like a green tower high into the clear sky. But after a little he was able to carry a rifle down to the woods, which swarmed with game.

This lazy life came suddenly to an end. He was sitting outside the door one evening reading and smoking after a long day in the woods, enjoying that state of delicious langour which honest physical exertion alone has the power to bestow.

The sudden crack of a rifle brought his thoughts back to real life in a moment.

From the top of the green wood, through which the setting sun was now shooting his level rays of red light, he saw a little thread of blue smoke rise, curling in the thin air. The boughs parted at the wood's edge, and two men stepped into the open. One carried a long rifle, the other bent under the body of a dead deer. Needless to say it was Maurice Blake and his inseparable attendant, who in a few minutes more were at the hut door.

Maurice Blake had good news and bad for Lord Edward. The war was over—the English troops were being recalled. Here were sad tidings for the ambitious young soldier and the devoted Loyalist. But, on the other hand, he was glad to learn that he would be able to rejoin his regiment, which was again encamped in the neighbourhood. In a week's time, Blake told him, they were under orders for the coast.

" Best stay here," he urged, " until they are actually

moving. You are more comfortable here than in the camp."

" I fear I must return," replied the other, somewhat sadly. " I am completely recovered, and have no excuse for further absence from my duty."

Blake looked disappointed. Then a bright thought struck him.

"You forgot you are my prisoner," he said, a little sharply.

"In truth, I had forgotten it," responded Lord Edward, somewhat dismayed at the reminder.

"Well," responded Blake, with a smile at his dismay, "you must give me your parole not to attempt to escape for a week. After that—well, it does not much matter what happens after that."

Lord Edward's parole was heartily given, and the two men sat chatting cheerily far into the placid night. Meanwhile Christy and Tony enjoyed themselves after their own fashion, on the principle of Jack Sprat and his wife. Tony did all the talking and Christy all the silence.

Betimes next morning Blake and his prisoner were entering the forest with the after-breakfast pipes between their lips, and their guns on their shoulders. Christy followed with long, silent strides. Never had Lord Edward Fitzgerald a more delightful day. His companion was charmed with his eagerness, and taught him a hundred secrets of woodcraft. A life spent chiefly in the forest had gifted Blake with a kind of sylvan second sight. No animal that put foot to earth could conceal from him its identity or whereabouts. But what Lord Edward chiefly marvelled at was the unerring accuracy of his aim. It seemed rather an effort of the will than of steady nerve and quick eye. Standing, running, or flying, it made no difference. Whatever he could see he could hit. Within rifle range he never missed.

Friendship is sometimes like love—a plant of quick growth. In less than a week these two foes were fast friends. They lay in the woods at night, and talked together under the quiet stars that peeped in through crevices in the leaves when the forest was fast asleep, and breathing heavily. Nor was it mere words they interchanged, but thought and feeling.

It was a hard wrench to both when the time came that they must part, probably for ever.

Their friendship grew closer as the time for parting came near. As they sat together the last evening at the hut's entrance, with the fair scene spread out before them in the glow of rosy sunset, Lord Edward's talk ran all on war and glory. Blake smiled at his eagerness.

"Glory or murder," he said at last, musingly. "Is there really any real difference between them? Were the British murderers when they marched their disciplined troops against our raw recruits? Were we murderers when we shot them down from the cover of the trees without giving them a chance?"

"Surely, you must feel the difference," cried out Lord Edward, earnestly; "though you cannot put it in words. War has been ever the delight of the noblest men. Through war and victory their names are held in honour for all time. There is no rapture in the world to equal the wild excitement of the battlefield."

"Have you ever been on that same battlefield when the fight was over? No? Well, I have; more than once. There is no delight, no excitement, then. I helped to fling the dead into their shallow graves after our late fight down yonder at Eutaw Springs. There was little thought of glory amongst us as we filled the great pit with the mangled corpses of thousands of brave and honest men, to whom God gave life and from whom man had taken it. They might have done good work in the world if they had not been sent out of it by this short cut. Close to the wood's edge I found the dead body of my oldest and dearest friend — Bill Saunders was his name. The bayonet of one of your fellows was driven up to the shoulder in his side. He was a great broad-chested fellow, blythe as a boy, affectionate as a woman. He had a pleasant little home away down in Kentucky. I was there when he bade his wife —a bright, brave, brown-eyed little woman—and his two prattling young ones good-bye. 'I will be a soldier, too,' said his three-year-old boy, 'when I grow big. When dad comes home he'll teach me soldiering.' Alas! he will never come home. The light of that pleasant home is gone out for ever.

"Are you sorry," he said, turning abruptly to his

companion, "that you had not the glory of that death? Do you grieve that it was not your sword instead of a bayonet point that bored the hole through which that brave and gentle spirit fled?"

Lord Edward started as if he had been accused of murder.

"Thank God, I had no hand in it," he said. "I trembled while you spoke to think that I might have made the widow and orphans desolate. But I may have made others that I know not of. Yet, surely war is not murder. I feel you are wrong, though I cannot well answer you. The voice and the history of the whole world are against you. All mankind are agreed that there is honour and glory to be reaped in righteous war."

"What is a righteous war?" asked Blake quietly.

"Ours was, if there ever was one," cried Lord Edward. "We were fighting for King and Constitution against the rebels. Of course, I do not mean," he added, remembering the ranks in which the other fought, "that all were conscious rebels. Many, doubtless, deemed their cause just."

"And ought, therefore, to be slaughtered?" asked Blake, a little bitterly. "But was there no danger that you Loyalists, as you call yourselves, were in the wrong? Who is the King for whose sake you are willing to slaughter men like my friend Saunders and myself? Did you ever so much as see him?"

"Never," said Lord Edward.

"Or know anything specially good or bad about him ?"

"Nothing good or bad."

Lord Edward looked a little foolish as he answered.

"Yet were you willing for this man's whim that a great country should be enslaved ; tens of thousands of honest men slain ; tens of thousands of humble homes made desolate."

"Surely," said Lord Edward, dismayed at the way his moral moorings were being pulled up, and his conscience turned adrift ; "surely you will admit that rebellion in itself is a bad thing and must be put down."

"Ask Tony there," returned the other ; "he is as good a judge as another. He, too, the gentlest creature on God's earth, has been a rebel in his day. The first time I ever laid eyes on him he was engaged in an act of desperate rebellion. He had got his legal lord and master by the throat, and was squeezing the life out of him with his bare hands. Two Loyalist bloodhounds were tearing at the naked limbs of the 'rebel.' A third Loyalist (human this one) whom he had flung into a swamp was fumbling for his pistol. If I had not come up at the moment and taken part with the rebel you would have lacked the kindest of nurses when your need was sorest."

Lord Edward was silenced for the moment ; then he broke out again abruptly—

"I cannot think why you should denounce war so. You are a soldier yourself, as brave and as fierce as any of us."

"When the bloody work is doing, the wild beast instinct that is at the bottom of all our hearts gets the better of me, I suppose," said Blake; "but I have no pleasure, be sure, in the thought of slaughter beforehand; no pride when it is done and over."

"Then why fight?" asked Lord Edward. "You blame me for fighting for loyalty. What do you fight for?"

"For freedom—the one thing worth fighting for," he responded, with such earnestness that he startled the other. His eyes flashed and his colour heightened as he spoke. "I fight for the freedom of my adopted land. Nor will I deny that the love of the land of my fathers inspires me, too.

"But you will pardon my Irish hastiness," he said more gently, noticing his friend's rising colour and misinterpreting its meaning. "I have no right to speak in such a strain to my English guest."

"I am no Englishman," cried Lord Edward Fitzgerald, proudly, "I am of the Geraldines—Irish to my finger-tips. In name, and race, and heart, Fitzgerald is Irish of the Irish."

Blake turned quickly, with something like veneration in his face and voice. His dark sunburnt cheek flushed to a ruddier brown; his blue eyes beamed with a warmer light. "Of the Geraldines," he said, wonderingly. "More Irish than the Irish themselves. The grand old race, who were ever true to the old land when her own sons failed her."

But the enthusiasm died out of his face in a moment, like light from the sky when the sun sets.

"It cannot be," he muttered, "a Geraldine in the army of England; a Geraldine in the ranks of Ireland's enslavers, battling against liberty in the Old World as in the New. The descendant of Silken Thomas has never surely sunk to this."

He thought aloud, unconscious of the insult his words conveyed. Lord Edward listened with flushed cheek. His hand dropped unconsciously on his sword's hilt, but, remembering his life saved, gratitude mastered his anger.

"This is cruel," he broke out, with a passionate sob, "when you have tied my hands with kindness."

Blake looked at him with surprise. Then he felt how harsh his own words were.

"Forgive me," he said, "I never meant it;" and he stretched out his hand as he spoke, "I promise you, my lord," he added, "I will never again touch on a topic that so pains you."

But Lord Edward would not let the subject be so put aside. "Believe me," he said, "I love the old land as dearly as any of my race, and would as willingly have died for her liberty. There is no longer need. Surely even here in the wilderness the glorious news must have reached you. Ireland is free at last. Grattan and the Volunteers have done the glorious work. I would have dearly loved to have had a hand in it, but I was a boy when it was done."

As he spoke he looked like a knight of the old days, eager for glorious adventure.

Blake gazed at him with an admiration in which there was pity too.

"Can a nation be called free," he asked, bitterly, "of which three-fourths of the people are as abject slaves as the black skins who pick cotton in the Southern States? I am an Irish Catholic, my lord," he went on with increased bitterness. "I am any man's equal here. What would I be in my native land—my 'free' native land, as you call it? What, but the bond-slave of every man who could boast of a newer and more fashionable faith. Do not wonder at me," he continued, for he saw that Lord Edward was surprised and even startled at the heat with which he spoke. "The old faith and the old land are all I have left to love or live for. All I know of my own story is told in a few words, mostly hearsay; the rest guesswork. Of my father I know nothing, except that he, too, was an Irish Catholic gentleman who came out here before I was born. My mother died at the hour of my birth. My father suddenly disappeared. Whether he is dead or living I cannot tell. No one can tell but Christy, and he keeps his secret stoutly, as he swore to keep it. He was my father's foster brother, and was alone trusted. He is at once my guardian, my comrade, and my servant— the last at his own command. I am quite alone in the world—an orphan and an exile. I have no friends, no relatives, no country. I long to go back to the dear old land, but slavery would not suit me. I should rebel, and get hanged. Can you wonder that I plunged eagerly into this war for freedom and against England? Can you wonder that I rejoiced to find a countryman in you, to whom my heart leaped out from the first, even when I stood in arms against you? Can you wonder that I grieved to find an Irishman in the ranks of his country's oppressors?"

"Not wittingly," cried Lord Edward, eagerly. "The allegiance of my heart is Ireland's. If ever she needs it, my sword will be her's, too, against the world. Believe me, I believed her free. I joined in the general huzzas at Grattan's triumph, without asking why. But how comes it that you know more about Ireland than I do?"

"Christy is largely responsible," replied the other. "He was a rebel himself, and he has made me one. He has filled my childhood with stories of my country's wrongs, and sufferings, and glory. Since I have grown to be a man I have read and thought of little else. From all I have heard and read I am convinced that Grattan's Parliament cannot last. I hardly wish it to last. I speak now as an Irishman, even more than as a Catholic. This spurious freedom, wrested from England's fears, is worse than worthless. Freedom and slavery cannot live together in the same land. To be really free all must be free. You cannot keep liberty long balanced on a point so narrow as Grattan's Parliament. It will topple over one side or another. England will recover by division and corruption the mastery she sacrificed from fear, unless united Irishmen strike together one brave blow for real liberty. Will the great lesson of unity be ever learned? Must the fairest and the bravest land on earth be a slave always? Why cannot we follow America's example? I should die happy if I might but make one in her army when Ireland meets her enslavers as she has never yet met them—on a fair field—to settle the question of her freedom or slavery for ever. I make no bargain with Providence for the issue of that fight. It is not needed. What Irishman dare doubt of victory in such a cause?"

The hot blood of the Geraldines coursed like fire through the veins of Lord Edward as the other spoke.

"When united Irishmen meet to strike a blow for freedom," he cried, with lion-like ardour, "I will not be the last in the charge."

"You will be first," said Blake, solemnly. "Your race calls you to the front."

His strong right hand fervently grasped Geraldine's as he spoke.

The two stood, hand clasped in hand, under the silent stars that now spangled the black sky. In their hearts they felt a sacred oath had been sworn, and the night wind that came stealing up from the far wood—the only moving thing abroad—seemed to whisper a sad amen.

Lord Edward, when he left, carried away Tony for good and all—never to part on this side of the grave. Maurice Blake rode with him to the British Camp.

At parting, the young Geraldine stretched a cordial hand to his first enemy, the grim silent Christy, who wrung it with awkward earnestness.

" Master Maurice has told me, my lord," he said. " If I had known you were of the old stock in the old land I would have cut my hand off sooner than it should shake a sword against you. May be yet— "

Before he could complete the sentence the chestnut thoroughbred, delirious with long idleness, tore them apart, and in two bounds was beside the great black charger " Phooka " that carried Blake so sedately.

Christy watched the two as they rode down the slope abreast in the slant sunshine, with Tony a little in the rear. The same thoughts came to his mind that filled theirs the night before.

" Pray God," he said. " The day will come when those two will lead us in our own land. There is a rusty pike in the thatch of a little cabin by the Shannon river at home, that will not be far behind in the first rush. It was in my grandfather's hands when they murdered him on his own threshold long ago, and I will carry no other weapon when the great day comes."

He watched the two young men, with his hand slanted over his eyes, until they disappeared around the edge of the forest. Then, with a curious mixture of tenderness and fierceness on his hard face he turned into the hut, and the wide landscape lay silent and solitary in the all-pervading sunlight.

CHAPTER IV.

" AND MAIDENS CALL IT ' LOVE IN IDLENESS.'"
Midsummer Night's Dream.

" Poor, honest lord, brought low by his own heart."
Timon of Athens.

A MONTH later found Lord Edward Fitzgerald tumbling across the Atlantic in the good ship *The Alacrity.*

Crossing the Atlantic was not then a six days' pleasure trip. Six weeks from shore to shore was counted a fast voyage.

Before a fortnight of the time was over he was deadly tired of the journey. In compliment to his wound, or rather in remembrance of it—for it was completely healed—he sailed in a passenger, not a troopship. He was the duller on that account. He knew no one on board, and was shy of making new acquaintances. The ship was peopled chiefly by dismissed British officials and disappointed place-hunters.

Lord Edward's notions of the merits of the war were further enlarged by the lamentations of this greedy crowd, who railed at the Americans for daring to do without them ; and eagerly looked forward to a speedy renewal of the conflict, and "extermination of the rebels."

There was but one man on board whose acquaintance Lord Edward cared to make. The ship's books told the name—Dr. Denver, and the name was familiar to Lord Edward. He knew the Doctor to be one of the shining lights of the profession in Dublin. He knew him to be a special friend and favourite of his mother's. He had a vague recollection of having seen that handsome old face when he had come in, a little boy, to dessert in the great dining-room at Carton. But beyond that the acquaintance did not reach.

It was in the Doctor's daughter, Norah, however, not in the Doctor, that Lord Edward was most keenly interested.

Norah Denver was, indeed, beyond expression, beautiful — fascinating alike in face and manner. Her father's old-fashioned, dignified courtesy was softened down in her to sweet womanly graciousness, that had an indefinable charm in it.

A great coil of soft brown, wavy hair crowned her shapely head, framing a broad forehead of pure white. There was a suggestion of resolute will in the shapely mouth and clear-cut chin, but her smile was of a winning sweetness, and her clear, shining eyes had all the frank candour of a child's.

Withal there was about her a gentle dignity which charmed even while it restrained.

Lord Edward, despite his shyness, had availed himself of the informality of ship life to get on speaking terms, with the father first, then with the daughter. His attentions, sanctioned by the narrowness of their little world and mutual dependence of its inhabitants, were graciously received by Norah Denver; and acquaintance imperceptibly ripened into friendship.

There was no touch of restraint in their intercourse. They walked and chatted on deck in the freshness of the morning and in the glories of the gorgeous sunset. Norah, with brush and pencil, captured bright glimpses of the changing beauty of sky and water, while Lord Edward praised and wondered. Despite of this, perhaps because of this, Lord Edward was not quite satisfied. He had a vague half-latent feeling of discontent. Their intimacy was too brotherly and sisterly for his taste. Those brave eyes looked too frankly into his own. There was no flutter of self-consciousness in her greeting. The colour never heightened on the soft cheek. The long lashes never drooped over the bright eyes when they met.

He felt it a kind of duty to himself to be in love with this beautiful and charming girl, whose life he had the good luck to save. But there was no hint of response.

Norah had lived in the gay Irish capital. She had lived, too, in the wildest part of the county of Kildare, where her father was known far and wide as "the poor man's doctor." To the peasants' mud-cabins, as "the Doctor's daughter, God bless her," she was always welcome. She loved the poor best.

She always stoutly maintained that the Irish peasant and his wife were the finest gentleman and lady in the world since Adam and Eve. She had a thousand stories to tell of their quaint humour, their tact, and courtesy, and unobtrusive tenderness. She had stories, too, of the savagery with which they were treated, and the misery they endured. Lord Edward, as he looked in her tear-dimmed eyes, felt his own cheeks burn with shame to know such things were in his own land, which, in his blank ignorance, he had boasted to be free.

He felt, too, while he listened, that he must and did love this girl, in every way so loveable—and yet, and yet—he never felt with her the foolish, wild palpitations which the mere sight of that stately, self-possessed young beauty—Lady Gertrude Glenmire—could provoke in those days when he first donned his uniform for the wars.

Even now that calm, fair face would sometimes look in upon his heart, and set it fluttering reproachfully at its own forgetfulness.

While Norah was present her frank, unaffected kindliness put love-making out of the question. He was content to be serenely happy. He found himself talking to her as freely as he had talked to Maurice Blake, under the high roof of the primæval forest.

But when she left him, he was angry with himself for the chance he had missed.

One evening late they sat together on deck, while with a pleasant rustling and rippling motion the good ship flew swiftly forward before a favourable wind. A full moon shone in the cloudless sky, glorifying the waters. It was no mere white disk, but a great globe of pure light—God's own lamp hung high in the heavens. The moonlight seemed to mingle with the young man's blood, filling him with soft and delicate desires. There was a tender embarrassment in his eyes and voice, which Norah was quick to notice, but quietly ignored. She listened with a smile of quiet amusement to the high-flown compliments with which he now and again broke the even tenor of their talk. At last she could no longer pretend to mistake his meaning, and frankly faced the situation.

"Lord Edward," she said, abruptly breaking in on a compliment, "will you grant me a favour—a very easy one to grant?"

"Can you doubt it," he replied, with tender passion in his voice that for the instant was fully felt. "I would die to please you."

"It is something much simpler than that," and she answered, smiling, "And I ask it for your own sake as much as mine—and yet I hardly know how to ask it."

She paused for a moment in evident confusion—then went on bravely.

"I want you to give up the foolish notion that you are bound to be in love with me because we have been so much alone together. You like me, I trust, a little. I like you and admire you; I cannot say how much. But of what is called love there is not the least bit in the world between us two, and there never can be."

He tried to utter a fervent protestation, but could find no words at the moment. She held up her finger in playful warning, and went on quickly before he could speak.

"It is the proper thing, of course, that we should fall in love," she said, smiling, "or would be in a romance. But we cannot set our hearts to what tune pleases the story-tellers. Best not try. It gives a touch of insincerity to our true friendship. Those pretty things you have been saying for the last half-hour must be very troublesome to you to devise. Forgive me, my lord, they are tiresome for me to listen to. I suppose"—she was blushing now a rosy red, but determined to have her say out—"when folk are really in love such soft nonsense is very pleasant. But this I know—it is not for us. Be my friend always, my lord, my true friend, as I am yours, but never make believe to yourself, or to me, to be my lover. This is the favour I have to ask."

Lord Edward heard her with something like relief, yet there was a little tinge of wounded self-love mixed with it, that she could talk so calmly.

He leaped up, and paced the deck two or three times before he could reply.

"I will trouble you with my love no more," he said, a little stiffly. Then her kind smile disarmed his petulance. "You are right and I was wrong," he added with all his own cheery frankness. "Friends,

"We cannot set our hearts to what tune pleases the story-tellers."

then, let it be, true and tried friends, and allies while life lasts."

With a kindly pressure of his hand, she silently closed the contract. From that hour the last shade of restraint passed from their friendship, and a few days later he found himself talking quite naturally to Norah of Gertrude Glenmire, while she listened and smiled.

Dr. Denver was a man whose friendship was hard either to win or lose. But he could not resist the brave, true spirit that looked out of Lord Edward's frank eyes, and spoke in every tone of his pleasant voice.

The Doctor was deeply interested in America. He was specially curious about the war. Lord Edward had many stories of his own experience, stories told without a touch of boastfulness, or of that mock modesty which jars still more unpleasantly on a listener's ear.

On his latest adventures he was, however, strangely silent. It was not till he and Dr. Denver had grown very intimate that Maurice Blake's name was incidentally mentioned, as they sat tranquilly smoking their after-dinner cigar, on deck in the cool of the evening.

The Doctor half-started from his seat with sudden surprise and interest at the name. " Maurice Blake," he repeated. " Did you meet a Maurice Blake in America, my lord? Pray tell me how and when. Believe me, I have special reason for wishing to know."

He listened with gradually growing interest as Lord Edward complied. When he came to Blake's brief, story of himself, Dr. Denver broke in once or twice with eager questions.

"How strange," said the Doctor musingly, when the story was finished, "if your new friend should prove the son of my old friend—Sir Valentine Blake, of Cloonlara—of whose sad story you may have heard something. Your father and he were friends, I know. It were still stranger if by mere accident on my return I should chance on something of the news for which my journey was made in vain. I will tell you what brought me to America, if you care to hear it. I begin to think you can help me.

"Some years before you were born," the Doctor went on, "I one night received a hurried summons to my hospital. A woman was dying, they told me, and begged to see me. I went, and found one whom I thought long dead, the dishonouring and dishonoured wife of my old friend, Sir Valentine Blake. No need to trouble your young ears with the sad story. She had fled with a false friend from the best and truest of husbands. She shamelessly flaunted her shame in the face of the city. There was a duel, and the wronged husband was wounded almost to death. The whisper ran of foul play, and of a pistol fired before the handkerchief fell. I think it must have been so, for Sir Valentine was famous for his skill, and the other escaped without a scratch."

"His son—if Maurice Blake be his son—inherits that quality at least," said Lord Edward. "His aim is miraculous."

"The rest of the story is short as sad," the Doctor continued. "Before Sir Valentine was again on his feet his guilty wife and her paramour both disappeared. The man was heard of now and again on a career of reckless vice through Europe. Of the woman nothing afterwards was seen or heard. Into what vile haunts she sank I cannot tell, but the rumour of her death was spread. It grew to be an accepted fact. My broken-hearted friend, Sir Valentine, believed himself a free man. But his freedom availed him little. He was filled with a fierce, unreasoning shame that almost touched his reason. He was a Catholic, and the penal laws had long galled his proud soul. His wife's dishonour made him desperate. It is said that he strove to organise a revolt among the broken-spirited peasants of Connaught, and failed. More than a year before that night on which I stood by his wife's death-bed, in the bleak hospital ward, he had fled to America, leaving his vast estate in Connaught in the hands of his twin brother, who, as time went on with no word from the wanderer, assumed the baronetcy without dispute.

"The wretched woman, who had dishonoured his name and broken his heart, sent for me, not as a doctor but as his nearest friend, who had been by his side on that most unhappy day on which he had made her his wife. She was dying now beyond all doubt, and she knew it. It was pitiful to witness the agony of her remorse. She begged me to beg forgiveness from her injured husband. She felt, she said, that she could not rest in her grave without it. From her own lips I wrote her agonising entreaty for pardon. She signed and dated it with trembling hands, and, tying it in a packet with her marriage certificate and marriage ring, implored me to deliver all safely to her husband, to whom it meant freedom and it might be happiness. I promised, and she thanked me fervently.

"Our conference lasted late into the night. When I called at noon next day she was in her death agony; she died almost as I arrived. I wrote at once to Sir Valentine, whose address I was the one man in Ireland that knew. I received a reply, that set my heart at ease. The very day after his wife's death—seven weeks before my letter was received— he had married a young American girl, to whom he was devoted with all the passionate tenderness of his noble heart. He freely forgave his dead wife. In his great joy there was no room for a bitter thought. He talked, in his letter, about returning to Ireland soon, and begged me to keep safe for him the packet of which I spoke.

"I heard no more. Though I wrote again and again, my letters were returned unopened. A score of years have not chilled my interest in my lost friend. It was in the wild hope of finding him I made this voyage to America, and failed. I heard nothing but vague rumours of his second wife's death and his frenzy and flight. Something was said of immense wealth acquired by a lucky purchase of land close to New York the first year he came out.

"There was talk too of a son; and the name Maurice was mentioned. This son lived, I was told, with his father's foster-brother in the backwoods the life of a trapper until the war broke out, when he joined the insurgents and greatly distinguished himself."

"It is the same; it is the same!" broke in Lord Edward, excitedly—"beyond all doubt the same. The foster-brother's name was Christy Culkin, was it not—a tall, gaunt man?"

"Yes, yes," said the Doctor, smiling at the young fellow's eagerness, even while he shared it. "Honest, uncompromising Christy. Hard and tough as a sprig of shillelagh which has been seasoned for three winters in the kitchen chimney, but with the living sap in his heart still. Assuredly it is the same."

The discovery was a new bond between them all. Norah was, if possible, more excited than the Doctor. She loved to listen to Lord Edward's generous praise of the son of her father's dearest friend. His strength, his skill, his courage, softened by his strange tenderness—above all, his passionate love for the old land —delighted her. To Lord Edward's surprise, she was far more interested in Maurice Blake than in Gertrude Glenmire.

So the last half of the voyage flew swiftly as the wind that sped the good ship to the Irish shore. The three friends, taking coach from Cork to Dublin, slipped safely through the highwaymen that infested the roads, and after a short four days' journey arrived in the Irish metropolis, then the brightest and gayest in Europe.

CHAPTER V.

*"A PLAGUE ON ALL COWARDS SAY I, AND A
VENGEANCE TOO."*
Henry IV. Part I.

> "But now he was returned and that war thoughts
> Had left their places vacant, in their rooms
> Came thronging soft and delicate desires."
Much Ado About Nothing.

> "Thurio, give back, or else embrace thy death.
> Come not within the measure of my wrath;
> Do not name Silvia thine."

THE gallant and noble young soldier, fresh from the wars, speedily became a lion in Dublin society. He was a gay young lion, and the bright Dianas of the Irish capital hunted him gaily. Sweet maidens, shy and sly, shot timid glances from under silken lashes, and the bright eyes of bolder beauties looked straight into his own with an audacious challenge. The life he lived was delightful—it was delirious. Youth and wit and beauty filled the gay Irish capital at the time. In the brilliant debates of the House of Commons he heard from the inspired lips of Henry Grattan the thrilling eloquence of freedom which has reverberated through a hundred years, and which even then stirred the crowd of brilliant, selfish place-hunters who thronged the benches, with something like generous emotion.

Lord Edward entered frankly into the social life of the brilliant capital, where wit and wine flowed with equal freedom ; where Curran, night after night, spread the intellectual feast with the careless, lavish generosity of wealth that was without limit. The coloured light of sparkling fancy played on all things in that bright society, changing them from what they were, and showing them by turns, fantastic, splendid, or grotesque, as the whim of the magician changed. At the theatre there were actors whose skill reached to the height of genius :

> " There Shakespeare's men and women lived in truth,
>   There gaily laughed the wit of Sheridan,
>   And gentle Goldsmith's genial humour smiled."

Life was, for the high-spirited young soldier, one round of enjoyment from morning till night, and, indeed, night and morning too often merged to minister to his enjoyment. Any other man than Lord Edward would have been spoiled by the flattery that followed him everywhere. Above all, the soft, delicious feminine adulation, so delicately administered, was most dangerous. But the simple modesty of his nature was an antidote against the subtle poison, and saved him harmless.

He took his pleasure gaily, and for a while unthinkingly. It is not to be denied that sadder and nobler thoughts, with which Blake, and after Blake, Norah Denver, inspired him, hid away in some inner recess of his heart, were not lost indeed, but half forgotten. As he floated with the current on the bright, warm surface of the stream, he had little thought of the chill and darkness that lay below. Freedom was the fashion in Dublin; the slavery of the people was placidly ignored. Where wealth and luxury flaunted themselves for ever before his eyes, scant blame was his that he could not see the abject want and misery on which the brilliant edifice was built.

Above all, his senses were dazzled and his heart made drunk by the bright eyes and beauty of his old flame—Lady Gertrude Glenmire. The passion which had smouldered in his heart through all changing scenes, was kindled to clear flame by the first glance of those bright eyes. He had neither the art nor the desire to hide his adoration. She received him very graciously, with a gentle tolerance of the ardour of his devotion that was like acceptance. She sedately paraded her conquest with a woman's pride. No one could doubt his passion that watched the rapture of his happy face as they sat whispering together, or swung around in voluptuous motion to the languishing swell of the music in the smooth whirl of the waltz, then a newly-arrived and welcome stranger in Dublin ball-rooms. Lady Glenmire was less demonstrative; but she was gracious, almost tender, especially when they were alone. Her calm voice took a softer tone, her proud eyes shone with gentler light, when he was by.

He lived and moved in the bright domain of love. He dreamt fair dreams of high enterprise and world-wide glory, rounded off by the perfect happiness of home. Every aspiration of his young soul took brighter tints from his love, as a lovely landscape from the golden sunrise. In that brief period of ardent hope he tasted such happiness as never twice falls to mortal's share amid the cold realities of life.

Norah Denver was the chief confidant of his love. Their friendship was not lost in the bright, full tide of passion that flooded his soul. He talked to her of Lady Gertrude by the hour, and she listened patiently, a little amused at first by his love raptures, till her amusement vanished in his earnestness. But he found her somewhat cold in her responses to his ecstasies. She never could be brought to see the celestial wings that sprouted from his angel's shoulders, nor the halo of heavenly light about her head. In Norah's eyes the fair Gertrude was a beautiful woman —very bright, very proud, very cold. She read her character with that keen instinct that women have, which shows in a moment, as with a lightning flash, what reason's slow search still fails to find.

The stately Gertrude, on the other hand, professed a great affection for "the Doctor's daughter," as she called her. " She was so wonderfully well-bred," Lady Glenmire was pleased to say ; " quite wonderful, con-sidering — and then her eccentric notions about the poor and the Papists, and all that sort of thing, lent a certain charm of originality to a character that otherwise, perhaps, ill-natured people might think a little insipid."

Just at this time, when Lord Edward burst like a comet on Dublin society, the Most Noble the Marquis of Dulwich shone there with steady light. Young, handsome, noble (in the sense in which the world uses the word), and of immense wealth, he was the centre around which the matrimonial system of the metropolis—marriageable maidens and match-making matrons—revolved.

Before Lord Edward Fitzgerald had flashed into society, Lord Dulwich had for a time bestowed his well-bred, coldly amorous patronage on Lady Gertrude Glenmire, who for her part held him on and off with half tolerant disdain. He was a young man with no touch of youth's folly or youth's enthusiasm—indolent, graceful, imperturbably dull, and supremely handsome. The smooth, white forehead was, perhaps, a shade too narrow, the bright eyes a shade too closely set, the red lips a shade too thin ; but the most hostile criticism could find no other fault with graceful form or clearly-chiselled features.

True, there was no special expression in his face, unless extreme caution can be called an expression. His languid pursuit of the dowerless Lady Gertrude, had been gradually cooling off when Lord Edward came so suddenly on the scene, and at once eagerly and openly monopolised the brilliant young beauty. The sight of Lord Edward's triumph, the flashing smiles that were showered upon him, seemed to stir

Lord Dulwich's dull blood to something like passion. Jealousy warmed him when love failed.

He renewed his abandoned half pursuit with something as much like ardour as his nature allowed. Lady Gertrude showed not the slightest change of manner, whether he advanced or retired. She politely tolerated him, neither encouraging nor repulsing his attentions. Lord Edward chafed a little against this toleration of a man whom he despised.

But afterwards, when alone with Lord Edward, Lady Gertrude would speak of the insult of this lofty patronage with such bitter scorn, and would flash to her ardent young lover bright eyes eloquent of love, and then all thought of pique and jealousy were burned up in the consuming ardour of his passion.

He had little doubt—indeed, he had been given no cause to doubt—that his love was returned. Half-a-dozen times he resolved to beg the full assurance from her lips. But somehow her "sweet unconsciousness" of his meaning—her sprightly sallies that sent the talk wandering off in gay channels, while the earnest words of love were just trembling into utterance—always balked his purpose until the opportunity was gone by.

One night Lord Edward had been to see Kemble at the theatre. The play was *Romeo and Juliet*, which is so warmed and illumined throughout with the fire of love. The great actor seemed to give eloquent voice and words to the young lover's own thoughts. In Juliet he saw his own love was personified. Through the changing scenes he knelt in spirit at her feet and worshipped her. The tragic close filled him with a strange grief, as if the tragedy were his own.

With a heart full of love thoughts he turned from the theatre in a delicious reverie—half joy, half sadness—that made him all unconscious of the squalour of his surroundings.

So he splashed unconcernedly through the dark and dirty streets, where the few dun oil lamps smoked and sputtered, his soul a myriad miles away (so great the distance of bright fancy from sordid truth), till the lights and noise of revelry bursting from the open doors of Lucas's famous coffee house recalled him to himself. It brought to his mind at the same moment a midnight appointment there with his friend Arthur O'Connor, afterwards a prime mover in the rebellion of "'98."

At a table close beside Lord Edward's, though he did not at first notice them, were seated, tippling claret, Lord Dulwich and a couple of the gaudily dressed bucks, "rough to common men but honeying at the whisper of a lord," who revolved perpetually around the wealthy nobleman, and plied him with coarse flattery, which his soul loved.

To Lord Edward, in his present mood, the crowded and noisy coffee-room was silent and solitary as vacant space. His soul was away at Gertrude Glenmire's feet, pouring out the full torrent of his love. He had neither eye nor ear for anything around him.

Suddenly, however, the name of his beloved, uttered in an arrogant voice that rang through the whole room, startled him from his reverie, as if a pistol-shot was fired off close to his head.

He listened, scarcely believing his ears. The voice was Lord Dulwich's. Lord Edward only just caught the name with which the sentence closed. Another voice, louder and coarser than the first, took up the theme, in words that cut him like a sword's edge.

" Be cautious, my lord," it cried, " be cautious, she's a tricksy jade with all her fine airs. She will come up to heel when you choose to whistle for her right enough, still——"

Here Lord Dulwich's voice broke in again, more angry and arrogant from the wine and flattery he had swallowed during the evening.

" Silence, Roche," he shouted. " Silence! I will not have you speak in that tone of a lady whom I admire. It is no fault in her, a merit rather, that she should aspire to the honour of my hand."

Lord Edward's right hand shook, so that the glass that he held to his lips sprinkled the red drops on the cloth. His face was pale as the white damask. His eyes blazed with passion, but he mastered himself by a tremendous effort. He put the glass down softly, and walked very quietly to the table where Lord Dulwich sat.

By his lordship's side lay a newspaper then much patronised by the Castle. His elbow rested on it. Without a word of request or apology Lord Edward laid hold of a corner of the paper and jerked it roughly away.

Lord Dulwich felt the rude jerk, and turning sharply around, caught sight of Lord Edward's pale face. For a moment he thought the young lord was drunk, and on that hint he spoke:

" How dare you," he broke out furiously, forgetting his drawl in his fury. "You insolent young——"

Here he met Lord Edward's eyes. The real motive of the deliberate insult suddenly flashed upon him, and he broke off abashed in the middle of a sentence.

But he had said quite enough for the other's purpose. Very deliberately Lord Edward drew off his glove, and, holding it by one finger, struck him twice across the face with it.

In an instant Lord Dulwich sprang to his feet and clapped his hand on his sword-hilt. The brace of bucks, both famous brawlers, were up with him, their ready swords half out of their scabbards. A fight seemed imminent—three to one—but behind Lord Edward, Arthur O'Connor appeared, with his customary quiet smile on his resolute face.

At the sight the swaggerers' swords clattered back into their scabbards.

Lord Edward was quite cool, now that his object was obtained. He bowed with stern courtesy to Lord Dulwich.

" You require satisfaction, my lord," he said gently, in reply to a hoarse muttering of his enemy, whose

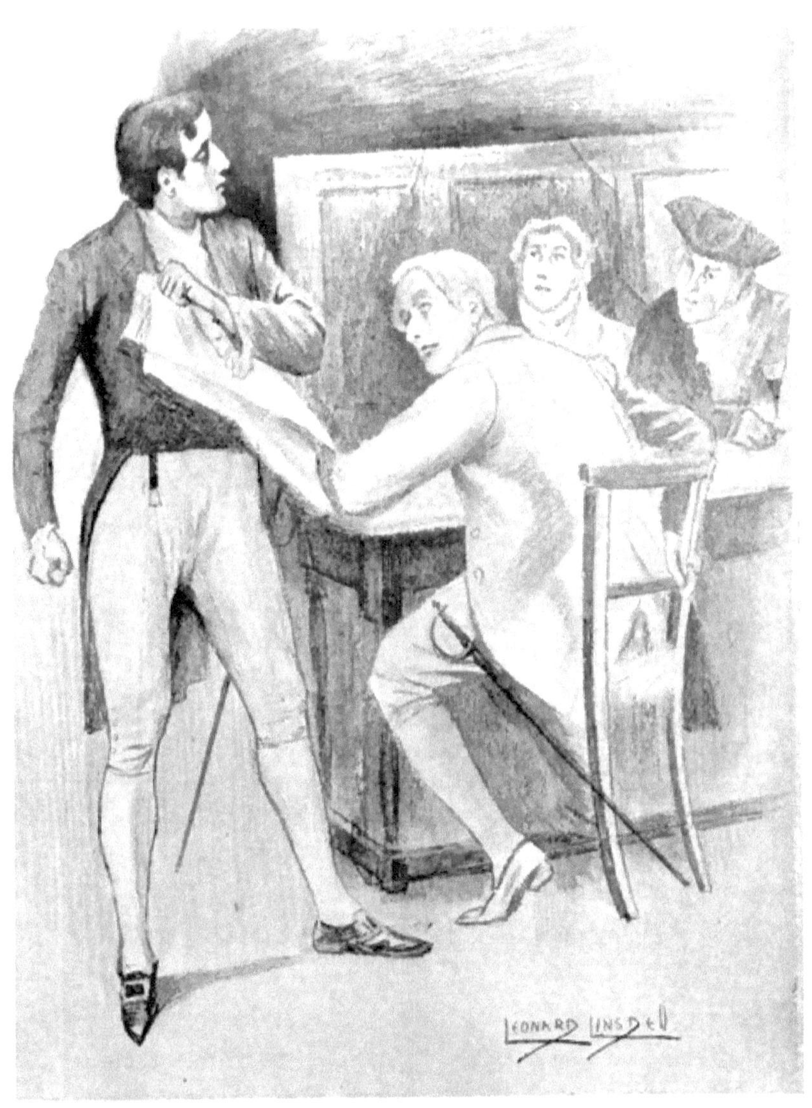

"Jerked it roughly away."

face was convulsed with passion. "You shall have it. My friend, Mr. Arthur O'Connor, will arrange with any friend of yours."

"Arthur," he continued to O'Connor, in a lower tone, "no accommodation is possible; let the meeting be to-morrow. I will tell you all later on. I know you will say I could not do otherwise than I have done. You will find me at my lodgings in Jervis Street."

With another bow, deeper than the last, to the astounded Lord Dulwich, he slipped away.

An hour later, O'Connor found Lord Edward pacing his sitting-room in Jervis Street in a fever of excitement. All the self-restraint which he had shown in the presence of the enemy had disappeared. Youth, and hot blood, and outraged love, and a feverish thirst for vengeance quite mastered him.

"Well, well, O'Connor," he cried, impatiently, as his friend entered.

"The meeting is to be to-morrow morning," O'Connor replied, still imperturbable; "at sunrise, in the Park, the weapons swords. Now, tell me why you fight. Surely not on account of that wretched newspaper you tore in pieces between you."

In a few words, Lord Edward told him the real cause of the quarrel.

"A duel to the death," said O'Connor, shortly. "I am sorry for it. His second insisted on swords. Of course you, as the challenged, had the choice of weapons. But he urged that your insult was so gross it was itself a challenge, and I could not gainsay him."

While he spoke he strode up and down the room impatiently, his coolness gone. Right well Lord Edward knew what was in his mind. As a swordsman Lord Dulwich had no equal, even in Dublin, where the fencing school and the pistol gallery were the chief fashionable resorts. It was generally rumoured that his valet was a fencing master, and that fencing was not merely the amusement but the occupation of his lordship's life. His reputation had hitherto saved him from many a challenge, which his dull arrogance might have provoked. There was no fencing master in Dublin that could save himself from the point of that deadly rapier. The most skilful amateur had no chance at all. Lord Edward himself had tried a bout with the foils more than once. But, though himself a brilliant swordsman, he could make no stand against Lord Dulwich. The button of that deadly foil slipped past his guard with clean sharp prod, while he could never once touch his dull, self-complacent opponent, who coldly exulted in his discomfiture. The narrow, restless strip of flexible steel covered Lord Dulwich as securely as a shield.

Clearly O'Connor had it in his mind that his friend would have but a poor chance for his life against this man, pitiless and malignant, as he was diabolically skilful with his weapon. His cold, dull nature, raised to a white heat of passion by the public insult, could be appeased only by the life-blood of the man who insulted him.

So O'Connor thought, and the thought filled him with fear and sorrow, for he loved Lord Edward Fitzgerald like a brother.

After a few abortive efforts to hide his fears, O'Connor left abruptly, with a promise to be punctual in the morning.

Lord Edward was glad to be alone. Yet, it is no disparagement to his courage to say that his thoughts were dismal company. He had faced death often on the battlefield, not merely without fear but with delight. But this was different — quite different. There was no fierce excitement to sustain him now. No wonder the warm blood of youth ran cold in his veins as he paced the silent room alone, waiting for the dawn and, with the dawn, death. He had little hope of escape. It would need a miracle to save him. He had tried his best in the fencing school against Lord Dulwich quite in vain. The other's deadly sword point had slipped past his guard again and again, impalpable as a lightning flash.

With the button off the foils, each thrust meant death. Right well he knew that Dulwich would not spare him, yet if one word of regret would have averted the duel, it would not have been spoken. Nay, the humblest apology from the lips of the man who had blasphemed the name of Gertrude Glenmire would have been spurned with scorn. But the thought of death was very bitter. He was so young and happy, and the world stretched out fair and bright before him, lit up with glorious hopes.

Love and glory mingled in his thoughts. His whole soul rebelled against the dull oblivion of death. The bitter thought to which the greatest of poets has given words ached at his heart.

> " To die ; to go we know not where ;
> To lie in cold obstruction, and to rot.
> This sensible warm motion to become
> A kneaded clod."

He strove to pierce the mystery of death into which he was about to enter, but his mind shrank back appalled from the thick darkness.

At length, late in the silent night, he grew weary with restless pacing and more restless thought, and sat down to a writing table in the corner of the room. His first letter was to his mother. Curiously enough, it was to her, not to the fair girl he so passionately loved, that his thoughts turned. He felt, in a vague way, that he was wronging her most by this duel, making her an ill return for her infinite tenderness. Her gentle, pleading face was before him. The lines of an old poem he had read and forgotten refashioned themselves into words in his mind—

> " As a fair pictured face whose eyes appear,
> With watchful love, to follow everywhere,
> So tenderly, so patiently, your care,
> Followed my life through every changing year."

Now for the love of another woman, he was about to break the close tie between them, and break her loving heart. With self-torturing fancy, he pictured his mother's agony when she gazed on his body, with a sword thrust through its bosom, while he, the cause of all her sorrow, lay there dull and still, with no power to utter a word of comfort.

His letter was an almost incoherent outpouring of protestations of love, and a passionate pleading for pardon. His last thought, he told her, would be hers, if it were doomed, as he feared, they should meet no more.

The letter to Lady Gertrude was shorter, yet far more difficult. It was not until he began to write to her for the first time in his life that he realised how formal after all had been their intercourse, and how far aloof it had been kept from any word of love. He felt it impossible to break out suddenly in hot protestations of passion. His letter in spite of himself ran at first into formal phrases that seemed so dull and cold in such an hour. But as he wrote the passion that was burning in his heart forced itself to the surface. He stood so near death that he could write with all freedom. His very despair gave power and pathos to his words. Standing by the grave's brink he told her simply and honestly of his great love.

The letters were directed and sealed ready for delivery by O'Connor, if the worst chanced.

The dismal thoughts that the writing had broken

for a time—the vague, cold shrinking from death, which even the bravest feel when death is faced without excitement—returned upon him. But, strange as it may seem, merciful sleep came and checked these dreary thoughts, even in full tide. Overtaxed nature gave way. His head drooped back upon the chair, his nerveless arms fell by his side: his weary eyes closed; the restless brain was at rest; his whole being passed into an oblivion as complete, while it lasted, as the death which he anticipated with so much awe.

He was awakened by a light touch on his shoulder, as he fancied, a moment afterwards. In reality he had slept for some hours. Arthur O'Connor was bending over him with a grave face. There were lights on the breakfast table, for the early morning was misty and cheerless.

"I have let you sleep to the last moment," O'Connor said, with an attempt at cheerfulness. "You will want all your nerve and strength, and please God they will yet carry you safe through."

He glanced at the letters on the writing table, and broke off abruptly—

"You will deliver them if need be," said Lord Edward.

"There will be no need," O'Connor tried to answer, but his sad thought so belied the words that he could not speak them. He only nodded as he thrust the letters into his bosom.

As silently they took their places at the breakfast

table. It was a dismal meal at best; but Lord Edward, whose spirits came back with the prospect of immediate action, was the brighter of the two. He strove to cheer up his friend, who, knowing the deadly skill of Dulwich, felt as if it were a funeral, not a duel, he was about to attend.

As they passed out into the raw, misty morning air a chill that was not altogether from the cold struck through Lord Edward's heart. He would never look on the sun again, was the thought that flashed through his mind. He longed to see once more the fair earth's face before he left it. He felt that the drizzling grey mist had cheated him out of his last hour of sunshine.

At the street door two sedan chairs waited, the bearers smoking short pipes and speculating in an undertone about the "jewel" for which some instinct told them their services were required.

Without a word, Lord Edward and his second slipped into the chairs, and the bearers, who had been already apprised of their destination, set off at a sling trot for the Phœnix Park, their heavy boots splashing dismally through the muddy streets.

They were first in the field, but they had hardly alighted on the spongy sod, and their chair-men withdrawn into the cover of the trees, when the splash of hurrying feet was heard at a little distance, and two other chairs came lumbering along through the murky fog.

The occupants alighted hastily, and walked towards Lord Edward and his companion, looming preternaturally large in the grey mist.

With Lord Dulwich was Captain Baker, one of his boon companions of the previous evening. Baker's pretensions to the title of captain (if he had any at all) were in the past tense. Nor was there any definite information forthcoming as to what regiment he had belonged to, or how he left it. But he was a well set-up, military looking man. His strong figure was a little fleshy, and his light blue eyes a little watery, and a brighter red than health generally gives flushed his handsome face. For the rest, he could rattle a dice-box, crack a bottle, or use sword or pistol with the best. Lord Dulwich had found him useful. Captain Baker flattered and fought for him before his face, and abused him as a cold-blooded skinflint behind his back, after the customary manner of the led captain.

Captain Baker was beaming all over with good humour. His rubicund face shone like the sun through the mist. The meeting was entirely to his liking. To be engaged in a duel with two lords as principals, and a man of the high position of Arthur O'Connor as second, was to him a rare social distinction. He had no fear for his patron, for he knew his unrivalled skill as a swordsman, and if he killed his man the Captain hoped to make their companionship in trouble profitable.

He beamed all round as he came up with his arm tucked into Lord Dulwich's, who on ordinary occasions would never have tolerated such familiarity.

"We are well up to time," he said, addressing O'Connor, who coldly nodded in return to his elaborate salute, "but, by G—, you are before us. Impatient to get to work, I suppose. Well, the sooner we begin the sooner we will get done."

He made a half-pass with his walking cane as he spoke, and then a motion of falling back, with his left hand pressed to his side in a way that was horrible suggestive.

Captain Baker laughed out loud at his own pleasant conceit, but Lord Dulwich frowned, and jerking his arm from his, stepped back a pace, without any response by word or motion to the formal salute of Lord Edward and his friend.

"Impatient to get his grip on the sword-hilt," said the Captain in a confidential undertone to O'Connor, nodding his head sideways towards his principal. "Your friend had best look out. He is in a dangerous humour. Means mischief, if ever a man did."

"My friend is quite ready," said O'Connor, sharply, yet not without an inward thrill at the thought of the almost certain death which Lord Edward was about to encounter.

"All right," replied the beaming Captain Baker, with undiminished good humour. "I have got the toothpicks convenient," and he took two rapiers in their scabbards from under his arm and presented them to O'Connor. "As the weapons are ours, the choice is yours."

O'Connor drew and examined the two splendid swords from Lord Dulwich's armoury. Even at that moment he felt a transient touch of admiration at the exquisite finish of the bright, tapering blades, whose points were as fine as a wasp's sting. He weighed them in his hand, and bent and measured them carefully.

There was not a feather's weight or a hair's breadth between them.

Courteously he held the hilts out to Captain Baker, who laid his hand carelessly on the nearest, and presented it with a bow and flourish to Lord Dulwich.

O'Connor handed the other to Lord Edward. "Caution," he whispered—"I need not say courage —and all will go well."

There was a tremor in his usually calm voice as he spoke.

But there was no tremor in the strong, resolute young hand that grasped the sword-hilt. As Lord Edward's fingers closed on the weapon, and he saw his foe in front of him, the fierce passion of battle at once took complete possession of his head, and left no room for other feeling.

The two men faced each other warily, and steel rasped on steel as their swords met, and they felt each other's deadly purpose along the quivering blades. For a second or so they stood as motionless as statues, the sharp points, which meant death, scarce half a foot from either breast, and the deadly will behind each sword to drive it home.

Even in that brief space Lord Edward, while he read in his enemy's eyes his fell intent, noted that his face was deadly pale, and that his thin, tight lips twitched convulsively as with concentrated rage. Lord Dulwich, he was assured, meant death.

He grew more than ever on his guard. Making his sword point spin in a half circle back and forward, like lightning, he feinted cautiously, in *tierce*, ready for a deadly thrust in return, which would test all his skill and quickness to parry.

But no return thrust came. Lord Dulwich gave ground a step, feebly parried Lord Edward's pass, and stood on the defensive. Surprised and fearing some trick of the game, Lord Edward stepped forward, engaged his sword, then in *quinte* lunged again.

The parade was feebler than before. Lord Dulwich's sword was held so loosely that it rattled against his opponent's blade. Utterly amazed, Lord Edward pressed forward now with determined purpose on his retreating foe. He glanced once more at the pale face, marked the white lips and stifly eyes. Then the truth dawned on him suddenly.

Lord Dulwich was a *coward*.

That marvellous skill of his was lost in craven fear. He, the matchless master of his weapon, was helpless as a schoolboy whose hand had never closed on sword's hilt before.

Lord Edward's anger vanished in a moment. Contempt took its place. He could not kill the coward at his mercy. He played with him for a while, and tortured him with terror. A dozen times the faltering guard left the craven breast open to a fatal thrust, but Lord Edward forewent his advantage.

At length he dexterously caught his foeman's blade in his own, and with a quick twist wrenched it from his feeble grasp, and sent it flying straight into the air. The sword fell on the sharp point, and buried itself halfway to the hilt in the sodden earth. Lord Edward drew it out, passed the mud-stained blade through his cambric handkerchief, presented the hilt to Lord Dulwich, and instantly stood again on guard. But Lord Dulwich dropped his point to the earth, and stepped out of reach of Lord Edward's threatening steel.

The whole incident passed like a flash. Now the seconds closed in on either side.

Before they could interpose Lord Edward spoke sternly.

"Sir," he said, addressing his shambling foe, and forgetting or ignoring his title, "this is no pleasant passage of arms between us two. It is a duel to the death. You must apologise or fight on."

The seconds, now near at hand, heard Lord Edward's words. Arthur O'Connor smiled that grim smile of his. The hand of Captain Barker, who, whatever his faults were, was no coward, went down on his sword hilt. He turned fiercely to his principal waiting his indignant defiance.

But no defiance came. Lord Dulwich was silent for a full minute. His pale face was distorted with passion. Fear and rage were struggling for mastery. Fear won.

"I humbly apologise," he said, and held out his hand scarcely knowing what he did.

Lord Edward looked at him for a moment with contemptuous wonder—ignoring the offered hand. Then, dropping the sword on the ground, he turned from the place.

O'Connor, still smiling, nodded to Captain Barker. "Our work is over," he said, and followed Lord Edward to his chair.

The unfortunate Captain was quite dumbfounded, all his fine swagger was gone. He shared the disgrace of his principal, and felt it the more acutely of the two. He turned his back upon the coward, who stood stock-still, dangling his sword. But the spark of honourable shame went out in a moment, finding no fuel in a heart sodden by a long life of meanness and vice. The Captain saw that the incident which proved his patron a coward had made him his master.

Turning sharp around, he clapped him on the shoulder boisterously, as he had never dared to do before, and bade him remember the raw mist was as dangerous as a sword thrust. "A drop of brandy is what you need, my lord, to take the chill off," he said, with no attempt to disguise the sarcasm in his voice.

Looking back, Arthur O'Connor noticed that Lord Dulwich carried both swords to the sedan chair, and that Captain Barker swaggered by his side with the air of a patron.

By this time the morning had begun to clear. A warm, white spot showed itself in the east, where the sun ought to be. The veil of mist lifted slowly from the green wooded slopes of the Park, and patches of faint blue were seen in the pale sky.

"We will walk, Arthur, if you do not object," said Lord Edward, who tingled all over with restless excitement.

The chair-men, who had watched the combat with the keenest interest, were dismissed with a handsome gratuity, and went trotting into town to spread the news of the "jewel," with what embellishments seemed good to them, and the two friends strode rapidly along the broad road that runs through the beautiful park.

Neither spoke for a little, though the companionship was inexpressibly pleasant to both. Arthur O'Connor was habitually silent. The delight that throbbed in Lord Edward's heart could find no words to utter itself. His passion had passed away, as the sword-hilt dropped from his hand. There was nothing of anger in the contempt with which Lord Dulwich was now regarded. The wild re-action from the dismal forebodings of an hour before, was full upon him. The young life which he had given over as lost, thrilled deliciously through his frame, even to his finger-tips. Never before had the beautiful world appeared so beautiful.

The sun breaking its way through the mist dissolved it in pure blue. The green sward, vivid from the recent rain, stretched away in wide slopes or in long vistas through the darker green of the trees. Across the valley the Dublin mountains began to outline themselves clear against the soft blue of the morning sky. Lord Edward's eyes drank in the scene delightedly, until he sighed in that vague pain—that excess of rapture—which all lovers of nature have felt in the vain effort to stretch their souls to the full possession of its beauty.

O'Connor heard the half sigh, and without a word he handed Lord Edward the two letters written the night before.

Without a word Lord Edward tore them to little pieces and scattered the bits in the light wind, where they went fluttering away behind him like a small snow storm.

" There go death and grief," he said, as he watched them—" welcome life and happiness."

" And love?" said O'Connor, with a note of interrogation in his voice.

Lord Edward blushed like a school girl in her teens—for the word had touched the thought that was in his heart.

F

"Yes, love!" he answered shyly, yet defiantly. "There is no shame, surely, in loving *her*.

"Oh! Arthur, that that coward"—with an emphasis on the word coward as if he would spurn it—"should dare to take her name in vain.

"Yet, do you know," he continued, after a pause, "I was a coward myself last night. I was a coward again this morning. But it was not life I feared to lose, but her love."

"You did not strike me as being so desperately frightened when your swords crossed," said the other, smiling.

"Oh! I was all right when I got hold of the sword. All the old fighting spirit came back with a rush, but never in my life have I thought of death as I thought of it last night."

"No wonder," responded O'Connor gravely. "I thought of it, too. If Dulwich's nerve was equal to his skill and his malice, I would be carrying home a corpse with a sword-thrust through its bosom, instead of walking by your side."

He laid his hand affectionately on the other's shoulder as he spoke, with a gesture that told more eloquently than words could, what had been his anxiety, and what was his relief.

"Thank you, Arthur," said Lord Edward, simply replying in words to the brief, kindly pressure of his hand. "But let us drop dismal thoughts and topics. I feel as if I had got a new lease of life, and mean to enjoy it. We will dine together to-day, wherever you will.   I am bidden to a reception at Mountjoy's in the evening.   Will you be there?"

"Will Lady Gertrude be there?"

Again the light blush came.

"I see," continued O'Connor, drily.   "I fancy you will be able to get along without my company in the drawing-room or garden of Henrietta Street."

CHAPTER VI.

*"THAT SHE SHOULD LOVE THIS FELLOW AND
REFUSE ME."*

Cymbeline.

"Look here, upon this picture and on this.
  Could you on this fair mountain leave to feed,
  And batten on this moor?   Ha ! have you eyes?
  You cannot call it love."—*Hamlet.*

THE day succeeding the morning of the duel
dawned the brightest of Lord Edward's life.
Every simple pleasure had a new zest for him.   The
happy escape of the morning, the anticipated rapture
of the evening, pervaded with delight the day that
lay between the two.   It is from hope or memory,
mainly, that happiness shines upon our lives, and his
was radiant then with that reflected light.

"One more glass of claret before you go," said
O'Connor—they had dined together at his cosy
quarters; "its colour is more rosy than your lady's
lips, and its breath more delicately sweet.   Aye,"
he added beneath his breath, "and the glow in its
heart is warmer and more pure."

"I will drink to her standing," cried Lord Edward.
"Drink, O'Connor, to Lady Gertrude, and wish me
success, old friend, for I try my fortune to-night."

"Lady Gertrude," cried both the young men together, and quaffed a bumper of the bright, red wine, and tossed the tinkling glasses over their shoulders, so that no meaner toast might ever more dishonour them. "She must have a heart of ice if she resist you," thought O'Connor, as he glanced admiringly at the figure before him, in its full court suit of rich velvet and brocaded silk, the handsome young face radiant with happiness and love.

He clasped Lord Edward's hand warmly and bade him God speed and good fortune, and the other went down the steps three at a time to the sedan chair that stood at the door, with, close at hand, the linkboy with torch alight, to guide it through the darkness.

Arthur O'Connor, left alone, filled himself another bumper of the rare, ripe claret, of flavour smooth as liquid velvet. "It will wound him sorely if she refuse," he murmured, "and yet I almost hope she may refuse. Better one hot, sharp pang of grief and anger than have that warm, loving heart of his slowly frozen in his breast, wasting its warmth on ice unthawable."

No such thought was in Lord Edward's heart, as his chair lumbered and swayed along through the dark thoroughfares towards Lord Mountjoy's stately mansion in Henrietta Street. He went to woo the most peerless woman that ever breathed on God's earth, and hope promised him the perfect happiness of success.

Henrietta Street's broad slope was filled with

stately equipages and all ablaze with flaming torches. The light and motion converged towards the door of the stately mansion at the head of the street, where in the great hall, marble paved in squares black and white, like a huge chessboard, Lord Mountjoy received his guests.

Here Lord Edward was cordially met and welcomed, and with the gay crowd passed up the broad staircase to the drawing-room. It was a scene to stir his young blood. Never a nation in the world understood better than the Irish the art of magnificent hospitality.

The spacious chamber was one great glow of colour and light, for in those days the gentlemen vied with the ladies in brilliant tints and flashing jewels. There was a murmur of feminine admiration as Lord Edward entered. The chair-men's tongues had been busy from early morning, and the whisper of that duel of his in the Phœnix with the most skilful swordsman in Dublin, had crept on and up until it reached the brilliant assembly at Lord Mountjoy's.

Bright eyes, blue and black, glanced admiringly at the slight, graceful figure of the lordly young hero who had risked life so gallantly for the smiles—so ran the rumour—of a woman.

"Welcome, my lord," said a deep, pleasant voice close beside. "Accept my congratulations on a danger met and conquered. Courage is the first quality Ireland expects from Irishmen."

It was a grave, middle-aged man, in sombre-hued velvet, that spoke; a man with a clean-cut aquiline face, and eyes that blazed like an eagle's, but with a winning smile for all that, and a pleasant softness in his voice.

Lord Edward blushed with pleasure, and bowed in silence, for a kind word from Henry Grattan was something to be proud of.

The little man with the brilliant, ugly face, and eyes like sparkling jewels, to whom Grattan had just been talking, broke in abruptly——

"If his tongue proves as sharp as his sword's point," he said, "and he wield it as dexterously, he will be a valuable ally, Henry, or a dangerous enemy, as the case may prove."

"I fear the sword is more my weapon than the tongue," said Lord Edward, modestly. "But sword or tongue, for whatever they may be worth, will ever be at Henry Grattan's service in Ireland's cause."

"A new volunteer movement," cried Curran, smiling. "Lord Edward is your first recruit."

"Pray God Ireland may not soon need to claim her sons' services again with voice and sword," said Grattan, very gravely.

His words, though quietly spoken, rang out with ominous clearness through the room, for a sudden silence had for a moment fallen on the assembly. All the pretty murmur of the ball-room was hushed.

Turning sharp around to find the cause, Lord

Edward saw his late opponent at the door at which he had himself just entered, and on his arm hung the proud and beautiful Lady Gertrude. Their entrance had startled the assembly into silence.

Lord Dulwich was, perhaps, a shade paler than usual, but faultlessly dressed and icily cool. He glanced with languid apathy around the room, and the looks of scorn that the proud-spirited Dublin girls flung at him were quenched in his cold unconsciousness. Yet it seemed as if a tinge of red crept into his pale cheek, as one saucy blue-eyed beauty of sixteen murmured under her breath, as he passed, the words of a gay new song much in vogue at the time—

> "For a laggard in love, and a dastard in war,
> Is to wed the fair Gertrude of our young Lochinvar."

Lord Edward's heart gave a great leap and stood still, as he saw those two cross the room together— the woman whom he so loved, the man whom he scorned too much to hate. But he was comforted to see that Lady Gertrude's lovely face wore a look of cold contempt, and that she scarcely spoke at all to her companion.

When the delicate music of the violins swelled softly through the great room and she swept by in the stately minuet, she flashed upon Lord Edward for a moment a glance and smile warmer and more appealing than she had ever granted him before, and his heart was flooded in a moment almost to overflowing with vague wild hopes and longings.

He waited his opportunity. It came soon. It almost seemed she made it for him. She spoke a few words quietly to Lord Dulwich, who bowed with that cold, impassive face of his, and left her side bound, doubtless, on some errand, real or feigned, for the imperious beauty.

A look and a gesture so slight that it could be noticed only by love's keen eyes called Lord Edward to the vacant place.

Lady Gertrude gathered up her rustling tabinet skirts of deep crimson to make room on the sofa beside her, and greeted him with a welcoming smile.

He was very pale. It was his way when intensely moved. His heart beat so quick and hard that he could hear nothing but its beating. He was dizzy with delight. He felt through every pulsation of his veins that she loved him, and his life-blood was warm with that delicious certainty.

Her greeting was calm and common-place, so far as words went, but there was a gentleness in her tones that seemed to give it a special meaning. Her beauty spoke for her with wondrous eloquence.

Then the music struck up again a languishing strain, and they rose and took their places in the minuet—the sweet, decorous, graceful minuet, so far removed from the swinging waltzes and jigging polkas of modern times—so befitting the timid sanctity of first love, which is less passion than worship.

As they danced, lending the poetry of motion to

the poetry of music, whispers buzzed about the room that Lady Gertrude had found a heart to lose at last, and that Lord Edward had conquered in more than a duel. The girls felt, perhaps, a little twinge of disappointment that he "was lost," and matrons a little thrill of delight that Lord Dulwich "was safe."

After the dance Lord Edward and his partner left the ball-room, and walked down the broad marble staircase together. Her small hand resting lightly on his arm made the blood course hotly through his veins.

But he had recovered from the first delirium of delight, and was able to fling back light answer and jest to her careless gossip about the doings of their little world. Never a hint was there on either side of the morning's duel, of which all Dublin was talking.

While light talk and laughter played about the surface of Lord Edward's mind, in its depths was formed the resolve that this evening should decide his fate. This evening, so he fondly hoped, would assure him of the love for which his soul so thirsted.

They sat and chatted in the panelled reception room, a little apart from the other guests, but still within range of curious eyes. He could not ask her there to be his wife. The question seemed too solemn, too removed from the common-places of the world. He longed for the open air and solitude.

"They passed out into the garden, and paced together down the moonlit walk."

So they passed out into the garden, and paced together down the moonlit walk. Lady Gertrude moved with him, docile as a child. They still talked lightly on gay topics that stirred the gay capital. But Lord Edward's voice at times faltered a little, and his laughter was broken by a sigh.

Halfway down the garden they came upon an arbour over which the bushy woodbine clambered, filling the space within with sweetness.

There was silence for a little as they sat close together on the rustic seat. Lady Gertrude, who had heretofore kept the conversation moving, made no effort to sustain it. Lord Edward could not speak. He was weak and trembling. He had often thought how eloquently he would plead his passion if such chance offered him. Now, he sat dumb. The silence grew painful. At last, with a great effort, he broke it in the old words that have been spoken so many million times and will be spoken so many more.

"Gertrude," he faltered out appealingly, "I love you. Oh! you must know how dearly I love you. Will you be my wife?"

He caught her hand and clasped it in both his own as he spoke. Very gently she withdrew it.

"Oh! Gertrude," he went on, for he found words now. "I · know I am not worthy of you. But my love is worthy of you, my darling. There is no such love in the world as mine."

She was still silent, and fear struck cold to his heart.

"Gertrude! Gertrude!" he cried in a pitiful voice, like one begging for life, "answer me, at least. Tell me my fate. Do not kill me by despair."

His voice seemed to touch her a little. Very gently she answered: "It cannot be, my lord. It grieves me to say it, but it cannot be. I feel proud of your love. I will feel glad of your friendship, but I can never be your wife."

"Do not speak so hastily, Gertrude," he entreated, with love's inconsistency. "I only ask hope—faint and distant though it be; and hope I will have until I hear from your own lips you love another."

"That you will never hear," she said——

He caught her hand again and she left it in his clasp—but she went on steadily, "I love no other; but hope for you there is none. Edward," she said more softly, "if I could love, I believe, I would have loved you; if I could have married for love I would have married you."

At this he would have raised the white hand he held to his lips, but she plucked it away.

"Hear me out. I speak frankly, because it is not likely that you and I will speak much together for the future. I am glad of the chance of a parting word. I have searched my heart. There is no love in it for you—for anyone—there never will be. To me the word is meaningless. You talk to me in a strange language when you talk to me of love. I have weighed this love of yours against wealth, power, and ambition; I found it wanting. In a way,

I am proud of the passion my beauty inspires. I am glad you have spoken of love. Now we must part till you have learned to forget it."

"No, Gertrude," he cried, the more passionately for her calmness. "We must not part. You wrong yourself—you wrong your own heart. I will not give up the hope that you may yet learn to love me."

They had risen, and were standing at the entrance of the arbour. She would have passed out. He made an effort to detain her.

"This is folly," she said, "and worse than folly. For both our sakes it must end. I take you at your word then. I am the promised wife of another."

"His name! his name!" Lord Edward cried, with fierce anger in his tones, yet not without hope that it was but a stratagem of Lady Gertrude to escape.

A voice answered that killed all hope.

"Gertrude!" it said, speaking out of the shadow of the summer-house. "I think the next dance is ours. I have waited to the last moment before disturbing you."

It was Lord Dulwich spoke. There was a cool tone of insolent authority and possession in his voice that stung Lord Edward with a sudden pang. It was the answer to his question. The next instant Lord Dulwich stepped into the circle of light, and, ignoring the other's presence, with a glance as cold and as unconscious as the moonbeam, he offered his arm to Lady Gertrude.

She paused a moment, half stretched her hand to Lord Edward, but, noticing how pale and rigid he stood, she dropped it to her side, and, with a gracious, stately inclination of her beautiful head, she took the arm of her affianced husband, and moved with him down the moonlit walk with face impassive as his own.

Only a faint quiver of his thin lips, and a touch of colour in his pale cheek, showed how keenly the coward enjoyed his cowardly revenge.

CHAPTER VII.

" THE PANGS OF DESPISED LOVE."

Hamlet.

" And writers say, as the most forward bud
    Is eaten by the canker ere it blow,
    E'en so by love the young and tender wit
    Is turned to folly, blasting in the bud,
    Losing his verdure even in his prime
    And all the fair effects of future hopes."

Two Gentlemen of Verona.

" How use doth breed a habit in a man,
    This shadowy desert, unfrequented woods,
    I better brook than flourishing peopled towns."

Two Gentlemen of Verona.

TO all outward seeming there was no change in Lord Edward Fitzgerald. His life ran its old routine course from day to day. In society the smile and gay jest were still constant on his lips. It has happened to men in the hunting-field, having fallen heavily and suffered grievous injuries, to remount and ride to the death, conscious only of a dull pain. So it fared with Lord Edward now. The savour and sweetness had gone out of his life. There was a dull, aching sense of something lost for ever in his heart, of which he was vaguely conscious even when he seemed most gay. Yet ever and again remembrance forced itself to the surface of his mind in a throb of keenest agony.

Slowly the news filtered through society that Lady Gertrude had " captured " Lord Dulwich. So society ladies were unkind enough to express it. Men and women were curious to see how Lord Edward would bear the news; for his passion had been no secret. It was hard to have curious eyes watching his face, and curious ears listening to his lightest words, but he never winced. His colour never changed, his voice never faltered, while all round him society prattled of the coming marriage.

He bore his wound bravely, silently, alone, making no sign; but day by day it grew harder to bear. Close observers might see that his eye was losing its brightness and his cheek its colour. In quiet despair he faced and fought his sorrow as resolutely as he faced the enemy in the field; but he struggled without hope. Life had no longer a purpose or enjoyment for him. He had the longing that the wounded bird or beast has for solitude and rest.

As the days slipped by that longing grew too strong to be resisted. He was sick of society, his Parliamentary duties he had neglected, his regiment was stationed abroad. There was no habit or duty for the anchor of resolution to hold to.

Without a word of warning or parting, even to his mother, whom he tenderly loved, he slipped down by coach from Dublin to Cork, got on board the good ship *Adventurer*, and turned his face once more to the New World, in whose lone wilds he thought his sorrow might find breathing space.

It was a breezy, sunshiny morning when they cleared the harbour. The fresh breeze blew out of the east. The gallant ship spread wide her woven wings, and glided over the bar, out across the measureless expanse of ocean. Swift and smooth she sped, as the sea-gull when he cleaves the air with motionless wings outstretched.

Very dismal was the contrast to Lord Edward between his outward and homeward voyage. Then everything delighted him—now nothing. His youth was struck down and stunned by the fatal blow. All its intense perceptions were dulled to careless apathy. The beauties of the sea and sky brought him not pleasure, but pain. Since he loved he could see no beauty with his own eyes only. Then was ever the thought of her by his side, sharing his admiration and delight. The ghost of that lost hope tortured him.

At times as he gazed out over the flashing expanse of water, when the sun sank in unutterable glory, filling the hollow globe of sea and sky with light and colour, he would turn to look into her eyes; he would stretch his hand to touch hers. Then sharp remembrance smote him, and his delight perished in pain.

A thousand dreams which he had dreamed of a happy home with Gertrude by his side made his waking more miserable. Home joys—a loving wife, the gay prattle, the tender touches, the fearless love of little ones—must never be his. Utter loneliness was his lot.

In the old days Lord Edward found solace from all troubles in books. His imagination made poetry and fiction a reality to him. He passed at once from the world of dull fact to the world of bright fiction. He left his troubles behind him when he opened a pleasant book, as the prince in the Eastern story when he stepped upon the enchanted carpet, and sped away to whatever pleasant land he chose. He lived in an enchanted world while he read. The people he met there were real to him. He shared their joys, and hopes, and sorrows, and forgot his own; but now for the first time even this solace was denied him. His fancy was chained to earth by the heavy fetters of despair. To read of faithful love and home joys was torture to him.

He found the greatness of his past love by the misery of his present desolation. Every thought, and hope, and pleasure, and ambition had been brightened by the magic of that master passion. How dull and mean they seemed when the passion died out of his life! His soul changed as the bright landscape, when dull grey clouds quench the sunshine.

> " His love had grown so softly in his heart
>   Through those bright days, he had not felt it grow;
>   He had not dreamed its roots had struck so deep,
>   Or that its branches cast so fair a shade.
>   But now it lay uprooted and o'erthrown,
>   Never to wear green leaves for ever more.
>   And, gazing on the ruins, he might see
>   How many birds had built amid the boughs,
>   How many flowers blossomed round the roots."

Let no one think his sorrow was less real because it dwelt in his heart only, and refused the test of common sense. It was not the real Gertrude—cold and selfish—he had lost, but the ideal Gertrude his love created — pure and true and every way loveable.

What are called the real miseries of life—cold, hunger, pain, imprisonment—had been light evils compared to the dull and deadly stupor of the soul from which he suffered. Men whose lives are weighted with all those evils are still loth to leave the world; but blighted love makes even death welcome. Despairing lovers are most prone to take up arms against their own lives. No other grief the sad world holds has been so fruitful of self-slaughter. To hearts that love has never touched such grief may seem fanciful. Those who have felt the pang will judge Lord Edward's misery by their own.

The long voyage passed as all things in this world —gay or gloomy—must pass at last.

He touched land on the 24th of June, being only twenty-eight days at sea—a miraculously short voyage at the time; but to him it seemed the longest year of his young life. From Halifax he proceeded down the river Shubennacadee through the primæval wilderness of forest to New Brunswick, where his regiment lay. The wild and solemn loneliness of the scene wakened strange thoughts in that young, lovelorn heart.

One vivid glimpse of his life and thoughts in that

wild pilgrimage through that primæval forest is given us in a letter written at the time.

"It was," he wrote, "as odd and as pleasant a day, in its way, as ever I passed. I wish I could describe it to you, but I cannot—you must only help it out with your own imagination. Conceive, dearest mother, arriving about twelve o'clock in a hot day at a little cabin upon the side of a rapid river, the banks all covered with woods, not a house in sight, and there finding a little old, clean, tidy woman spinning, with an old man of the same appearance weeding salad. We had come for ten miles up the river without seeing anything but woods. The old pair, on our arrival, got as active as if only five-and-twenty, the gentleman getting wood and water, the lady frying bacon and eggs, both talking a great deal, telling their story, as I mentioned before, how they had been there thirty years, and how their children were settled, and when either's back was turned, remarking how old the other had grown; at the same time all kindness, cheerfulness, and love to each other. The contrast of all this which had passed during the day, with the quietness of the evening, when the spirits of the old people had a little subsided, and began to wear off with the day, and with the fatigue of their little work—sitting quietly at their door, on the same spot they had lived in thirty years together, the contented thoughtfulness of their countenances, which was increased by their age and the solitary life they had led, the wild quietness of the place, not a living creature or habitation to be seen, Tony and myself, sitting with them, all on one log. The difference of the scene I had left—the immense way I had to get from this little corner of the world, to see anything I loved—the difference of the life I should lead from that of this old pair, perhaps at their age discontented, disappointed, and miserable, wishing for power—my dearest mother, if it was not for you, I believe I never should go home, at least, I thought so at that moment."

As Lord Edward lay awake that night, not within the narrow limits of the hut, but out in the open air, on a bed of freshly-pulled sweet-smelling spruce, staring at the starlight and listening to the waters' ripple and the leaves' rustle, the impulse was strong upon him to pitch his tent in those pleasant places, and live his life out there. But with the dawn the fancy faded. The impetus of habit, which is, after all, the master motor of our life, carried him forward.

With the hearty good wishes of the kindly old couple, who had made their peaceful home in the wilderness, Lord Edward and Tony embarked in the bark canoe, and, with a touch of the paddles to guide, not help their progress, they swept swiftly down the shining current between the great curved ramparts of dark verdure that rose on either hand.

The freshness of the morning was in the air ; the

sun had risen high enough to brighten, not scorch, and showered its golden *largesse* on leaf and water. Even Lord Edward's sad thoughts took brighter colouring from the brightness of the scene around him, as he sat musing in the prow of the little skiff.

A dozen miles down stream they swept around a curve, close to the right bank, under the over-hanging branches of a great tree, that seemed to spring almost from the water. Just at an angle of the bend, a heavy log splashed down in the wake of the little boat, flinging the water over them. The instant after a second log, more surely aimed, went crashing through the bottom of the canoe. The water leaped and bubbled up like a fountain through the breach. The frail boat swept around and around in the current, and, turning over, emptied its contents into the stream.

As they clambered, dripping, from the stream, a dozen wild figures dropped from the branches, or sprang from the underwood, around them, and before they could stir a finger in resistance they were seized and bound.

They were not treated cruelly, nor even roughly, except so far as haste caused roughness. The Indians were plainly in a hurry to be gone. Taking no trouble to conceal their trail, they pushed rapidly forward for some miles under the dark roof of the tangled forest, through which only a stray sunbeam glanced.

The eyes of the captives were dazzled by the sudden flood of sunshine when they came at last to the borders of a wide, lone prairie, which stretched away to the horizon's brink, its green floor thickly sprinkled with wild flowers. Here and there a few dark, round clumps of trees showed like islands in this limitless ocean of brilliant colouring, on which the noonday sun beamed down from a sky of cloudless blue.

But Lord Edward had no thought or desire of escape. He rather enjoyed the excitement and uncertainty of his position. It stirred the dull apathy that lay so heavy on him, as the mist is stirred and broken by the fresh breeze. The long, swift gallop across the boundless plain roused in him more of the spirit and buoyancy of youth than he had ever felt since his high hopes were laid low that fatal night.

All day those wild steeds stretched forward with untiring speed. As evening drew on apace they still galloped into the red light of the sinking sun, the soft, western wind blowing fresh in their faces.

At length a low bank, as it seemed, of dark clouds showed up against the clear sky line. It grew and took form and colour as they rapidly approached. Soon they found themselves once more within the circle of the forest.

The wood was more open here, and they could walk their horses through without dismounting.

They heard the refreshing murmur of running

water through the trees. A few moments more brought them to the edge of the chief village of the Great Bear tribe, to which the party belonged.

It was a primitive and a pleasant scene they came upon set in the great circle of green woods, and lit by the red rays of the setting sun.

The lesser trees had been cleared away from where the village stood. Only a few of the giants of the forest remained to shelter the dome-shaped huts of the tribe, which showed like huge beehives scattered thickly over the clearing.

In front, the ground sloped down to the banks of a clear stream, which came gleaming out of the dark woods to plunge into darkness again a little farther on. Along the river banks the young Indians sported—now in the water, now out—like creatures of both elements. Their gay cries filled the summer air as they shot their arrows, or flung their lassoes, or sent their birch canoes gliding over the shining surface of the stream, or plunged fearlessly into its cool depths. The sound went with the river as it ran, and mingled pleasantly with its plaintive murmurings.

Lord Edward, as the party rode slowly by, thought he had never yet seen childhood so bright, so unrestrained, so filled with the joyous spirit of youth. It cheered him to watch their sports. How different, he thought, from the pale and squalid spawn of humanity which he had seen in the back slums of great cities, where sunshine never came.

Here was no hard task or sordid surrounding to crush the life out of young hearts. Here was nothing of the heavy burden which unpitying civilisation lays on the shoulders of poverty. Their life from first to last was undiluted enjoyment, lived out in the free air of heaven. The sports of their youth was the occupation of their lives.

He had scant time for moralizing, however. The party rode straight through the opening glade to the very verge of the wood on the further side, where, larger than the others and more artistically constructed, stood the wigwam of the chief. It jarred strongly on the peaceful thoughts which the sylvan scene inspired, to mark the festooning of dishevelled scalp-locks—fair, and black, and grey—upon the door posts of the hut.

The chief received the party and their captives with face as stolid as a bronze statue, though he had had no warning of their capture, or their coming.

His braves had not been on the war-path. They were at peace with the pale-faces. The canoe and its occupants had been captured in that same spirit of wantonness which makes the kitten catch what it sees moving.

At the very first moment of entering, Lord Edward noticed a strange figure standing in the shade, a little way behind the chief, with a long rifle resting on the hollow of his arm. He was a man of huge frame, but gaunt as a greyhound. The tallest Indians seemed boys in comparison. He had no weapon but his rifle, and his dress of tanned deer-skin was free from all Indian frippery. His features were finely formed, but seamed with innumerable wrinkles, so deep and clearly cut that they appeared carved with a chisel's edge on stone. His hair and beard were iron grey, and his keen blue eyes peered out from under a thick thatch of grey eyebrows.

A wild strange figure, yet sadness rather than sternness was the impression he conveyed. Though the sun had burned his skin brown his features betrayed his race.

He moved a little forward as the chief spoke in his own tongue, the Indians making way for him respectfully.

"The chief welcomes the stranger," he said, speaking to Lord Edward. "You are brothers."

He spoke English clearly and with the unmistakeable accent of culture, but he spoke slowly and with something of hesitation, as if unused to the sound of his own voice.

Lord Edward bowed his acknowledgments as gravely as if he were in a Dublin drawing-room.

Meanwhile, the chief had been speaking somewhat angrily, as it seemed, to the leader of Lord Edward's captors.

But in a moment he turned to his young captive, with a courteous dignity that seemed strange amid such surroundings. The gaunt old man again interpreted. "Great Bear," he said, "is at peace with the pale-skins. But his young men are rough and foolish," here he glanced angrily at the leader of the expedition. "They mistake friends for foes, and men for deer and fishes. My brother will forgive. He is free to go or stay. The doors of the wigwam or the paths of the forest are open to him. Let him choose. The horse is ready at the door, but the venison is cooked within. My brother will stay?"

Lord Edward stayed. The thought of that wild, strange life had an overpowering fascination for him. Excitement raised him from torpor.

There was something, too, in the voice and manner of the old man that caught his fancy. Lord Edward had the strange feeling that every one has sometimes felt—that all this had happened to him before.

The surroundings of the wild forest and Indian village seemed curiously, vaguely familiar. The whole scene appeared to be some fragment of a half-forgotten dream, which might vanish in a moment. Lord Edward feared to move or speak, lest he should destroy the wonderful delusion.

No dream, however, but pleasant and substantial reality were the smoking-hot steaks of venison served to them later on, whose tempting savour needed not the persuasive eloquence of a long day's fast in the open air to commend it. No dream, but a pleasant reality, were the couches of soft skins stretched on the floor of the hut reserved for their use.

The fatigue and excitement of the day were

atoned for by the sweet sleep that solaced weary brain and limb. They lay in the quietude and un-consciousness of death, to awaken to renewed life and vigour with the glint of the sunshine, and sparkle of the water, and the fresh breeze that came rustling from the woods in the first glow of the morning.

CHAPTER VIII.

"DAFFED THE WORLD ASIDE AND BID IT PASS."
Henry IV. Part I.

> " Whate'er you are ;
> That in this desert inaccessible,
> Under the shade of melancholy boughs,
> Lose and neglect the creeping hours of time."
>
> *As You Like It.*

> " Who thought there was no more behind,
> Than such a day to-morrow as to-day,
> And to be boy eternal."—*Winter's Tale.*

> " What is a man ?
> If the chief good and market of his time
> Be but to sleep and feed? a beast, no more.
> Sure, he that made us with such large discourse,
> Looking before and after, gave us not
> That capability and God-like reason
> To fust in us unused."—*Hamlet.*

FOR some days Lord Edward lived this strange primitive life with a forgetfulness that was akin to delight, so bitter had remembrance grown. He joined in the wild sports of the Indians with youthful emulation, and gloried to hold his own amongst the best of them. It was a renewal of thoughtless, happy boyhood. In the soft evening as he smoked placidly in the doorway of his hut looking towards the river, a dreamy, delightful reverie stole over

his soul like a rosy haze, softening the harsher out-
lines of the landscape. Action and duty, even
blighted love, were half-forgotten—he lived for the
careless pleasure of the hour, and " thought no more
behind, than such a day to-morrow as to-day, and to
be boy eternal."

The ice of stoicism once broken, the Indian chief
treated him with the frank demonstrative friendship
of a school-boy. His slim young daughter —
" Laughing Water,"— as graceful as a fawn, and
almost as shy, glanced with timid admiration in
her soft dark eyes at the handsome young pale-
face chief.

Of the strange old man with the wild, gaunt
figure, and cold courtly manner, who had so roused
his interest, Lord Edward saw but little.

With Tony, however, the recluse was more familiar.
These curiously assorted comrades had long walks
together, while Tony's tongue rang on incessantly as
the restless stream, and the other listened silently as
the dark still forest.

From his faithful servant Lord Edward gleaned
that the old man had come amongst the Indians
many years ago, and lived amongst them since,
an adopted son of the tribe, second only in authority
(if second) to their titular chief. Ever and again
he visited the fringes of civilisation, and returned
to his tribe with horses laden with the wealth the
Indian prizes—rifles and powder and ball, and the
simple medicines that sufficed for a life so natural

and healthful, that old age or violence alone brought disease or death.

He preached peace perpetually to the tribe. He never joined them upon the war path. But once, when the village of the tribe was attacked in the night by a hostile band, far outnumbering them in fighting men, he took the lead in the brave and successful defence, and his long rifle wrought such havoc amongst the discomfited foe, that the terror of it long afterwards kept the village safe from attack.

"Thundercloud" he was called by the Indians, both on account of the solemn gloom of his appearance and the fatal flash of his rifle, which never missed its aim.

The life in the woods, in its wild and free simplicity, was very soothing to Lord Edward's wounded spirit. He rather dreamed than lived. But like cold water on a sleeper's face was the awakening thrill, when the news came that it was resolved to adopt him into the tribe. He quickly learned, however, that it was an honour to be conferred, not a vow to be enforced. He would still be free to go or stay.

Next day at noon, down by the river side, the solemn ceremony of adoption was performed, with all those curious rites, quaint yet grave, that the Indians love. The certificate of his adoption, curiously engrossed on parchment, is still preserved. The copy, in the Indian language, will be of interest

to every reader who follows the strange adventures
of the young Irish hero.   It is as follows :—

> "Waghgongh Sen non Pryer
> Ne nen Seghyrage ni i
> Ye Sayats Eghnidal
> Ethonayyere Karonghyontye Iyogh Saghnontyon."

Translated it runs :—

"I, Chief of the Six Nations, give the name of *Eghnidal* to
my friend Lord Edward Fitzgerald, for which I hope he will
remember *me* as long as he lives.   The name belongs to the
Bear Tribe."

Henceforward he was known by his name of adoption, "Eghnidal," amongst the tribe, and took rank as
a "brave."   Poor Tony remained still an alien, with
no rank at all, but neither his appetite nor sleep were
disturbed by the slight.   Ambition was no failing of
Tony's.

Day followed day in careless, unthinking ease, and
Lord Edward's life grew daily more delightful, more
hard to leave.   It was active idleness, pleasure un-
purchased by toil or pain.   No harsh duty crossed
the path of delight.   The mind was called upon for
no effort, the will suffered no strain.   The excitement of the hunt, the freedom and solitude of stream
and forest, the ever-varying beauty in which Nature
had clothed the wilderness, charmed him.   His life
seemed to have again merged into a delicious dream,
which he had no power or will to break, knowing
that he should waken to remembrance, and labour,
and pain.

In the shock his heart had suffered, the springs of self-reliance were strained. His ambition was so interwoven with his love that it almost died with it. All things that stirred or charmed him in the old days seemed vague and remote. Rest and oblivion were what his soul craved. There was nothing in the world he thought worth toiling for.

The strange charm of the life he led might have caught and held him to his life's close. He might have chosen for himself, or rather, with enervated will, have allowed fate to choose for him, the simple, easy, empty, purposeless life of the wild man or wild beast. The saddest and most glorious chapter of Irish history might never have been written, if a strong, stern will had not interposed and saved him from ignominious oblivion.

He sat one evening smoking dreamily in the doorway of his wigwam, looking out on the stream that flowed red in the slanting sunbeam, and listening to the happy cries of the children whose voices came up fitfully on the wind.

His musings were vague as the soft vapour that curled round his head, melting in the summer air, but as soothing withal. A shadow fell at his feet—a figure crossed between him and the rosy sunset. Dropping his gaze, which had been dreamily drinking in the beauty of the sky, he encountered the keen blue eyes of the man whom the Indians called Thundercloud.

"Lord Edward Fitzgerald," he said, with that

old-fashioned courtesy which seemed so strange amid such surroundings, "if you can pardon my intrusion I would fain speak a few plain words with you."

Lord Edward was for a moment startled to be so addressed. The language and manner of the outer world brought the outer world sharply to his mind, but he merely bowed his head and made room for the other on the bench on which he sat.

The elder man accepted the seat without a word. Hiding his face with his hands, he seemed lost in thought and forgetful of the purpose for which he had come.

Lord Edward began to grow impatient at the long silence, when his companion, lifting up a face paler and more haggard than ever, with traces of much suffering in it, spoke again abruptly—

"When do you go hence, my lord?"

The young dreamer had no reply ready for the sudden question. He had not thought of it. He had lived from day to day, bidding each morrow welcome as it came.

"This is no place for you," the other went on, more eagerly than before. "You must not waste your young life and energy here in unthinking ease. Your life is a trust, my lord, not given for self only —it is a sacred trust, the one thing real in a world of shams—to be used, not wasted, while it lasts."

"To me," Lord Edward replied rather ungraciously, for the words set the old wound throbbing again in his heart, "life is the hollowest of all shams—a burden, not a delight—to be borne as easily as may be until it can be cast aside."

"Your life is you," was the stern retort. "Here or hereafter you have or are nothing but that. Each hour wasted is part of yourself lost. Will you step down from your high place? Will you swop fate with the beasts, or with men just rising from the beasts? Will you change even the noble suffering of soul for low delights of the body?"

"Oblivion is better than sorrow," said Lord Edward, sadly. "Why suffer when one may be at ease? Forgetfulness is the best thing the world can give me."

The recluse gazed kindly at that young face, flushed with sudden pain. For the first time since he had come amongst them he caught his hand and grasped it tight while he spoke again.

"It is your passion and grief that speak now," he said, "not reason. Believe an old man, they are fleeting, though while we suffer they proclaim themselves eternal. In energy, not sloth, the real remedy lies. Fight the enemy and beat it. Do not live its languid prisoner for ever."

"My first relief was here," replied Lord Edward. "Energy had gone out of my life, and only pain remained. Here the pain was softened by forgetfulness. What calls me back again to the sorrow of the world from which I have happily escaped? Here I may dream my life pleasantly away, and die

when death comes without keen regret.   Here is
God's beautiful world; here is man as God made
him before what is called civilisation spoiled him."
He pointed as he spoke to the tall trees that
curtained the burning western skies, to the glowing
river, and the young Indians sporting on its margin.
" The selfishness, the greed, the falsehood, the cruelty,
of the civilised world are missing here."

" Are all found here," retorted the other sadly.
" Do not harbour so foolish a delusion for a moment.
The evil passions, which are the seeds of sin and
misery, are in all human hearts alike.   It is the
virtues of civilisation that are lacking here, and not
its vices.   Cruelty, and selfishness, and falsehood—
believe me, for I know—can lodge in a wigwam as
in a palace.   But of purer love, of larger humanity
and self-sacrifice, there is little or no trace."

" They are not needed," said Lord Edward stubbornly, for his conscience rebelled against his words,
" where all are free and equal.   Man's vices make
the evils that man's virtues partially relieve.   From
oppression patriotism springs.   It is cruelty that
evokes benevolence.   But the virtues fight fitfully
and lose; the vices fight constantly and win.   So
luxury and misery divide the civilised world between
them.   You speak of love," he went on with an
increased bitterness, which showed the source from
which his fine, youthful misanthropy sprung.   " It
is the mockery of the many and the torment of the
few.   A foolish, bitter, self-wounding passion, which

tortures even while the heart that suffers owns its folly."

With a pitying smile the recluse listened to the fine phrases with which the young lord denounced the whole human race, because a heartless woman had jilted him.

He spoke again very gently. "Poor boy!" he said. "In your grief and passion I find my own wound again. Do not, as I did, listen only to the specious lies your pain and anger tell you, and so wreck your life. You have seen but the bright surface of savage life. You know nothing of the horrors below. Has there been no time when the life you left also seemed full of happiness and truth?"

Lord Edward was silent.

He remembered how bright the world seemed, and how good its men and women, while he still dreamed that Lady Gertrude loved him; how suddenly he realised all its wickedness at once when she turned from him.

"Life is not all sport and sunshine, believe me," the warning voice went on. "Even here in the woods I have seen horrors of cruelty, when hunger or revenge roused the wild beast in the wild man, horrors which it would freeze your blood to hear. But even were this wild life all you fancy, its joys are not for you. Would you sink to the brute's level? The beast that ranges wild over the plains, the deer that drinks in the evening at the river's brim, the bird that flutters through the tree-tops, the bear that haunts the summer woods and snores away the winter, has all the joys you envy the savage man, till bullet or arrow cuts their life short like his. Are you content to go down to the level of the beast?"

"Is it crime or folly to shun pain?" said Lord Edward, evading a more direct reply.

"Yes. Folly, and crime, and cowardice, if you play false with your manhood to escape it. Better the noble sorrow than the low delight. You cannot sink your soul down to the brute's level even if you try. It was not for this that high duties and glorious hopes were given you. Your soul will rebel against the degradation you would impose, and torture you. May you never know such torture."

His voice faltered. Even in the darkening twilight that was now softly drawing its grey veil across the glowing sky Lord Edward could see that he was deeply moved. He started from his seat, and paced up and down for a moment or two; then paused as abruptly as he had risen. When he spoke again it was with no trace of the emotion that had shaken him, only his voice was lower than before.

"I had not meant to speak of myself," he said. "Lord Edward Fitzgerald, something I have gathered of your history from that faithful follower of yours, something also, strange as it may seem to you, from other sources. I have patched out what I have heard with guesses, which, I think, come near the

" Better the noble sorrow than the low delight."

truth. Your words to-night confirm them. Your heart has been sorely wounded—it will revive and live."

Lord Edward shook his head sadly, with all the profound confidence of youth in its own wisdom.

" Sorrows are not eternal," said the other, " though youth thinks them so. When night first falls on bright hopes, youth fondly fancies there can never be day again, but the sun will rise again to-morrow— it may be, brighter than before. Believe me, the pains you have suffered are but a child's ache compared to mine. Your warning came in time. Even now your reason tells your loss was a blessing. Bitter shame and disgrace mingled with my agony. Yet, in time, even that agony wore itself away, and happiness came too perfect to last. My second loss was more terrible, because more real. I lost a love, the purest and dearest that ever breathed on this earth. The weight of the blow stunned my reason, and broke the springs of my will. I fled like a coward from the battle, where I was so wounded. Bitterly have I paid for my cowardice. To the sweet oblivion I first sought and found in the woods has come a terrible reaction. The worst paroxysm of wounded love was easier to bear than the constant soul-subduing monotony of a purposeless life. I am here alone with my remorse ; my imprisoned soul feeding on itself."

There was deep pity in Lord Edward's heart as he listened. His own sorrow seemed petty in comparison with the tragic grief of this strange man, who showed his own wounds for a warning.

There was silence between them. The village was asleep. The white crescent of the moon, keen-edged and shining as a curved sword, shone coldly in the blue-black sky. The night was hush as death. The thought came in Lord Edward's mind how placidly, beautiful and cold-hearted Nature smiled at poor mortals' suffering.

A low, despairing sob shook the strong figure stooped beside him ; the moonlight shining on the white hair.

The young man's heart was flooded with compassion. "Let us leave together," he said. "If this life be bitter to you, abandon it. Come back to the world where your place lies, and your work still waits for you."

The face that raised itself from the bony hands might have been carved in grey stone, so ghastly it looked, and so hard.

"No! no! no!" he said, and each word sounded like a moan of despair. "For me there is no escape. I have chosen my lot and must abide by it. As well might you try to transplant yonder deep-rooted tree, and bring back its lost life and verdure."

He pointed as he spoke to a blasted oak by the river's bank, that stretched its huge branches, bare and white, casting black shadows.

"Habit and despair bind me here. The chain galls, but it holds. I cannot now stretch forth my hand to clasp the duties and joys of life that I cast from me so recklessly. But you have the youth and vigour that cast off sorrow lightly. Be warned by my fate. Depart!"

"Whither?" asked Lord Edward, dolefully. "No duty calls; no career opens for me; I am sick of soldiering, which was once my delight."

"Has your own heart no answer? On your name and race has Ireland no claim?"

The gaunt figure was erect as he spoke, and the grey eyes alight with excitement. His voice took a bolder tone.

Something in voice, face, and eyes suddenly made clear to Lord Edward a vague resemblance that was haunting him. There came back to him in a sudden flash the eager words of Maurice Blake, in those far-off days that now seemed to belong to another life, and the vow they had silently sworn in the solemn starlight.

"How strange," he cried, wonderingly. "You speak almost the words a dear friend of mine once spoke to me. The voice, tone, and thought bring vividly to my mind"——

But before he could close the sentence with the name of Maurice Blake the other rose abruptly. With a gesture, that was like a blessing, he laid his hand on Lord Edward's shoulder; then, without a word, he vanished into the thick gloom, moving towards the forest.

Lord Edward sat far into the lonely midnight,

buried in thought, while Tony slept the sleep of unconscious content in the interior of the wigwam.

The noise of the running water, which alone broke the silence of the still night, mingled with his musings. The energy of life and hope, of ambition, had been revived in his heart, which throbbed strongly and fiercely now, forbidding sleep. But his vague, restless thoughts could shape themselves into no definite resolve. No way of life opened before him. The crisis of his disease had come and gone. The fantastic fever begotten of his sore heart-wound vanished, and his judgment was cool again. He could smile at the folly of the vision of love that had so charmed him, as the awakening man smiles at the incoherent dreams that troubled his sleep.

Back to the world he felt his path lay. Then, once more custom took control of his movements, and insisted on the completion of his interrupted progress to the British barracks at New Brunswick, where his regiment was encamped.

The night was melting into dawn when he dropped asleep. Next morning found him still resolved and eager to depart. The Indian chief heard of his sudden purpose without a sign of surprise, without a hint of remonstrance. Grave courtesy absorbed both.

"My white brother," he said, "is free; where his will calls him he goes."

By noon Lord Edward and Tony were riding through the depths of the silent forest, many miles

from the primitive settlement of the Indians. The
river was their guide — untiring and unerring — a
guide that would neither loiter nor mislead. Tony
had much to tell of the quaint customs of the
Indians, with whom he had mingled more familiarly
than his master, but his talk ran chiefly on "Thundercloud."

"A strange man," said Tony, with something of
awe in his tone, for Christianity had not got the old
superstitious leaven out of his blood. "A strange
man. Speaks very little, knows very much. Would
listen always to my talk of you and Christy, but
above all of Master Maurice. At times he would
drop a few words that seemed to show he knew
more about you all than I could tell him. He spoke
of Master Maurice as a father might speak of a
son."

A careless word will sometimes kindle a train of
thought, as a careless spark kindles gunpowder.

It came on Lord Edward's mind, with swift
certainty, that "Thundercloud"—the strange Indian
recluse—was no other than the missing Sir Valentine
Blake, of whom Dr. Denver had spoken. He marvelled at his own blindness that had missed the plain
truth so long. The strange coincidence of circum-
stances, the resemblance in face and voice, even in
thought, to Maurice Blake were proof conclusive.

His hand was on the reins to wheel round in his
tracks and return, but the thought checked him—
"To what purpose?" What could he do, what say

that he had not said? He remembered now with what emotion the old man had turned and left him, when the name of Maurice Blake was on his lips. Why should he probe further, and to no good purpose, a wound that plainly was deep and sore?

So he did not turn, but rode steadily forward plunged in thought, with Tony's words sounding in his ears with no more meaning than the incessant monotone of the stream.

CHAPTER IX.

"THE AIR BITES SHREWDLY; IT IS VERY COLD."
Hamlet.

"Myself must hunt this deer to death."—*Henry VI.* Part ii.

"Return with me
And push distraction and perpetual shame
Out of the weak door of our fainting land."—*King John.*

TO tell of Lord Edward's life in the barracks at New Brunswick would be foreign to the purpose of our story. The all-pervading military discipline, which made the very atmosphere of the place, imparted the powers of self-restraint, which served him well in later life. It taught him, if he could not check, at least to hide from careless eyes the fiery enthusiasm of his nature. The responsibility which, in that lonely station, was thrown on the officer, and the readiness of resource the situation in command called for, fitted him for the perilous part he was hereafter to play as leader of an oppressed people, to whom fortune alone denied victory.

His letters at this time, written with sweet, playful humour to those at home, show how lightly his emancipated spirit now sported with the fancy which so seriously enthralled him a little time before. He wrote :—

" I ought to have been a savage, and if it were not that the people I love and wish to live with are civilised people, and like houses, I really would join the savages.

" There would be then no cases there of looking forward to the fortune of children, of thinking how you are to live ; no separations in families, one in Ireland, one in England ; no devilish politics, no fashions, customs, duties, or appearances to the world, to interfere with one's happiness. Instead of being served and supported by servants, everything here is done by the people one loves, and the mutual obligations you must be under increase your love for each other. To be sure, the poor ladies are obliged to cut a little wood and bring a little water. Now, the dear Ciss and Mimi, instead of being with Mrs. Lynch, would be carrying wood and fetching water, while Ladies Lucy and Sophia were cooking or drying fish. As for you, dear mother, you would be smoking your pipe. Ogilvie and us boys, after having brought in our game, would be lying about the fire, while our squaws were helping the ladies to cook, or taking care of our papouses. All this in a fine wood, beside some beautiful lake, which when you were tired of, you would, in ten minutes, without any baggage, get into your canoes and off with you elsewhere."

One would like to linger over this busy, and not

unhappy, period of his life, of which many details remain to us, but the chief action of his career cries " Forward."

The military genius of Lord Edward was stimulated by a military life. Daily and daily he mastered more and more completely the details of his fascinating profession. Daily his active and penetrating mind showed him more clearly how these details could be combined for stupendous results.

More and more his old brilliant dreams of victory and conquest beset him. He pictured himself at the head of a nation's armaments, wielding its powers as Jove's arm wields the thunderbolt. The clash, the struggle, and the triumphs of the battle-field delighted him. He dreamed of great armies beaten, and vast territories overrun, his name on all men's lips, in all men's ears, at once the glory of his country and the terror of her foes.

His cheek flushed and his heart beat faster at these glorious visions. The cost of victory—the plains strewn with mangled corpses, the myriad happy homes made desolate, were quite forgotten. The young soldier's eyes could only see the glories of war, not its horrors.

But there were times, too, when the nobler instincts of his nature rebelled against the dull routine of the life he led, and the hard, hurtful splendour of the dreams he dreamt. Ever and again the scar of the old love wound would rankle at his heart.

Then he would start on long expeditions in the unknown land, alone or with little company. The solitary communion with Nature soothed his troubled soul for a time. But the restlessness increased upon him, and grew daily harder to appease.

He longed for adventure with a spice of danger in it, and fortune threw what he longed for in his way.

He volunteered for the command of a wild and dangerous expedition—from Frederickstown, where his troops lay, to Quebec, and was accepted. Forthwith he embarked on the strangest piece of inland navigation ever attempted.

One hundred and seventy miles he must pass through the primæval forest. To miss the way (where no way was visible) was to meet death. Lord Edward commanded the little troop, which consisted of an officer, younger than himself, and two men of the rank and file. Tony, of course, was of the party. Their food supply was coarse and scanty, for the double question had to be determined, what was the least that could sustain them through the journey, and what was the most that they could carry. For guide through the illimitable waste they trusted to a pocket compass. On the delicate quivering of the little morsel of magnetised iron the lives of these four men were staked with perfect confidence.

Boldly they plunged into the still depths of that illimitable tangle—more blood-chilling than the fierce ocean at its wildest—in whose recesses death lurked, with hunger and cold for his attendants.

It was mid-winter when the expedition started. The snow lay thick upon the ground—soft, dry, and powdery as white sugar. The sky was of clear, distinct blue in the daytime, with vivid flushings at sunrise and sunset. At night a myriad stars burned cold and bright in the great black vault.

In Indian file the party marched, their broad snow-shoes sinking half a foot or so in the soft drift, where a man without such support would have gone down to his waist. Lord Edward walked first for the most part. The others followed, stepping carefully in his track. The pressure of each man's foot made the track firmer for him that followed. The last man walked almost on solid ground.

At night they cleared a narrow circle of the snow, and spread the ground thickly with soft, sweet-smelling spruce leaves. A huge fire was kindled in the centre—firewood, at least, was abundant in those regions.

Within the radiant and glowing circle, hemmed around by the cold, they ate their frugal meal, of which steaming hot coffee was the chief luxury. Pipes were smoked and story and song interchanged. Then, with a pleasant chorus of "good nights," they turned on their soft, sweet-smelling couches to taste that perfect repose which only hard work can buy.

I

They were up with the first ray of morning, to rekindle the smouldering fire with armfuls of wood, just as the rekindled sun, peering over the globe's rim, threw a red glow across the white world.

Snow and frost! frost and snow! It grew very monotonous at last; trudging along, all day, and every day, as it seemed over the same white ground, through the same interminable woods. At times the very air appeared to freeze into clear fluid ice, chill and motionless. At times there was a thin, cutting breeze that blew out of the trees and sky a cloud of frozen dust, powdered them all over white, and made them glitter in the sunshine like the figures that delight children at Christmas time.

They had been twenty-one days on the expedition —each day as like another as the miles of white forest. Their food supply was running out, and it was thought necessary to shorten the rations to make sure of their holding on to the last. They had at first grown a bit tired of corn and grease, which were the chief staple of their repast. But the first hint of scarcity converted both into luxuries—not the quality but the quantity of the food was thenceforth considered.

Of game they saw little and got none. The tracks of wild animals were, indeed, abundant, but the animals themselves were missing. There had now been a hard frost and no snow-fall for a fortnight. They could not tell if the tracks they met were fresh or old, and they dared not start from their line of march in pursuit of game that had perhaps vanished from the place a fortnight ago.

Lord Edward, as chief of the expedition, felt the food dearth most keenly, for his comrades' sake rather than his own. The thought of their peril often broke his rest at night when a hard day's march enjoined sleep.

One such night he lay with eyes wide open, and senses alive to the sweet smell of the spruce bed and the quiet beauty of the night, while his comrades, soothed by the kindly ministrations of "nature's soft nurse" were as still as the earth's bosom where they lay, and as insensible.

Lord Edward's troubled thoughts yielded to the magic of the night's beauty. The moon shone placidly from a clear far sky, touching the tree tops with light, and marking the silver ground with black tracery that waved with the swaying branches as the light breeze softly stirred them, making no sound. His thoughts as he gazed on the vast still sky were away from earth. In one of those supreme trances when the soul seems for a moment to pierce a little way to the mystery of the invisible world which surrounds it, and to which some instinct tells us the road leads skywards.

His quick ear, which kept sentinel while his thoughts wandered, caught the sound of a light rustle in the woods. Instantly he was down on earth again with all his bodily senses keenly on the alert. Very quietly he drew his rifle to him, and slowly and gently cocked it. The moon shone coldly on the barrel as he stretched it in the direction whence the sound came.

Suddenly out of the darkness of the thick wood the huge black quivering shadow of a deer's head was projected flat on the white ground. The body followed, the long legs striking back right into the shadow of the trees.

It was a weird and ghastly sight, to send a thrill through the heart of a watcher in the still moonlight, but Lord Edward felt no such thrill. He knew there was a substance behind that shadow. As he steadied his rifle across his arm where he lay and waited for the substance to follow the shadow into the light, the savour of hot grilled venison steak was the homely anticipation that absorbed him.

But there is many a slip between the game and the bullet. The high-piled camp fire at this instant fell in with a crash. The black shadow vanished suddenly as ghosts vanish, and only the keenest ear could detect the rustle through the snow as the frightened moose deer fled away into the night.

Lord Edward called up his sleeping comrades. Here was a chance of fresh meat not to be neglected. But the meat was alive on four swift, strong legs, and must be caught before it was cooked.

They reconnoitered the spot where the shadow vanished, and at the covert's edge found a deep track stretching away through the woods. Very quickly their simple belongings were bundled up,

"The black quivering shadow of a deer's head was projected flat on the white ground."

their snow-shoes strapped on, and they were away in pursuit.

The trail was easy to find. There was a broad, deep furrow where the resolute deer had ploughed his way, belly deep, in the loose snow dust.

The trail was easy to find, but it was by no means easy to follow. The snow-shoes of the party sunk deeper than ever from the quick motion. The front man who laboriously beat down the track for the others, had to be constantly relieved. Every half hour or so there was a change along the whole line, so that the labour might be more equally divided. But Lord Edward, light and active, insisted on more than his share of the toil as the leader's right.

So they plodded rapidly and doggedly forward along that white furrow from red sunrise to redder sunset. But the stout deer ploughed his way still faster; and from sunset to sunrise their strained eyes caught no glimpse of moving thing in the still white forest.

By endurance, plainly, not speed, the brave prize was to be captured.

Wearied, but hopeful, they camped round their huge fire that night, and ate more freely of their scanty store, and drank success to their strange chase in cups of scalding coffee.

Before dawn they were up and away again. By sunrise they had come where the wood was more open, and a broad expanse of white ground flushed pure red in the morning light.

Young Lieutenant Langley, who headed the party at the moment, peering out into the crimson haze, thought he saw two black branches stuck up from the white, bare ground, and quiver and wave in the dead calm.

At the same instant he felt Lord Edward's hand heavy on his shoulder.

"Down, Artie, down!" the leader cried, in an excited whisper. "It is he—only three rifle shots away. With caution we may creep on him."

Crouching and cautious, the party moved stealthily as spectres over the white ground.

It was no use. The quick ear of the deer caught the faint rustle in the snow; the keen eye marked the string of dark figures sharply outlined on the white. Before half the distance was over-passed the slender branches that stuck up out of the snow were violently shaking. For one moment they caught the full outline of the great deer as he leaped from his repose. The next he was tearing through the snow like a swift ship through the water, throwing up as he went a cloud of frozen foam, that glistened and sparkled with myriad colours in the glancing sunlight.

With a shout of excitement they pressed forward, as the trail of foam lengthened out before their eyes. But the moving cloud distanced them, despite their utmost efforts.

Stepping carelessly, in his haste, young Langley's snow-shoes interlocked. He fell forward on his hands and face in the deep, soft drift, and the whole party came tumbling after and over him.

They gathered themselves up, laughing, from the frozen bath, shaking off the clinging white dust, like so many water-dogs fresh from a plunge. But the useful lesson was learned once again that by steadiness, not speed, the moose deer was to be captured, if at all.

On they went, steadily, with eyes straining through the forest, for yet another peep at their quarry.

About noon Lord Edward noted a thin, dark line leading down through the wood on the right hand towards the deer's trail.

As he came up he discovered with dismay the distinct impression of snow-shoes like their own, following the deer's trail like themselves. The party stood stock still for a moment in surprise and disgust. The sharp breeze which they had scarcely felt in their excitement, seemed now to warp their flesh with cold. It was wonderful how tired and hungry they felt suddenly. The same thought was in all their minds. There was another competitor for their live venison, and he had got the start of them.

Lord Edward bent down and examined the track carefully.

"More than one man has passed here," he said; "the weight of two at least was needed to press the snow so hard. Come along, my boys," he cried out with sudden cheeriness. "They have kindly made a path for us. We will catch them and the deer yet if we make haste, and at least share the venison we started."

His words put new life into his party. They reckoned confidently that the great advantage of a ready-made path would soon bring them level with the men and deer they pursued.

An hour later they noted (at first with joy) that the snow lay less thickly on the ground, and they moved forward more easily and more rapidly than ever.

But very quickly they realised that what was good for them was better for those in front.

The deer's track was no longer an even continuous furrow, ploughed breast deep in the snow. His deep footprints clear apart showed where he had leaped more lightly forward. Soon their snow shoes began to be a hindrance, not a help.

The men in front must have found the same, for the tracks of their snow shoes suddenly changed to Indian mocassins.

Quickly taking the hint Lord Edward and his party discumbered their feet and pressed forward with an energy born of despair.

Shallower and shallower the snow grew. The frozen earth began to show through it in patches. Then the snow began to show in patches on the frozen earth, then in specks, then it vanished.

The deer's trail was now hard to find. They could only creep forward cautiously, with their eyes on the ground, seeking here and there some slight mark to guide them. They had noted before the trail was lost that his strides had grown shorter. Their last hope was that, wearied out (as they were) with the long day's chase, he might take cover and rest.

They no longer moved in Indian file, but spread, fan-like, to miss no chance of catching the faint trail, which grew fainter and fainter as they advanced. An arched tree root caught young Langley's careless foot. He fell forward with a crash, his rifle discharging itself into the offending tree.

At the sound, right out from the cover beside him, not fifteen yards off, sprang the persecuted deer. It was a last chance — a rare chance for the deer. Young Langley had stumbled to his feet, and the man behind him dared not fire.

For one long moment the line of the deer's flight was covered by the body of the one man whose gun was empty.

Then the deer broke a little to the left, and the rifles rang out one after the other like the roll of a kettledrum. But they were snap shots at long range—Lord Edward's the longest. The deer still bounded swiftly forward—the swifter for the sounds. In despair they watched him flash along the clear space from great tree trunk to tree trunk. He was just vanishing out of range, when Lord Edward, with something that sounded like a curse, flung his rifle on the ground At that moment a tongue of flame flashed out so close beside that it startled him, a sharp report rang through the crisp air, the distant deer leaped five feet sheer into the air, and fell on his side dead.

With a cheery laugh, Maurice Blake broke from the thick cover, his smoking rifle in his left hand, his right stretched cordially to greet Lord Edward, who, with a cry of glad surprise, sprang forward to grasp it.

Christy Culken followed, as imperturbable and sedate as if they had only parted yesterday, yet with a twinkle of humour in his eye.

"An old friend," said Lord Edward, to his astonished comrades. "I may venture to invite you all to this supper of his providing. It is not the first time his rifle has fed me."

Soon a huge fire was blazing cheerily, flashing its fierce light into the dim recesses of the wood, and killing the stinging cold within the wide circle of its genial influence. Very speedily, for hunger makes haste, the venison steaks were hissing on the live embers, and the warmed air was redolent with the grateful savour.

It was a Homeric banquet, and they fed with Homeric appetite. "When hunger was appeased and strength restored," they sat or lay amid the soft spruce within the ambit of the fire's glow, and told wild tales or sang gay songs, waking the echoes of the woods and flouting the pale moon and solemn stars with uproarious merriment. For the full meal of venison after the long fast exhilarated them like wine.

Then sleep claimed her due from fatigue. One after another the party fell off into deep slumber. But Lord Edward and Maurice Blake, who lay close beside each other in the thick, sweet-smelling leaves, their blankets wrapping them warmly, were too excited by their meeting for sleep to come easily or soon. As silence settled around they dropped into more serious talk of what had chanced since they met. Maurice Blake's story was short. His life had run in the old groove. When peace came, he resumed his wanderings in the woods, but the old life palled on him. Though he hated war, he was fain to confess he missed the excitement of the war out of his life.

Lord Edward, in whose soul the young dreams of military glory were re-awakening, smiled, pleased at the confession. It seemed as if Blake guessed his thoughts.

"It was not war but work I wanted," he added, hastily. "Work and human sympathy. I feel my life was not meant to be wasted killing venison and eating it. Even the grandeur of the forest palls on an empty or discontented soul."

"How strange," cried Lord Edward. "I have heard that gospel ably preached to me in the very heart of the wilderness, and I have much to tell you of that same preacher. Then he ran shortly through the incidents that had chequered his life since he and Blake had grasped hands at parting. Shyly and slightly, he touched on his own love sorrow, but he dealt at length with Dr. Denver's story and his own startling experiences amongst the Indians. He made no secret of his belief that his strange monitor, the gloomy hermit of the woods, was the lost Sir Valentine Blake, the father whom Maurice had never seen.

Blake listened with breathless interest. There was a long silence when Lord Edward's voice ceased.

" I feel quite sure it is so," said Blake, at last, speaking very low and earnestly. " Some instinct tells me you are right, but I have no claim to break in upon his lonely life until he calls or comes to me. Still the words he has spoken are for me as well as you—for me more than for you—they are spoken from a father to his son. They are the echo of the voice of my own heart."

There was another pause. This time Lord Edward broke it.

" Whither are you bound ? " he asked Blake.

" For Ireland," the other replied with a curious tremor in his voice as it dwelt lovingly on the name· " Let me confess," he added impetuously. " I had some hope of your company. Do you ever think at all of that talk of ours on the night before we last parted, when, as it seems to me, we swore fidelity to the old land? Often the remembrance has come to me reproachfully by the silent camp-fire in the lonely woods, and has set me pacing restlessly all through the night. You have been in Ireland since we last met ? "

"I have," said Lord Edward, sadly. "I have seen her misery without the power to help it. I have felt weak and bewildered, and ended by swimming with the current, with eyes and ears close shut."

"I will not believe," Blake broke in, "that you saw misery without trying to soften it—that you saw wrong without trying to right it."

"I felt helpless—that is all. There was no point where I could set the lever—no power I could apply to raise the people. There was no use, I thought, grieving over what I could not remedy· I tried to forget, and I did forget. I grew absorbed in my own life, and I paid the penalty of selfishness. I drifted, and my drifting has landed me here. Our life's course is fashioned before our lives begin," he went on gloomily, with a touch of that dreary philosophy, old as the hills and false as the seas׳ which youth borrows from disappointed love, and thinks new and true: "Our lives are made for us like our minds and bodies. We can change none of the three. We revolve in a narrow self-conscious circle from day to day, but the great orbit of our existence is shaped by mysterious powers which we neither know nor can control. We are what we are, and will be what we must be."

A half-conscious admiration of his own cynical wisdom mingled with the bitterness with which he spoke.

"I deny it," cried Blake in earnest protest, "God has made us masters of ourselves for good or evil.

He has given us power to shape our own lives. On our own heads are the folly, crime, and punishment if we mis-shape them."

The earnestness in his voice touched Lord Edward, more than he cared to show.

"Give fate her due," he cried lightly. "At any rate she has tied your life and mine together. For the third time we have met by the strangest chance in the heart of this lonely forest, far from all the beaten tracks of human footsteps."

"The thought that our lives are fated to run together," Blake replied, "has often been in my own heart, and has been very pleasant to me, but our meeting here has not been chance. I knew of your expedition and came to seek you. When I crossed the trail of the moose I knew he was hunted, and guessed who the hunters were. I knew, too, that where the snow ceased there was danger of losing him. I followed the deer and you followed me, and so we met."

"Not soon to part, I trust," said Lord Edward, with something of his old boyish enthusiasm.

"Most sincerely, I hope so," Blake replied.

"I had the offer of long leave," the impetuous young soldier continued, "as I started on this expedition. I have a great mind to take it. I have caught home sickness from you. I am tired of the loneliness of barrack and forest alike. I want familiar places and faces. Will you have my company to Ireland?"

" It is of all things what I most longed for," replied Blake.

" It is a bargain then ?"

" A bargain," exclaimed Maurice.

Half rising from their rough couch, the two men clasped hands once more. Then, with a murmured good-night, they nestled snugly down amongst the spruce, drew their blankets closer, and dropped into a dreamless sleep that lasted to the dawn.

The trouble of the expedition was over. Blake knew the forest as a cabman knows a city.

His rifle and woodcraft combined provided them with food, dainty and abundant, as regularly and assuredly as the most careful housewife that ever haunted the meat market for city epicure. Their painful march was thenceforward turned into a holiday expedition.

CHAPTER X.

"ARE YOU CONTENT TO BE OUR GENERAL?"
Two Gentlemen of Verona.

" Another of his fathom they have none
To lead their business."—*Othello.*

" Farewell the plumèd troup and the big wars
That make ambition virtue.   Oh, Farewell."—*Othello.*

AFTER a few days spent pleasantly enough in the quaint old town of Quebec, Lord Edward and Blake started together on their homeward voyage, which passed without adventure. Landing at Gibraltar, they thence travelled leisurely on to London, seeing all that was worth seeing by the way.

By both the trip was afterwards remembered as about the happiest time of their lives. The brilliant emotional nature of Lord Edward had a singular charm for his more sedate but not less earnest companion. The war fever was again hot on the fiery young Geraldine. A great Continental war was in the air, and his imagination was dazzled by its stupendous possibilities. Blake, who knew enough about the science to be, at least, a discriminating critic, was amazed at the military genius he displayed —the mastery of detail, and the power of bold and colossal combination which together mark the great general.

Lord Edward's excitement was contagious. Blake was at times quite carried away by it, as the other eagerly discussed the moves of that fascinating game of wholesale murder, in which science exhausts itself to kill, and glory heaps up rewards for massacre and misery.

But Blake's humanity still quickly hastened to the rescue, and fought many a brave battle against Lord Edward's enthusiasm.

On their arrival in London Lord Edward stayed for some little time at the house of his uncle—the Duke of Richmond—with whom he was on very cordial terms.

Blake, for a few days, loitered admiringly through the wonderful metropolis—most wonderful to a man whose life had been lived in the lonely woods. Then his Irish impatience mastered him. With letters of introduction to some of Lord Edward's patriot friends —Arthur O'Connor amongst the number—he crossed, in rough weather, over the tumbling waves of the Channel to Ireland, which he longed to look upon as a child the mother loves but has never seen.

Meanwhile the Duke was delighted with his nephew. He had seen him last a boy, and now found him a man. Sorrow and experience had given a certain firmness to a character which nature, perhaps, had made too gentle. In those days every man was a soldier, and knew something of military science. The Duke of Richmond was no exception. His nephew's proficiency in what he styled the noblest profession, delighted him. He thought he saw his way to do a service at the same time to his kinsman, his party, and himself. He had some talk with Pitt, with whom he was intimate, in which Lord Edward's name was mentioned. Very coldly the great minister admitted that a brilliant young general was specially desirable for the Spanish campaign ; but he looked a chilling doubt when he was told that such a general was to be found in the Duke's nephew.

"I can trust your judgment in port, Richmond, if not in nephews," he said in reply to the Duke's invitation to dinner. " I will come to drink one, and test the other, any day you please."

There was for Lord Edward a pleasurable excitement in the thought of meeting the great Minister of England. In Pitt's character and career there was something specially fascinating for a young man. He was the young champion who had wrested all privileges from age and experience. He had deserted his own youth—cast it aside like its follies and delights. He had seized the helm of the greatest empire of the world with a boy's hand, and steadily and fearlessly steered it through a storm that shook the world.

A small party sat down to the admirably served little dinner at the Duke's. There was the great Commoner himself and his inseparable friend

Dundas, the host, Lord Edward Fitzgerald, and Lord Castlereagh, who was at this time beginning to make himself useful to Pitt, as the jackal makes himself useful to the lion.

Lord Edward had the great but nervous honour of a seat next the Prime Minister. At first he was tongue-tied by modest admiration. Nor was Pitt's stiffly dignified manner at all likely to put the shy young soldier at his ease. But as the good wine flowed freely, after the fashion of the time, the sunshine which the purple grapes had stolen in the bright southern summer a quarter of a century before, and had treasured safe through cold and darkness in its crimson life-blood, began to thaw the ice of ceremony.

Dundas, indeed, was more silent as he drank. The Duke of Richmond kept his manner of stately courteousness. He was, perhaps, a shade more deferential to the Minister, a shade more pompous to the others; that was all. Lord Castlereagh grew blander and blander under the mellowing influence. The sleek servility of his tones when he addressed the Prime Minister became more and more apparent. A softly-purring cat he seemed, whose sharp claws were hid in velvet cushions, but who might scratch as well as purr if a safe chance offered.

Towards Lord Edward, Castlereagh conceived that antipathy which the sleek vermin of the brute world have for their natural enemies, though seen for the first time. It was dislike, tinctured with fear. It may be that his servility awakened some touch of scorn in Lord Edward's simple and manly nature; but he was conscious of no special feeling concerning him. No instinct told him how their careers should clash in the time to come, and the meaner nature triumph over the nobler.

He was too interested, too excited, by Pitt's presence to waste much thought on Lord Castlereagh. The good wine, mellow, but potent, set his young blood aflame. A few well-contrived questions from the Prime Minister completed the charm. The smouldering fire of military enthusiasm was again kindled to a blaze. He talked freely and brilliantly, because he was master of the subject.

In the great Minister himself the greatest change of all was wrought. Something of his abandoned boyhood seemed to return to him as the liquid sunshine made summer in his blood. He chatted to Lord Edward with a frank abandonment, which was at once delightful and encouraging to the young soldier.

They talked much of the American war. Pitt's interest was keen on the subject, remembering how this suicidal strife had embittered the last days of his great father's life—how, even when the hand of death was heavy upon him, his fiery indignation had kindled his failing powers into a final blaze of surpassing eloquence. Lord Edward was encouraged to give a brief but vivid description of the campaign. He placed the troops, and showed the moves of the great game, as a master of chess expounds the problems of that most elaborate of pastimes.

Very skilfully the Prime Minister drew him on to tell of his trip through Spain. It was wonderful how Lord Edward had caught up and carried away with him the character of the country through which he had passed. It seemed a power more like instinct than observation. A hasty glance told him more than a duller mind could gather from a day's study of the maps. So, if small things may be compared with great, we have seen ladies who, with one scornful flash of the eye, take in a rival's costume in all detail, from boots to bonnet.

About Cadiz the Prime Minister was full of curiosity, which Lord Edward, flattered by his attention, strove to satisfy. He told of the strong points and the weak in its defences. The military engineers, to his thinking, had trusted too much to its natural strength, and given science no fair play. He laughed at the suggestion of Castlereagh that it was impregnable to British soldiers. He assailed and captured it there and then, planting his guns and marshalling his troops on the shining surface of the mahogany.

The enthusiasm of the young soldier and his military aptitude delighted the great War Minister. More than once his keen eyes telegraphed their approval to the Duke of Richmond, who smiled superior at this triumph of his own judgment.

" Richmond," said Pitt, at last, turning to the Duke

with a touch of that abrupt and domineering tone by which he had maintained his position from the first in spite of his youth, "you are right this time. Your nephew is a military paragon. I wish I had known of this before. Military genius is not so plentiful that we can afford to waste it these stirring times fighting backwoodsmen in the Colonies"—in England they still spoke of the "American Colonies" —"or drilling recruits in Canada. We can get lots of common place young fellows with pluck and muscle from Eton or Harrow for this common-place work. A soldier who can think as well as fight— who can carry maps and fortifications, and military combinations in his brain—is meant for something better than to lick an awkward squad into shape, or make one in a dashing cavalry charge. We must 'take the goods the gods provide us,' as glorious John has it, and use them to advantage.

"Lord Edward Fitzgerald," he went on, addressing the young soldier, who had listened amazedly to this outburst, "I am glad that it is in my power at the same time to do good service to you, and to England. An expedition is in preparation against Cadiz; will you accept the command?"

Dead silence fell on the company as this startling offer was made. It was in Pitt's customary style, sudden, dazzling, but guided by an unerring judgment of men.

Lord Edward Fitzgerald was himself the most amazed of all.

"'Lord Edward,' said Pitt, 'an expedition is in preparation against Cadiz, will you accept the command?'"

"But, sir," he faltered out, "I hold only a major's rank. Such command "——

"You shall be promoted by brevet," Pitt broke in, "to the rank of lieutenant-general. Your commission shall be made out immediately. You accept?"

To those present the question seemed formal merely. Delight and gratitude for an offer so dazzling were taken as a matter of course. To their surprise, Lord Edward appeared to hesitate. The suddenness of the thing stunned him. Here all at once was the gate opened to that bright career of military glory of which he had dreamed afar off. The path lay straight before him ; the dazzling prize was full in view. He felt his ability to seize it. His pulses throbbed with delirious exultation. Yet was there a whisper far down in his heart, the echo of nobler thoughts that even at that jubilant moment troubled him. He faltered out a few broken words of acknowledgment of the great honour.

"And you accept?" said Pitt again, in a tone that took acceptance as assured.

For the life of him Lord Edward could not answer "Yes."

"Pardon," he pleaded, "what must seem my folly and ingratitude. Most heartily I thank you, but I need a little time to think. I am conscious how silly it must seem, but there have been times when I almost foreswore the profession of arms. There have been times when my whole soul has revolted against war. The soldier's trade seemed to me at such times more degrading than the hangman's, who at least only slaughters the guilty. I have killed men better than myself in my time for no reason I can give, except that I was sent out to kill."

Dundas laughed out loud, but not unkindly, at this appeal. Lord Castlereagh tittered softly, and there was an insulting undertone in his laughter that jarred upon Lord Edward.

The Duke of Richmond did not laugh. He glared and frowned in mixed wonder and anger at the boyish absurdities of his nephew, who had thrown away such a gallant chance as comes to a man only once in his lifetime.

But the chance was not gone yet. Pitt's manner was kinder than before, as he replied, speaking now with that quiet, overmastering authority which was one of the great secrets of his success.

"I understand your scruples, my gallant young Don Quixote," he said; "and, what is more, I admire them." This with a sharp look at Lord Castlereagh, whose merriment was stilled in a moment. "But they would lead you gloriously astray. It is dangerous to set up a new private personal morality of your own. In all nations —even the people beloved by God—war was, and is, regarded as honourable. A hundred times it is approved, and even enjoined, in the Old Scriptures. In the promotion of great designs we must not be too particular as to the means. Be there mud or blood in the path, we must tread it to the desired goal. Through griefs, and wrongs, and slaughter, if need be, great objects are accomplished. If the good outweighs the evil, it is all we can hope for in life, where good and evil are so mixed. So the world moves, and we, perforce, move with it. We may march fast or slow. We cannot stop. Your place, my lord, is with the first. Will you lose it for a foolish scruple?"

He spoke with an authority not to be resisted. Lord Edward's scruples were silenced, if not killed.

"I take your offer," he said, "with gratitude. I will strive hard to prove myself worthy of your confidence."

"I do not doubt it," said Pitt, very kindly. "Your services will be my praise. You cannot choose but share your glory with me."

He filled a bumper of port as he spoke, which glowed like liquid ruby in the cut crystal.

"The future conqueror of Cadiz!" he cried, raising the glass to his lips. "Richmond, you will pledge me in that toast?"

"The future conqueror of Cadiz!" cried all—Castlereagh more earnestly than any.

It was late when the party broke up, for those were times when all men sat long and drank deep. The feet of the distinguished guests were a little unsteady on the marble steps as they descended, and their hands heavy on the broad banister of black mahogany.

After the guests were borne away by the patient chairman, Lord Richmond sat for some little time before his final glass of port, pouring mellifluous congratulations into the unheeding ears of his nephew, who, with difficulty, escaped at last to his room.

On close to the dawn Lord Edward lay awake, wearied with the thoughts that coursed each other tumultuously through his brain. He was elated, indeed, but not content. The uneasy whisper at his heart troubled him still, though he refused to listen to it.

"I was right," he kept on saying to himself half aloud, "and Blake was wrong. Destiny rules our lives. I could not turn aside. Fate has forced me into the position I longed for. There is no resisting fate." He slept a little, but his excitement pursued him into sleep in incoherent dreams. He dreamed he was leading his men to an assault, when suddenly his horse wheeled round, and he went charging into the midst of the British troops. He awoke angry with his folly; swore he would dream no more, and slept again a deep, unconscious slumber.

He was late to breakfast next morning, and the Duke of Richmond was seated. The Duke's greeting when he came in, though a little pompous, was very kind.

"A letter from the Prime Minister delivered this morning," he said, with a poor assumption of unconcern, tossing it across to Lord Edward as he spoke. "Read it."

Lord Edward took, and read—

"Dear Richmond,"—(so the letter ran)—"Your nephew may possibly desire a formal repetition of last night's offer, to show it was the Prime Minister himself, and not your good port, that spoke. Let him be assured his commission shall be made out with all convenient speed. The result, I am sure, will do credit to his military genius and my discernment. By-the-bye, I understand from Castlereagh that Lord Edward still holds his brother's (the Duke of Leinster's) borough in the Irish Parliament. I assume, of course, that his vote and interest will be at the service of the Government.—Yours,   "W. P."

The blood rushed hotly to Lord Edward's cheek as he read the letter. He felt it was the end of his appointment. Never for one moment did he dream of so bartering away his independence. The very suggestion he regarded as an insult. He suspected (but his suspicion was unjust to the Prime Minister) that this political servility was meant, from the first, to be the price of his promotion. "I did not know the borough had been kept for me," he said, looking up quickly.

"Oh! yes," the Duke replied ; "Leinster brought you in all right. Lucky, was it not? You have the double chance to serve the Government in peace and war."

"No," the young soldier said quietly. "My appointment is hereby revoked," he went on, while the Duke regarded him with blank amazement. "I might with honour accept a favour from the Prime Minister, but not a bribe. My voice and vote—since a vote has been given me—belong to Ireland, and will be devoted to Ireland's liberty."

The Duke for a moment was too amazed to reply. He thought his nephew had gone mad. He could find no meaning at all in his words.

" But you have pledged yourself," he stammered out at last.

" I pledged my sword," said Lord Edward. " I did not sell my honour. He that demands both can have neither."

CHAPTER XI.

"OUT, OUT! BRIEF CANDLE!"—Macbeth.

"A little more than kin, and less than kind."—*Hamlet.*

"If I quench thee, thou flaming minister,
  I can again thy former light restore
  Should I repent me ; but once put out thy light,
  Thou cunningest pattern of excelling nature,
  I know not where is that Promethean heat
  That can thy light relume."—*Othello.*

LORD EDWARD'S firmness changed the Duke of Richmond's surprise to anger. He argued, expostulated, stormed at last in unducal rage. All to no effect. Lord Edward's resolve was not to be shaken, and uncle and nephew parted as they had never parted before—in anger.

Though deeply pained, Lord Edward was no jot stirred from his purpose. When his uncle left him he wrote a letter to the Prime Minister, respectful, but at the same time brief and firm, declining the appointment. He had a duty, he said, to discharge in the Irish Parliament, "to which all other considerations must yield."

In that hour the Rubicon was crossed. Lord Edward was committed thenceforward to the glorious fatal career of an Irish patriot. For a nature like his, his path once chosen no turning back was possible, nor faltering by the way.

A few lines of kindly farewell he wrote and left for his uncle. Believing the Duke's anger would grow fiercer the longer they were together, that very night he took boat for Ireland, where Maurice Blake awaited him with a hearty welcome.

Dublin society, which had lost Lord Edward a careless boy, found him a thoughtful man. Yet his character had rather grown than changed. What it lost in gracefulness it gained in strength. It put forth new powers—it bore new fruit. The old charm of gaiety, truth, and courage remained. But grave thoughts and stern resolves were at work beneath the sunshiny surface of his nature.

He was now zealous in his attendance in the House of Commons. For the most part he gave a silent vote with the party of patriots led by Henry Grattan; but there were times when cruelty or corruption stirred him beyond endurance, and he flamed into indignant speech.

Maurice Blake was kept by his religion from a seat in the House of Commons; but in the outside organisation, which even then began to supersede the Parliament in the confidence of the country, he worked with a will.

The "Whig Club," which Grattan had founded, had already fallen from its high popularity. On its ruins "The Patriots' Plot," as it was then half jocosely called, was founded. Thence rose the famous society of " United Irishmen," in which by degrees all the patriotic manhood of the Irish race was included, and which treachery alone prevented from the achievement of Ireland's independence, under Lord Edward's leadership.

The whole time of the two friends was not given over to Parliament and politics. Even if Lord Edward had not loved society as he did, he would have found it impossible to escape the allurements that beset him. Blake, too, first for the sake of his friend, the Duke's son, afterwards for his own sake, was made welcome to the hospitable mansions of Dublin.

Young, handsome, a master of all weapons and all sports, with a refinement of manner which ran in his blood, and which his wild life had not tarnished, he rivalled even Lord Edward in popularity.

But Blake had not Lord Edward's love of company. There was one door-step, indeed, on which his foot was frequent, and Lord Edward quizzed him about the dangerous heart affection that carried him so often for a remedy to the famous Dr. Denver, and Blake winced a little under his badinage.

Some months after their arrival, both were bidden to a dinner at Lord Mountjoy's. Lord Edward, remembering his last experience there, felt the old wound throb, and was at first tempted to refuse ; but a moment later he made up his mind to go, on the principle that one holds a burned finger to the fire to burn out the pain. He guessed he would meet Lord

Dulwich, but he knew he would not meet his wife, as gentlemen only were invited.

Having made up his own mind to go, he insisted on making up Blake's, too, and the other yielded, as a good-natured elder brother yields to the whim of the younger.

The dinner was in magnificent style, even for that magnificent time. The dining-room was like a conservatory, with the scent and colour of fresh flowers. A miniature fountain splashed and sparkled in the centre of the great round table, where twenty guests were comfortably seated.

They ate off solid silver. They drank the rich wines, amber and crimson, from goblets of the old Waterford glass, whose clear-cut facets sparkled like diamonds in the light of the hundreds of wax-tapers in silver branches that illumined the room.

These were the days of reckless extravagance. Irish lords and landlords spent money as if a gold-mine were hidden in every acre of bog. The wretched, ragged, starving tenant, toiling his life away in squalid poverty, was the "slave of the lamp," by whom all these wonders were produced for those careless and idle Irish Aladdins.

Yet surely luxury was never more subtly blended with refinement than in those sumptuous Irish entertainments, where good taste and bright wit were honoured guests.

Lord Mountjoy was a model host, whose smiling welcome made every guest feel instantly at home.

The form of the table contributed to the unchecked flow of conviviality. The guests were not linked in conversational handcuffs with next neighbours, however ungenial. Each one could choose for himself round the great curve of the festive board.

In the earlier stage of the dinner the talk turned lightly on light topics of fashionable life. It was skirmishing before the general engagement. Jest and counter-jest flashed across the table, like the play of the harmless sheet-lightning that "gives delight and hurts not." Curran and Sheridan were of the party, and the wit, polished and bright, that has since dazzled the world, flashed freely from their lips in unrestrained extravagance, like the girl in the story who talked diamonds after the fairy blessed her.

But as the feast advanced the talk grew, if not less brilliant, far more serious. When the cloth was removed and the decanters began coursing more rapidly than ever round the broad expanse of shining mahogany, politics, as usual, mastered and killed all other topics of conversation.

Politics ran high and hot in Dublin at the time. Between the placeman and the patriots the feud was fierce.

All shades of opinion were represented around that table, from the rebel to the Castle hack. Good breeding and ability were all that Lord Mountjoy demanded from his guests.

Grattan was there, and Flood, and Lord Castlereagh, bland and smiling, and Lord Clare, lowering and haughty. Blake and Lord Edward Fitzgerald sat with only one between them. Almost opposite, with a sting from the old wound, Lord Edward recognised his defeated enemy and successful rival —Lord Dulwich. Richly dressed was his lordship. The long, white fingers that protruded from the deep, lace cuffs flashed with jewels, and the pale, impassive face was coldly handsome as ever.

By his side sat a young man who was in every way a contrast. His dress was rich too, but careless; his face handsome but flushed; his black hair curled close round a forehead narrow but smooth and white; his black eyes flashed with restless excitement. His mouth was the feature in his face that caught attention; the lips were thick and blood red, and the teeth sharp and white, and the smile not pleasant to see.

As the wine warmed their blood men spoke out more freely the faith that was in them. Martial law on the one hand, and rebellion on the other hand, found warm advocates. Words were spoken that, embodied in an indictment, would have brought many a speaker to the gallows.

With unfailing courtesy the disputants argued each that the other and his friends must be exterminated. Their politeness was the wonder of it. There was no harsh word, no angry tone, no insulting gesture. The genius of the duel presided at the discussion, sword and pistol in hand! Each man knew that a rude word might mean death.

They were brave men there, none braver, but death was not to be incurred without grave reason, even by the bravest. With the older men courtesy had grown so much a custom they could not be rude if they would.

With the younger men it was different. Their tongues were less under command. He who sat beside Lord Dulwich especially gave free rein to his. He flashed quick sarcasm around him, and now and again his words almost touched the limit where, in those days, the only answer was a sword-thrust or a pistol shot.

Others took their cue from him. There was lightning in the air. All round the table the uneasy feeling grew that it would never clear without a storm.

Their host noticed without seeming to notice, and quietly led the talk into a safer channel.

"A glass of wine with you, Mark," he cried down the table, courteously, to the young man, who in the excitement of discussion, had let the claret jug rest in front of him longer than custom allowed. "Do not play the dog in the manger with the decanter. Fill and pass."

"May I join in, my lord?" said a pleasant voice at the young man's side.

"Certainly, Sir Miles," cried Lord Mountjoy. "Mark, fill your father's glass to the brim. I will season the wine with a good wish for both of you —May Mark Blake have the good sense to be proud of his father, and Sir Miles good reason to be proud of his son."

Mark Blake winced a little as the words were spoken, for the tone smacked somewhat of reproof. He tossed off his bumper of claret a little impatiently, and was silent.

The names caught Maurice Blake's attention and Lord Edward's at the same moment, and the same thought was in both their minds.

Here, perchance, was one of the strange coincidences of which life is full. The heart of Maurice Blake, who all his life long had never before looked upon the face of a kinsman, beat hard and fast with new-found emotion. Surely by no race in the world are the ties of blood more closely felt than by the Irish. Amongst them the words "friend" and "relative" convey the same meaning. His isolation had given this feeling a special sanctity for Blake.

Some instinct told him here were kinsmen at last. Only by a strong effort could he restrain himself from claiming kindred and friendship there and then. The feeling was strongest towards him he thought his father's brother. That kindly and courteous face was infinitely attractive to the young man, whose heart had so long hungered for a father's love.

But for Mark Blake, even while he longed to join hands and claim cousinship with him, he felt a touch of repugnance. The leopard is sleek and graceful, and beautiful and sportive, but there is an instinct which warns against caressing it.

Lord Edward was scarcely less excited than his friend. In the handsome face of Sir Miles the young man's eye and memory were quick to trace a resemblance to the grave, gaunt hermit of the woods, whose words had helped to mould his own life. Trait after trait came out of feature and expression as he looked. The voice, too, though modulated to gentlest courtesy, had at times a touch of that solemn earnestness he remembered so well.

Resemblance carried his soul away with it, leaving his body still seated at the hospitable table of Lord Mountjoy. He was again alone in the wide woods, over whose tops the white moon shone, and dark forest and bright stream mingled their murmur in his ears.

His own name spoken loudly startled him from this reverie.

"Lord Edward Fitzgerald is my authority," cried a titled young Republican—Viscount Neterville. "Those Americans were neither cowards nor boors. He says they were as brave in battle and as generous in victory as the best of our fellows."

"Lord Edward is no judge of boorishness or cowardice," retorted Mark Blake, for it was he who had entered upon this new controversy. "He shared his own good qualities with the enemy."

He spoke softly and smoothly, but there was a touch of irony in his tone that nettled Lord Edward. The whole company looked to him for an answer.

"I ask no one to accept my opinion," he said very quietly, "but I hope no one will dispute my word." Then very briefly and modestly (naming no names) he told the story of his first and second encounter with Maurice Blake—his defeat, his rescue, his careful tending, and his unconditional release.

A murmur of applause ran around the table, in which all joined except Maurice Blake, who inwardly chafed at his own praise, and Mark Blake, who was coolly incredulous.

Mark's look ruffled Lord Edward. "The man that finds meanness or cowardice in the American ranks," he said, quickly, "must bring with him what he finds."

The other flushed at the words, but replied more gently than before :

"I accept your statement, of course, my lord," he said, "but you will be kind enough to allow me my liberty of judgment. You have not shaken my belief that these rebels are little better than white Indians, as cruel, as cowardly, but more cunning. The fellow you speak of had doubtless some end of his own in view when he spared your lordship's scalp."

"You forget, sir," retorted Lord Edward, angrily, "that he conquered before he spared me. I do not love boasting, but if Mark Blake thinks this an easy task for a coward he is at liberty to try. The man of whom I spoke," he went on, still more hotly, "is my friend, whose honour is as dear to me as my own, and "—he had caught sight of a malicious smile on Lord Dulwich's face—" I at least number no cowards amongst my friends."

There was a low buzz of applause as he spoke. It was felt the retort was deserved. Lord Dulwich turned pale, and was silent, and Mark Blake flushed angrily, and for a moment seemed struggling with some angry retort. It was but for one moment. To do him justice, he at least was no coward; but he was no fool. He felt the social verdict was against him, and hastened to get right.

"Forgive me, Lord Edward," he said; "I spoke hastily and without thought. I will confess that your friend and conqueror"—there was the faint suspicion of a sneer in his smooth rich voice—" was a hero of ancient chivalry, the peerless knight of the tomahawk and scalping knife. Your praise shall be his passport to my most respectful admiration. But you will permit me to wonder how such a paragon found place amongst this rabble rout of rebels and assassins."

This time it was Maurice Blake that spoke, very slowly, very quietly :

" The man of whom you speak, sir, though his good fortune gained him the friendship of Lord Edward Fitzgerald, was least amongst the brave American citizen soldiers whom you are pleased to calumniate."

A pistol shot fired at the table would not have startled the company more than those few words, so coldly spoken. They meant a duel, and a duel to the death.

Mark Blake was not the man to twice withdraw his words the same evening. He was a noted pistol shot—cool and cruel on the ground. He had been out thrice, two of his antagonists had been disabled, and the third—a handsome young Trinity student— shot through the heart. There were ugly stories afloat of a sister's name spoken slightingly and her brother's cane broken across the face of her traducer, but they never took definite shape, and the public heard only of a falling-out at cards.

When Mark Blake returned from the short trip abroad, which was the formal atonement the out- raged law demanded, there was no more trace of violence than of remorse on that handsome, smiling, evil face of his.

He was smiling now, as amid the sudden silence that had fallen on the company he spoke with easy and almost careless politeness across the table to Maurice Blake.

"By whom," he said, "if I may venture to inquire, have I the honour to be called a calumniator."

"By the friend and brother-in-arms of the brave men you have calumniated," retorted Maurice Blake, sternly.

There was a cold light in the other's eyes, but the smile was still on his lips.

"I have much pleasure," he said, "in repeating my opinion, but I beg to withdraw the exception, which only respect for Lord Edward induced me to make. If I have failed to make myself quite clear, my friend, Lord Dulwich, will explain my meaning." He turned as he spoke, and whispered a word or two in his lordship's ear.

"Lord Edward," said Maurice, "may I trespass on your kindness?"

Lord Dulwich had already risen from his place, and was moving towards the door, cold as an icicle. Flushed and excited, Lord Edward leaped up, flinging his chair back with a crash on the floor. He caught his friend's hand and pressed it for a moment, then hurried after Lord Dulwich, who paused at the door and held it open for him to pass.

With a nod, so short that it was more an insult than a salute, Lord Edward acknowledged his courtesy, and the two enemies walked side by side, but silently, down the marble stairs, on their mission to settle when and where and how their respective friends might most conveniently kill each other.

In the dining-room there was a thrill of excitement as they left, an excitement not altogether painful. A duel was one of the institutions of the time, jealous of its institutions. There was scarcely one at the table who had not been on the ground. The older men were connoisseurs in affairs of honour, and were critically satisfied with the progress of the quarrel. So far the game had been played according to the rules. The prologue had been fairly spoken, the exciting drama was about to begin, to the accompaniment of sword clash or pistol shot.

But no trace of the subdued excitement that prevailed was visible. Fashion forbade. Wine and wit flowed freely as ever. Laughter was louder than before, while death made ready to join their company.

None was gayer there than Mark Blake. Nor was there any trace of affectation in his gaiety. His manner was too easy for acting, as he leant over a little to half whisper a good story in the ear of his neighbour, a grizzled and bloated old campaigner, who broke out into a hoarse horse-laugh at the finish.

Lord Dulwich's rising left a vacant seat between Mark Blake and his father, but the son did not take it. He scarcely glanced at the old man, whose face, despite the stately stoicism of his school, had grown a shade paler, and whose hand shook as he raised the wine to his lips, which quivered even while they smiled.

Maurice Blake, alone of the company, neither felt nor made any pretence of unconcern. He leant back in his chair, letting the wine stand untasted in his glass before him. The trouble he felt was written plainly on his face. The hot spark of anger had died out, and its ashes were regret. Within an hour he had met a kinsman for the first time in his lonely life; within an hour more he must take his life or lose his own.

The face of his foe's father, in whose features his keen eyes could read the sorrow he so bravely strove to hide, saddened him most of all. So he sat gloomy and silent, cursing the hot temper that made death the penalty of a few rude words spoken hastily.

All round the laughter and wine flowed freely, and the younger men, seeing him sad and silent, whispered slightingly of his courage ; while the elder, glancing now and again at that calm, stern face, augured ill for Mark Blake.

Meantime the two seconds were settling the fatal formalities in the library. Lord Dulwich had dropped into a great chair, cushioned in crimson velvet, and stretched his thin, white hands to the cheery blaze of the fire, which shone through with a pink tinge. Lord Edward paced the room with hasty steps.   In a moment or two he came up to where the other was seated listless and silent.

" Well," he said abruptly, " when ? "

" The sooner the better," drawled Lord Dulwich, who had a keen relish for the work in which he was engaged.

" To-morrow morning, then," said Lord Edward. " Will eight in the Park suit? " With a touch of malice he fixed the same hour and place as their own meeting.

But Lord Dulwich gave not the faintest sign that he remembered they had ever met, except as casual acquaintances.

" Impossible," he said coolly. " Mark Blake starts with his father for Cloonlara an hour earlier in the morning. He bade me insist that they should fight to-night."

"Be it as you will," returned Lord Edward, "my friend asks no truce."

"The weapons pistols," said Lord Dulwich. "We claim the right to choose."

Lord Edward, knowing his friend's equal and consummate skill with both weapons, nodded assent. "And the distance?" he said.

"I should please my principal best, if I said the span of a pocket handkerchief," responded Lord Dulwich. "But it is a duel we arrange, not a murder. You know his skill. For humanity's sake I am anxious the distance should be a long one."

Lord Edward guessed what was in his mind. He knew by repute Mark Blake's skill as a pistol shot. Lord Dulwich, knowing nothing of Maurice Blake's, hoped to give his friend a long, safe pot shot at his opponent.

"I fully appreciate Lord Dulwich's humanity," said Lord Edward, with a scornful smile twitching the corners of his mouth. "I have already had some reason to admire the constitutional antipathy to bloodshed, which does him such infinite credit."

The shot told this time. Lord Dulwich flushed a little and bit his lip hard, but there was no change in his voice.

"Twenty paces, then?"

"Twenty-five, if you will—"

The ready acquiescence startled Lord Dulwich a little. He assented with a gesture.

"But how about light?" asked Lord Edward. "The dining-hall is scarcely twenty paces in length, and out there"—he drew back the silken curtain as he spoke, and looked into the garden, "Out there the stars are no more than pin-holes in the darkness. A man might safely play blind-man's buff with pistol-bullets all the night."

"I have thought of that, too," replied Lord Dulwich, calmly. "Let each man carry a lighted taper in his hand. He need only see his own pistol sight and the target. If the pistol barrel is pointed straight, the bullet will find its way home in the dark."

He spoke so callously—touching his breast with a white forefinger as he spoke—that Lord Edward's gorge rose.

"Be it so," he said sternly, and turned to the door.

Re-entering the dining-hall, each of the seconds spoke a word or two to his principal, telling him of the arrangements that were made.

The novelty of the fight gave it a keener enjoyment for the general company. Half a dozen silver candlesticks were caught up from the dining-table, and the bearers, their gay silks and bright jewels gleaming in the light, headed the brilliant mob that streamed in procession down the broad staircase out into the cool dark night.

The final arrangements were quickly made.

Duelling pistols for self or friends were part of the furniture of an Irish mansion in those days. A splendid pair, of the hair-trigger variety, were kindly placed by Lord Mountjoy at the disposal of his guests to kill each other withal.

But at the last moment it occurred to the seconds that it was almost impossible to arrange for a simultaneous fire. Midway between the two men would be pitch dark. A handkerchief dropped as a signal would be invisible to both. It was agreed, therefore, that lots must be drawn for first shot.

Two slips of paper were prepared and committed to Lord Edward Fitzgerald.

The longer gave precedence.

Lord Dulwich drew.

Lord Edward with a sinking heart found the shorter slip remaining in his hand.

His friend must stand the helpless target of the deadly aim of a man who knew neither fear nor pity. Lord Dulwich smiled, delighted as he noted how pale his former opponent was, and how his hand shook and spilt the powder as he loaded the pistol for his friend.

Then the ground was placed and the men set.

Each held in his left hand, level with his face, a massive silver candlestick, with a wax light in it. His right hand grasped the pistol butt. Their seconds stood close by, but out of the range of fire. All other lights were extinguished, and out of the darkness the mob of gentlemen, quivering with

"The lights shone full on the pale faces of the two men that stood waiting
there so quietly to kill or be killed."

excitement, watched the strange game played for lives.

The night was dead calm. The candles were topped with two cones of pure white flame that never so much as shook in the still air. The lights shone full on the pale faces of the two men that stood waiting there so quietly to kill or be killed.

Looking from the darkness into the light, the spectators could see every line of their faces with fascinating distinctness. Both were very pale, but it might be that the black setting of the darkness made their faces seem so white. The features of Maurice Blake were impassive as a marble statue and as grave; not a muscle quivered. His right hand hung by his side with the pistol in it; his left held the taper steadily that was to light death to him. With steady, fearless eyes he looked his doom in the face.

There was an evil smile on Mark's lips and in his eyes as he slowly raised his pistol. The light shone on the bright barrel and on the silver mounting of the weapon as it moved. The spectators held their breath. A short fervent prayer formed itself in Maurice Blake's heart as he saw the gleaming barrel rise slowly to position. Half way up it wavered a little. It almost seemed as if his foe meant to torture him. For one moment the pistol was levelled straight at his heart, then it moved again. Slowly and steadily it rises; now it points directly at his head. Then the bent arm that held the weapon stiffened itself like steel. Then there was an awful pause — the silence of death. All eyes were fixed on the levelled weapon held so steadily, and the calm pale face of the man who looked death straight in the face. The waiting was agony. It seemed as if the shot would never come.

Out sprang the flash through the darkness, out rang the report through the still air.

Maurice Blake heard the sharp hiss of the bullet as it cut through the thick curls close to his ear.

He was on his feet still—he was safe. His heart, which had stopped beating for a moment, with one great throb sent the blood rushing through his veins.

His enemy had done his deadly best and failed. It was his turn now.

" Ready !" cried the seconds.

There was no pausing for aim. In an instant the pistol was raised, levelled, and discharged.

But just at that instant the taper that Mark Blake held went out.

There was a smothered cry from the onlookers, for it was thought he was hit and down. The seconds, hastening to the spot, through the dim light could see him standing steadily with the quenched candle fast in his hand.

A second cry, this time of surprise, from Lord Edward, brought the spectators around them.

The quickest-witted amongst the company relit

the wax candles they had brought from the drawing-room, and half-a-dozen points of light now danced about restlessly in the darkness.

Mark Blake was unhurt. So much he confessed, a little sullenly, in reply to eager questioning.

Then there was an awkward pause, and a strange look on all faces. The question was in every mind, how came the light quenched, with not a breath of wind stirring? How came it quenched just as the shot was fired?

Mark Blake said not one word to explain. He stood silent and stock still, like one dazed. His manifest confusion increased suspicion. The thoughts in the men's minds began to shape themselves on their lips in whispers. They fell away from Blake as timid people from a fever patient, with elaborate show of carelessness. Lord Dulwich made no attempt at defence. He believed Mark capable of the cowardice of which he knew himself capable. So he fell off with the rest, and took part with the whisperers against his friend.

At this moment Maurice Blake approached with the pistol still smoking in his hand. He, too, heard the whisper, " How came the candle quenched?" and divined its meaning.

It was Lord Dulwich spoke the ominous words under his breath.

Maurice Blake tapped him on the arm sharply with the pistol stock.

" Look at the candle," he said in a voice that was

heard by every one on the ground. "Look at the candle itself, and you will see."

Lord Edward Fitzgerald was the first that caught his meaning. He snatched the quenched candle from Mark Blake's hand, and lowered the top to the lights which half-a-dozen eager hands held to him.

There was no more mystery about it. The bullet had cut a furrow through the wax and chipped the top of the wick off like a knife.

There was a low murmur of applause at a shot that seemed a miracle.

Then Mark Blake spoke out impetuously, " I have to thank you for life and honour," he said, "and to ask pardon for words that cast a slight on courage like yours."

He flung down his pistol as he spoke, and caught his late foe's hand in his and wrung it heartily.

At the same moment Sir Miles Blake approached, his handsome old face all aglow with pleasure at his son's safety. His eyes kindled with affectionate pride as he heard his frank speech. He caught Maurice Blake's hand in his turn and shook it heartily.

"Lord Edward Fitzgerald tells me you, too, are a Blake," he said, " I was always proud of the old name, but never prouder than now."

Maurice murmured something in return, for he was deeply touched by his old kinsman's kindness.

But Lord Mountjoy's mellow voice cut short all interchange of compliments.

"Your pardon, Miles," he said, clapping his old friend affectionately on the shoulder. "We will drown old angers and christen new friendships in a bowl of punch."

"Gentlemen," he cried to his guests, "The fireworks are over. Let us return to business."

His words sent the company trooping gaily back to the dining-room, where a huge silver bowl, with elbowed handles, smoked like a furnace, filling the room with rich vapour.

It was liquor richly and curiously compounded, of which the receipt is lost as completely as the ambrosia which the jolly gods drank on Olympus. A rich amber it shone against the white metal of the bowl, which was smoothed and worn like the hard stones on the seaside by the washing of many tides.

Lord Mountjoy dipped splashing in a ladle that was a smaller bowl with a handle a full yard long. Soon a goblet of the genial liquor steamed before every guest. It warmed their brains and hearts, and set their tongues wagging. Serious topics were banished when the punch-bowl appeared. Besides, the pistol shots like a thunder-clap had cleared the air, and good stories and jolly songs were the order of the night. If the singers took liberties with the tune, or the story-tellers with the truth, there was no one so critical as to grumble. The listeners in their turn had their revenge in kind.

Maurice Blake sat next Sir Miles, who charmed him more and more. The old man had that grace of perfect manner, which is the rarest of all accomplishments and the pleasantest. It belongs, indeed, only to honest and kindly natures, but not to all the honest or kindly does it belong. Like a well-fitting garment it shows the gentle soul. Not all such souls wear such manners, but only those can wear them, whether of peer or peasant, who are gentlefolk at heart. The old man's talk was brightened by quaint humour which gleamed the brighter for its quaintness like gems in antique setting.

Sir Miles had been in America. How Maurice Blake's heart throbbed when he learned from a few words carelessly dropped that he had gone in a vain quest of a lost brother. Their common knowledge made a common interest for them. The younger man's hearty earned towards the elder, with something of the affectionate respect due to the father he had never seen.

It was hard to resist a cordial invitation from Sir Miles that he should join them next morning in their journey to Cloonlara. He longed to visit the old home of his race. He did resist, however, until he had consulted with Lord Edward, and assured himself that the good work they had in hand could nowhere be better helped, and nowhere needed help more, than amongst the poor and oppressed peasants of Connaught.

So he closed hands with Sir Miles on his kindly invitation.

Mark Blake, indeed, professed himself delighted

at the news, but his delight seemed a little affected and overdone. His friendship for Maurice appeared to have evaporated in the first frank outburst of gratitude.

A whisper from Lord Dulwich knitted his forehead in a quick frown, but his face cleared in a moment, and, clinking glasses with Maurice Blake, he drank his safe arrival and long stay in Cloonlara.

With a strange, bitter feeling Mark Blake remembered that toast in later days.

CHAPTER XII.

"PERFECT GALLOWES."

The Tempest.

"A murder which I thought a sacrifice."—*Othello.*

" He uses his folly like a stalking horse, and under the presentation of
that shoots his wit."—*As You Like It.*

" But see, his face is black and full of blood,
His eye-balls further out than when he lived,
Staring full ghastly like a strangled man."

Henry VI. Part II.

CLOSE up to the dawn, Lord Edward and
Maurice Blake sat in earnest talk. The shock
of the explosion of the French Revolution had been
felt, and the flame seen as far as Dublin. Lord
Edward was eager to be away to Paris.

"It is Liberty's school," he said to Blake. "I will
learn the lesson there and teach my countrymen
on my return."

"Pray God you learn and teach no other lesson,"
said Blake. "For me there is a limit even to liberty.
I draw the line at rebellion against God.

"Look to your heart," he went on in a lighter tone.
"The French girls, I hear, have bright eyes."

"I have had the fever and am safe," retorted Lord
Edward, laughing, for he could now jest about a
wound that was agony a year before.

"You have only had the blue-eye epidemic," said Blake, with a smile. "Dark-eye, they say, is the more fatal form of the fever. You may bury your bachelorhood in Paris unless you have a care. Heads and hearts are in jeopardy in that gay capital, if rumour runs right."

"I warrant I will keep my head on my shoulders and my heart in my bosom till we meet again," cried Lord Edward, as he clasped his friend's hand heartily in parting.

A couple of hours later found Maurice Blake, blythe and gay as if an all night's sitting refreshed, not wearied him, true to his appointment at the door of Sir Valentine Blake's house in Dominick Street. He was mounted on the famous black horse which Lord Edward had so admired in the old days in America, and which he had carried with him to Ireland.

Sir Valentine's spacious travelling coach was at the door, with four horses harnessed to it, and the postillions already in their saddles.

The old man welcomed him cordially, and his son was, in outward manner, at least, scarcely less cordial.

Sir Miles Blake looked pale and wan in the searching morning light, and his breath came short as his son helped him a little carelessly into his great coat, lined with the velvety skins of the otter, which then infested the rivers and lakes of Ireland. Something of the pained surprise which Maurice felt must have been written on his face, for Sir Miles replied to it.

"An old man, sir," he said, "and a weak. The doctors tell me I carry death about with me here." He touched the region of the heart as he spoke· "Not a pleasant travelling companion, but I must humour the fellow, or he may strike at any moment. Last night's excitement has made him restive."

"Heart disease," whispered Mark Blake, in an aside whisper, a little callously Maurice thought, as he helped his father into the spacious carriage, and took his place beside him.

The plan of the journey had been arranged the previous night. It was needful that Sir Miles should travel in short stages with long rests. Maurice Blake, to whom experience had made the saddle as comfortable as an arm chair, preferred to make the journey on horseback.

It gave him, too, a chance of a hundred diversions to the right hand and the left, and of seeing the country and people in whom he was so deeply interested.

He generally managed to catch up with the party at the inn where they stopped for the night. Christy Culkin had a seat on the box.

For Maurice Blake the week's journey was full of strange and sad experiences. It was lovely weather, in the early autumn, which is the very tit-bit of the Irish climate. The bright sky and fair green land

made the contrast sharp and sad with the misery of
the people.

At first the country folk were a little shy with
Maurice Blake, but his frank, kindly manner, and his
quick sympathy, speedily won their hearts. They
told him the story of their lives. It was still the
same story, though told with many tongues—told
with a simplicity that vouched its truth—told, too,
with touches of quaint humour that made the pathos
of it more pathetic. There was scarcely a life that
had not some tragedy in it. Now it was a home
destroyed by a landlord's whim ; now it was some
dear one maimed or slain for devotion to the old
faith. These incidents stood out in sharper pain
from lives of blank, hopeless ignorance, and misery
enforced by laws which Burke so well described in a
sentence that is immortal :—" A machine of wise and
elaborate contrivance ; as well fitted for oppression,
impoverishment, and degradation of a people, and
the debasement, in them, of human nature itself, as
ever proceeded from the perverted ingenuity of man."

What amazed him most of all was to find so
much vitality, so much virtue, survive amid such
abject misery. He grew daily prouder of his race
as he fondly pictured to himself what freedom
might do for a people whom slavery was powerless
to degrade. A word or two he dropped here and
there of hope. He told them of the wild outburst of
liberty in France—of the breaking of chains and the
lifting up of peoples.

He was listened to by young and old with bated breath and kindling eyes. But the chorus of "Glory be to God." "The Lord be thanked," "Praise be to the Vargin," showed how closely the thought of freedom and the old faith were blended in the Irish heart.

Secret hints he got of old muskets carefully preserved in thatch or chimney, and of pike heads and handles that would come together, with strong arms and stout hearts behind them, whenever "the boys" were called out to strike a blow for the old land.

He had wandered during the last day a good deal from the main route, and had spent the last night by himself in the chief inn in Ballinasloe, not unwilling that Sir Miles should be untroubled by the care of a guest on the first day of his arrival at his ancestral home.

That night, as Maurice Blake sat in his room alone, sipping his claret thoughtfully before the fire of peat and bog deal that roared and blazed cheerily in the huge grate, there was a clatter of horses' hooves up the street, and a resounding rattle of the knocker at the door. It wanted but a few days of the great October fair in the town, and the house was full of visitors. Half-a-dozen were drawn out into the hall by the clamorous knocking.

Some stirring news was on foot. The hotel was instantly in a commotion. Maurice Blake could hear the surprised and excited exclamations as the tidings passed from lip to lip.

A moment after there was a knock at his own

door, and, almost before he could call "Come in," a waiter entered, eager, it was plain, to have the first chance to tell the news.

He had a basket of turf in his hand, and he made an elaborate pretence of mending the fire, which needed no mending.

"Yer honour heard the news, of course?" he said quite carelessly, but his quick eye and pale face belied his carelessness.

"No," said Blake with some impatience. "But I heard the messenger who brought it. He seems to have set the whole hotel humming like a hive of bees. What is the news? Out with it, like a good fellow."

"Yer honour knows Lord Clearanstown?" said the waiter, still making the most of his intelligence.

"No," answered Blake again shortly. "Well?"

"Yer heard tell of him, anyhow," persisted the other.

"I heard nothing good of him," said Blake. "I have heard many curse him and none bless. But what of him now? Speak out, man."

The waiter had got his cue. He wanted a hint how his tale should be told, and how it was likely to be received.

"Lord Clearanstown is shot," he said, dropping his words out slowly. "He was shot dead last night at his own hall-door as he stood smoking his cigar, with a sodger on one side of him and a bailiff on the other, planning out a great clearance. Shot dead,

and no one caught for it. He'll clear no more. He's cleared himself now, and it was time." The little man grew hotter and hotter as he spoke. "Saving yer honour's presence," he said to Blake, who listened to the outburst with amazement, "the bloody tyrant put me sister and her childer out with the rest of the neighbours in the winter time, and her husband only wan short week in his grave. I have no call to be sorry for him anyhow. They say it was a boy whose sister he wronged that done the deed. Troth, it's many a dacent girl he brought to ruin, more shame to the fathers and brothers that listened to him so long."

"It is not by murder the country will right itself," said Blake, "though the system," he added, half to himself, "is the more accursed that makes murder look so like a virtue."

"True for you, yer honour," said the waiter, with a look of penitence. "That's the mischief of it, intirely. But if there was not someone killed now and again, it's murdered intirely we'd all be."

He left the room and closed the door with a deep sigh, but there was no trace of sorrow on his face as he went down the stairs two at a time to talk over the details with "morose delectation" among his fellows in the kitchen.

When Maurice Blake breakfasted in the public sitting-room of the hotel next morning, the talk still ran on the murder, and highly edifying were the comments he heard amongst the landlords and

land agents with whom the hotel was crowded for
the fair.

"It's the fault of the Government, sir," said a thin,
angular-faced man, with a nervous twitching of the
mouth, and a hunted look on his face. "They should
put their foot down and keep the people under it.
This talk about toleration has done the mischief.
I'd hang anybody that mentioned it. A tolerated
Papist is a murderer. I'd as soon open a wild
beasts' cage and call that toleration. The instinct
of these fellows is blood. Nothing but bars and
bolts can restrain them—not those always."

"Don't you think the landlords are a bit hard
sometimes—just a little bit?" said a chubby little
man, who stood with his back to the fire, and smiled
in a deprecatory way as he spoke. "Lord Glenracket
comes over to Ireland once a year for a week for the
partridge shooting. This year the shooting was not
up to the mark. He was twenty brace short of the
average bag, and he ordered me to clear out the
village of Mulawaddy. 'It will be a lesson to those
damn poachers, Joyce,' he said to me quite carelessly
as we parted.

"Well, I have served the notices to quit, and there
has been a cross-fire of threatening letters from the
village. I believe the fellows mean mischief. I
wrote to Lord Glenracket about it; and the only
reply was, 'If the blackguards think they can
intimidate me with threatening to shoot my agent,
they will find themselves much mistaken. I would

sooner give up my partridge shooting next year altogether than submit to such dictation.'"

"It is not the landlords that are too hard," broke in another, "but the agents are too soft. That's where the mischief is."

It was a stout, middle-aged man that spoke this time, a man with watery eye, a large, laughing mouth, and a face that told at once of good living and good humour. His voice, too, was rich and husky. "The only way," he went on, "is to keep the Irish tenant's nose to the grinding-stone, if you want to keep him out of mischief. There are not a dozen men on our estate in Connemara that have not been evicted a couple of times, at least. My plan is to keep their backsides always to the bog. I push them back as they reclaim. It keeps them out of harm's way."

"Were you never fired at yourself?" said Joyce, in a tone that suggested such an immunity was little less than a miracle.

"Just once," replied the other, with a good-humoured laugh, as if he were telling the best story in the world. "It was a close shave, too. The driver on the car was shot dead; but I do not think the outrage is likely to be repeated. I turned out the village nearest the spot where that shot was fired, and forbad the tenants to give shelter to man, woman, or child. I heard three of the children died on the road that night. I don't think they were particularly obliged to the bad shots that brought the trouble on them."

"But they may hit you next time," said Joyce, a little maliciously, "as they hit Lord Clearanstown, and then they are all safe."

" Aye, but they may miss me," said the other, still laughing ; "and if they miss they know I won't. A notice to quit carries straight at long range."

" Popery is poisoning the country," broke in the man that spoke first, fretfully ; "and Sir Miles Blake is largely responsible. It is whispered there is a Popish priest at Cloonlara, and it is even rumoured that he sometimes says Mass for the tenants. How can law and order prosper when such things are allowed ?"

"Make your mind easy. They won't be allowed long," said the jovial man cheerily. " Haven't you heard that Lord Dulwich is coming down with a big detachment of Yeos to put his part of the country in order? He has a fine reputation for pitch-caps and half-hanging. This business of Clearanstown will be a signal to begin."

" But isn't he a friend of young Mark Blake, of Cloonlara ? " asked Joyce.

" As thick as pickpockets," said the other. " But neither of them are a bit the worse for that. Young Mark is a fine young fellow, and will be a credit to the country when he comes by his own. He keeps the tenants in rare order even now, since his father has given him up the box-seat and the ribbons. He 'll go the pace, and no mistake, when he owns the coach."

everywhere, always on the run. He never yet was seen to walk. His speed and endurance bordered on the miraculous. Sometimes when stories were told of the distance he had accomplished in a day and night, travelling without rest or food, the old folk crossed themselves as they sat round the fire, and whispered that "Thady was not right; the good people had some hand in him, surely."

Amongst the Castle authorities, too, there was a vague suspicion that Thady was "not right" in another sense, and it was hinted that though he told much—for his tongue was as active as his legs—still he knew more than he told.

Maurice Blake had seen him in the yard of the hotel an hour before he started, and was amazed to find him now a good twelve Irish miles away from his starting point.

The poor fool was draped in rags from his bare head to his bare feet—"a thing of shreds and patches." Yet, as with careless ease he confronted the officer and yeomen, even the rags could not hide the graceful figure, lithe, slender, and active as a greyhound's. If it were not that the light blue eye wandered and flashed so wildly, the pale, thin face might almost have been counted handsome.

The group thus gathered into a recess where the road bulged into the wood under the broad shade of a spreading beech, seemed to Blake so curious that almost instinctively he reined his horse to a walk.

They were so engrossed in their talk, and the

horse's feet fell so softly on the turf, they noticed nothing.

They talked loudly, and their talk turned on the murder of Lord Clearanstown. The officer was plainly pumping the "fool."

"You heard tell of this business about Lord Clearanstown, Thady," he said coaxingly.

"Clearanstown *enagh*! Is it of the corpse you mane?" asked Thady, abruptly. "Troth an' I did that so. I was in very near at the death, as I might say. I seen him before his body was well could or his soul hot."

"You expected the news, then," said the other, leading him on.

"Begad! it's tired expecting it I was for many a long year, but sure it's an' old sayin' an' a true wan, What's everybody's business is nobody's business."

"You wouldn't be sorry, Thady, if he was sent to heaven a few years ago?"

"Lord Clearanstown in heaven," said Thady, with a comical look on his face. "Well, if the likes of him's let in the place 'ill be crowded."

The two soldiers laughed, and the officer looked a bit vexed. The fool was getting the best of it.

"Where is your religion, Thady?" he said, a little tartly. "What about the mercy of God, and all that kind of thing?"

"The mercy of God is too good to be wasted on the likes of him. It's kept for dacent sinners, who have a touch of good left. What's the use of keeping a divil at all if he doesn't git old Clearanstown."

There was another laugh, and the officer thought it safer to let theology slide.

"Ye have no notion who took this job in hand in the long run, Thady?" he said. "It would be a pity anything would happen the decent boy."

"Don't trouble yerself," retorted Thady, with a cunning look. "He wouldn't come to you for a karackter, anyhow. It's a pity now I can't give you his name and his address. It's himself that would be proud to see you knocking at his hall door. Faith, with the hurry that was on him he forgot to lave his visitin' card after him when he was done with Lord Clearanstown."

"But you saw him, Thady? You saw him? Tell us what he was like? He was a brave boy, anyhow."

"Faith, I never laid eyes on him," Thady said sorrowfully. "I was late for the fair—the baste was sould and delivered to the devil before I came up."

"The fellow knows more than he'll tell, unless I can squeeze it out of him," muttered the giant, drawing a strong cord from his pocket and fiddling with the running noose at the end of it.

"I suppose, Thady," he went on, "you wouldn't care to pay his lordship a visit in his new quarters?"

"No fear of that," retorted the fool quickly, "it's to heaven I'm going, no less."

"Perhaps I would be able to give you a lift on

"One end of the rope was drawn tight over his shoulder; from the other end
his victim dangled."

your road," said the other, still playing with the rope.

"I'd be sorry to take your honour out of your way," replied Thady with a simple look that set the soldiers laughing again.

Maurice Blake did not hear the reply. He had passed out of earshot and rode forward smiling to himself, not a little amused, at the dialogue he had listened to.

He had not gone fifty paces when one shrill yell of agony and terror cut the still air like a knife.

He glanced back over his shoulder. Then with a quick wrench of the reins he turned his horse right round on his hind legs as on a pivot, and clapped the spurs to his sides.

A dozen bounds brought him back to the group by the roadside.

Not one moment too soon. The giant had converted himself into a living gallows.

One end of the rope was drawn tight over his shoulder; from the other end his victim dangled at his back. His followers roared with laughter at the gruesome sight. The struggles of the poor fool had almost ceased—his face was livid, his tongue and eye-balls horribly protruding.

Blake's sword was out in an instant. With a quick back stroke he cut the taut rope in two and the keen edge bit through the uniform and scored the great brute's back.

The sharp sting was his first warning of the rescue.

As he wheeled sharply round his broad face was almost on a level with the horseman's.

Standing in his stirrups, Blake raised his sword again for one downright stroke, that must cleave the huge head like a pumpkin. But the giant was unarmed and unready. He could not strike a helpless foe. More than once afterwards Blake regretted the blow had not fallen, and the brutal Hempenstal gone down under his sword.

The giant stood stock still, half dazed by the sudden attack.

The rescued victim was quicker of wit and limb. He bounded from the ground like a ball, seized the hilt of his enemy's huge sword, plucked it from the scabbard, and, lifting it with both hands, stood beside his preserver on the road, quivering with an excitement that was not fear.

At the first onslaught the two yeomen had fled howling down the road.

With a face in which fear and rage were blended, the disarmed and discomfited giant skulked slowly after them.

In a moment Thady was absorbed in admiration of the captured sword.

"It will make an illegant scythe," muttered he, "when a nate handle is put to it, and the blacksmith gives it a bit of a bend."

Then, the end of the rope that still dangled from his neck caught his eye, and from that he looked up at Blake.

"Ye spoiled me cravat," he said, with a look of intelligence so keen, yet so momentary, that Blake was more puzzled than ever to know what to make of him. "But I'm not blaming you for that same. It was too tight to be comfortable." The words were foolish, but there were tears in the wild blue eyes as he spoke.

"Are ye going my way?" he asked abruptly, after a pause.

"I must know what your way is first," said Blake, willing to humour him. "You have turned back on your way to heaven."

"I have been through purgatory," retorted Thady promptly, "but I came out the wrong door."

"Cloonlara is my road," said Blake, "if you know the place."

"Know it?" said Thady; "aye, begad, as well as the fox knows his earth. Straight for it I was going when they made me turn off on the cross road to heaven. Hurry on, now, and I'll wait and show you the way."

Giving the rein to his horse, Blake set forward at a brisk trot. Without an apparent effort Thady kept close beside him, leaping forward as lightly as a hound, the end of the halter, which still dangled from his neck, flying back in the wind.

Ten minutes' run brought them to the entrance of the avenue of Cloonlara. On huge pillars of grey stone, over whose tops the tall trees could just peep, were hung two great gates, so finely worked that they looked like gigantic spider's webs spun in wrought iron. Surmounting the pillars two monster tiger-cats, each with forepaw raised threateningly, guarded the entrance. On the arch that spanned the gates from pillar to pillar, cut deep in the stone, was engraved the proud motto of the family, *Virtus sola nobilitas.*

The bell that hung at the entrance was set dangling by Thady, and an old dame, with smooth, grey hair, and dress of decorous black, issuing from the Gothic ivy-clad gate-house close at hand, gave them entrance to the demesne.

Before they had gone a hundred yards a rabbit suddenly dashed across the avenue. With a cry of childish delight Thady was after it in an instant, breaking through the thick underwood in his eagerness.

Blake saw or heard no more of him for the day. Next morning he found him at last, apparently quite at home among the horses and stable-boys, in the great yard at Cloonlara.

Another hundred yards, at the top of a gentle ascent, Blake pulled his horse to a walk, and flung the reins on his neck, absorbed by the peaceful beauty of the scene.

What folly it is to try to paint light, and shade, and colour, trees, and sky, and water, all that makes the world lovely, with mere poor, colourless words. It is like Olivia's dry catalogue of her own peerless charms. "Item two lips indifferent red, item two grey eyes with lids to them, item one neck, one chin, and so forth."

So Maurice Blake felt, as his eye ranged delightedly over the vast expanse of sloping lawn and waving wood that stretched away to where the Shannon, broadening into a lake, shone in the sunshine. The fair expanse was full of life. The burnished pheasants fluttered up from the glossy laurels or the thick ferns, just touched with autumnal brown, that skirted the avenue. The rabbits spotted the green sward as thick as daisies, and flashed white and grey almost under his horse's feet. Through the vistas of the woods he saw the deer trouping in file long drawn out, or feeding quietly under the shade of some huge old tree that grew by itself in the open, as if disdaining meaner companionship.

Twenty minutes' walking, and suddenly a turn in the avenue gave him a full view of the old mansion house, which stood on a gentle rise ; the vivid green lawn in front stretching in terraces to the wood's edge, through which a bright salmon stream plunged boldly, leaping and flashing down to the lake.

A broad and stately pile was this ancient mansion house, built for the most part in the Roman style, with Ionic porch and pillars, but with turret and balcony and bow windows to boot, of which the Romans had never dreamed.

The inevitable tiger cats guarded the corners of the building, their stone limbs and tails cut clean out against the blue of the sky.

As his horse's hoofs crunched the gravelled sweep in front of the entrance, Christy Culkin walked down the broad stone steps, as demurely as if he had lived his life in the place, held the reins for him to dismount, and led his horse away.

Mark Blake met him half way down the steps, and Sir Miles welcomed him at the door.

So he passed over the threshold into the great square hall, panelled rich with brown oak, and full of trophies of war and chase, and found himself for the first time in his wild, wandering life under the roof of his father's home.

CHAPTER XIII.

" YOU SHALL NOT LACK A PRIEST."
Merry Wives of Windsor.

" A child of conscience."—*Merry Wives of Windsor.*
" Ready to starve and dare not touch."—*Henry IV.* Part II.

SIR MILES BLAKE lived very quietly for a
rich Irish landlord of those days. His feeble
health forbade excitement, and inclination seconded
the command of prudence. As for Mark, he for
the most part took his pleasure elsewhere than at
home.

So it chanced that there was but one other visitor
at Cloonlara when Maurice Blake arrived. They all
four met at dinner. Mr. Spenser O'Carroll, to whom
Maurice was introduced, was of slight, graceful
figure, with a face fresh, eager, and bright as a boy's.
It seemed a mere freak of nature that his light brown
hair was touched with grey. He looked a youth just
verging on manhood. With amazement Maurice
Blake learned, later in the evening, that this seeming
youth was a Catholic priest, full fifty years of age.
Born in Ireland, educated in Paris, Father O'Carroll's
French training had given a surface smoothness
to a nature eminently Irish—Irish in its depth and

strength of sentiment; Irish in the poetry of its patriotism; Irish in the purity of its devotion to religion. His was a wild and strange life—quite unsuited, one would have thought, for that slight boyish frame and gentle, cultured spirit. But the very qualities that seemed to make his weakness made his strength. He was a boy in temperament as well as in appearance; he laughed at hardship and danger with a boy's enjoyment. A high-strung devotion, which sordid minds never know, sustained him through the most terrible ordeals.

There was a price on that handsome young head. It was valued at £500 in the Castle market. He had lain like a fox for days and nights in a cave in the hillside when the yeomen were encamped at the foot, with gallows set and halter ready to save the trouble of a trial. He had said Mass for his persecuted flock, starving for spiritual comfort, in mountain gorge or lonely ravine, when every wind that came moaning by whispered the coming of their persecutors, whose coming meant pitiless slaughter.

With the authority which his holy character gave him he blessed the babe at the font, he blessed the husband and wife at the altar; above all, he brought the blessing and comfort of religion at the death bedside to the ears and hearts of the repentant sinner. The story ran that in the guise of a recruit he had visited and confessed a dying Catholic prisoner in the barracks of the yeomen. His youthful appearance often stood him in good stead. He had been once arrested and tortured to make him confess his own whereabouts.

"That boy" was never suspected to be the notorious "Papist priest," who for years had disturbed the country side, celebrating Mass, hearing confession, instructing the ignorant, consoling the living, encouraging the dying, "in open flagrant violation of law and order."

It was rest and recreation to Father O'Carroll when the round of his unceasing duties brought him within range of Cloonlara, where welcome and security always awaited him, and where secret chambers and passages rendered detection impossible.

They were a pleasant little party that were gathered in the great hall. A smaller table had been drawn close to the bright wood fire that burned cheerily in the low grate, changing the chill of the autumn evening to a genial glow. Fire, table, and party were curtained round with a huge crimson upright screen, that made a room within a room.

Within this citadel of comfort the four were seated. Comfort begot sociality. When the dainty dinner had disappeared and the wine came, their talk played freely on a hundred topics, striking light from all. Literature, art, politics, and religion were discussed in turn, the discussion growing more serious as the evening wore away to night.

To Maurice Blake that evening was one of the pleasantest of his life, none the less pleasant because at first he sat a silent but delighted listener to the others. Talk was a fine art in these days, and priest and baronet were adepts in the art. It had not degenerated, as in our modern days, to a mere crazy patchwork of slang, slander, and scoff. "From grave to gay, from serious to serene," it freely wandered. Hand-in-hand with bright jest and pleasant story and badinage came wisdom, doffing her solemn mask and sombre garments, and making merry with the rest.

Mark Blake, too, talked well and appreciatively on such topics, though more coldly than the others. There was a sub-acid pungency in some of his observations that gave zest to their earnestness, as olives enhance the flavour of wine.

By degrees the talk slipped round to living topics —to the laws under which they lived—their relentless savagery ; the people amongst whom they lived— their long-suffering patience, and their child-like good humour.

On this theme the priest was as one inspired. His love of his people was an absorbing passion. His pictures were from life. His stories moved to smiles and tears. So simple were they, so sad, or so truly they pictured the life of his people, whose quaint humour, whose odd turns of phrase and thought, whose light-hearted playfulness in the intervals of misery are no more than the sunbeams on the surface of a life whose depths are dark and cold.

Sir Miles and Maurice Blake listened enthralled, but Mark now and again dropped a phrase or two carelessly, almost contemptuously, that jarred painfully on their earnest mood.

"You remember the Wickhard evictions?" said the priest to Mark, who nodded assent. "Well, amongst the victims was an old man of eighty years—Pat Dunn was the name—who died that night in an outhouse where he was thrown.

"He had lived alone with his grandson, a child of twelve; and when the old man died, the poor lad stole away, when the corpse was carried to an outhouse to await its burial. For two days he disappeared, and early on the morning of the third, the boy was found fast asleep at the great gate of the Wickhard demesne. My lady's coach-and-four had almost rolled over the forlorn little creature as he lay there in the mud. The horses shied, and so saved him. Some strange freak of compassion seized her ladyship as she saw the desolate little waif lying so still, almost under the horses' feet. He was a pretty boy, for all the rags and mud. Her ladyship was touched by the sight. Her one son had died about the same age, and she had consoled herself since with the conversion of Papists. Now the mother's instinct in her stirred. She had the poor waif lifted gently into the carriage, for he was so weak with fatigue and hunger he could not stand.

"Then the horses were wheeled round, and she drove straight back. The poor child's story touched the great lady's heart. For two days and nights he had wandered through wood and mountain in foolish terror of being taken by the police. No food but haws and blackberries had passed his lips. 'Then all the sense went out of him,' he said. 'There was no strength in his legs, nor light in his eyes. He staggered like a man that had drink in him.' He could not tell how he came lying there in front of the gate.

"Who can say what vague thoughts and longings were in her heart, as she patted the pale cheek of the desolate boy. This thought, at any rate, be sure, was surely amongst them. Here was a chance to win a young soul from the blind superstitions of Popery.

"The child was carried to the kitchen, and set before a comfortable fire that warmed his numbed limbs. A basin of wholesome broth was prepared, and bread broken into it. Her ladyship meant to feed him with her own white hands. The hungry longing in his face pleased her. There would be a novel pleasure in relieving it. The boy watched her eagerly with grateful, longing eyes. Then the poor weak little hand fluttered over the forehead and breast in the sign of the Cross. Lady Wickhard caught the gesture, and understood it.

"'What are you doing, my boy?' she said. 'You must not do that.'

"'O sure, I'm only blessin' mesel', ma'am,' said the child, feebly. 'There's no harm in thanking the good God for the bit and sup he sent to me. I couldn't set to ating without blessin' mesel'. I 'd as leve ate mate on Friday very near.'

" Lady Wickhard shut her lips tight with anger. 'What a blind idolator that poor boy is,' she thought.

" ' What if it were Friday?' she said.

" He looked at her sharply, with a quick suspicion in his eyes. 'Is it? Is it?' he whispered.

" Then an evil thought came into her head in the disguise of a duty. She would cure him of such superstition once and for all. She nodded her head.

" To her amazement the feeble hand put away the tempting food.

" ' Not that! not that!' he said. 'A crust of dry bread, for the love of God, and a drop of water, but not that.' But she was earnest and determined in her duty. It was for the boy's own good, she told herself. He steadily refused the food. She coaxed, she even threatened—all in vain.

" Then she set the savoury mess beside him so that the steam of it should be in his nostrils, and so left him. An hour later she stole back into the kitchen. The food was then untouched. The boy lay very quiet, leaning wearily and patiently back in the chair. His eyes were half-closed: the face seemed paler even than before. Her heart relented: something of admiration took the place of her impatience.

" The child had conquered. With her own hands she got some hot bread and milk ready, and brought it to him. She raised the little hand that lay so quietly on his lap. It dropped from her grasp limp and lifeless. Startled, she touched his face with her hand. It was stone cold. The heroic spirit had gone to its reward. The child was dead."

There was silence when the story ended. Then Mark Blake laughed a little bitter, scornful laugh.

"What folly!" he muttered, half aloud. "What silly, cruel folly to preach or practise! Did our merciful Mother Church, father, really command this poor child to starve itself to death?"

"No," said the priest shortly. "The poor child was in this mistaken—the sacrifice was not demanded. But was his self-devotion, therefore, the less noble? He died for his faith! This, to your thinking, was folly, and the martyr was a fool; but the soldier who dies on the battle-field for his king—a weak, wicked mortal like himself—is a hero!"

The priest spoke with warmth.

Mark Blake replied, still sneeringly, "Whence had you your story, reverend father?—for to me it borders closely on the marvellous."

"From the lips of Lady Wickhard herself," returned the priest. "For her, at least, that sad death was no theme for laughter. Her thoughts and hopes turned towards the faith that could inspire such devotion. She sent for me, and I came. She has returned to the faith of her fathers, and now, through the broad acres that call her mistress, the poor are at peace."

It was plain that between the priest and the heir of the house no love was lost. If rumours spoke truly, Mark Blake's life was wild and reckless—"sparing neither man in his hate nor woman in his lust." The priest, it is likely enough, knew something of this, and the other hated him for his knowledge, and feared him too a little, it may be.

Mark bit his lips hard, to keep back the bitter retort—for his father's face was turned to him in grave surprise and rebuke.

"Forgive me, reverend father," he said at last, in a tone that might be jest or earnest, as it was taken. "I will trouble you no more. With your permission I will retire to my evening devotions—and do penance," he muttered aside to Maurice, "for my blasphemy against the sacred mystery of chicken broth and bread and milk."

The time was approaching midnight, and the others rose with him. Mark showed his guest to his room.

"That priest will drive me mad," he said, as they mounted the broad stairs together. "I trust Lord Dulwich's bloodhounds may catch the sly fox. He keeps the country side in a ferment with his mummery. A gentleman cannot look sidelong at a pretty peasant wench, but he is ready with bell, book, and candle. He spoils all sport—curse him again. You are a Protestant, of course?" he added abruptly, turning to his companion.

"No," answered Maurice sharply. "I am a Catholic."

"Like myself," retorted the other with a careless

laugh. "Well, good night, and do not forget your night prayers."

Maurice Blake was too excited by the strange new life into which he had got a glimpse, to settle at once to sleep. The fire burned brightly in his room, but at the further window behind the shadow of the deep curtain the moon threw a beam of pure white athwart the darkness.

Maurice, as is the fashion of youth, deserted the prosaic comfort of the fire-light for the unsubstantial splendour of the moonshine. He threw open the window, and stepped out on the little stone balcony that projected from the angle of the wall. The view was superb. From his perch he could see over the whitened tree tops away for miles to the broad flash of the lake, slumbering calmly in the still moonlight. It was a rich land and a fair. Can it be wondered that the thought came into his mind that all this vast heritage by right of birth should be his own? Can he be blamed if he dreamed a dream, brief as bright, of what his life might be with happiness to have and share, amid such scenes.

A fair face looked in upon his soul, with eyes tender and truthful, and made him dizzy with delight.

The cool night wind that began to creep in from the lake roused him from his reverie. Then came back the remembrance of the high and stern duty to which his life was vowed.

He cast away his cigar, that fell with a long trail

of sparks through the night, closed the window, and drew the curtains close, shutting in the cosiness and shutting out the moonshine, and ten minutes later was asleep.

It was a pleasant life he led at Cloonlara, and he enjoyed it keenly. In all forms of manly sport he was marvellously proficient, and proficiency begets delight. His shot gun was as deadly to the wild duck, snipe, grouse, and partridge, as his rifle had been to the big game of America. His horsemanship won the admiration of the hard-riding county folk, who reluctantly confessed the supremacy of the stranger.

Sir Miles was his guide through the pleasant ways of literature, as Mark was the companion of his field sports. Yet while his respect and affection for the older man, who treated him like a son, grew daily deeper, the instinctive repugnance he felt for Mark Blake from the first never totally disappeared.

Sir Miles treated him as a son, Mark as a brother. He had a manner when he liked almost as charming as his father's. Even in his bluff frankness there was a touch of refinement. The hardest substances take the finest polish, and his heart was as hard as flint, and as cold. There was no place in it for pity or love. Like the flint, too, a short, hot spark of anger was the only warmth which his nature knew.

He was so frank, so cordial, so full of cheerful spirits at times, that Maurice would half forget his distrust, when a look or word for the most part to

some poor wretch who implored help or pity, revealed
the wild beast nature under the cover of the smooth
and charming manner he could so well assume.

For some time back Sir Miles, broken with sickness, had entrusted the management of the vast
estate almost entirely to his son, and by degrees the
tenants were beginning to realise the change of
government, though Mark was somewhat kept in
check as yet by his fear of his father's resumption of
the reins.

It would wrong Maurice Blake to suppose his
secret mission was forgotten or neglected. He lost
no chance of making himself acquainted with the
people, in which task he was well seconded by
Father O'Carroll, who readily consented to become
a member of their association.

"As a priest," he said smilingly, "I am already
ex-officio a traitor, and worthy of the worst punishment the law has at its disposal. On their own
showing I am no worse by becoming a rebel."

CHAPTER XIV.

"I DO LOVE THAT COUNTRY GIRL."

Love's Labour Lost.

" Call it not love, for love to Heaven is fled,
  Since sweating lust on earth usurped his name :
  Under whose simple semblance he had fed
  Upon fresh beauty, blotting it with blame.
  Love comforteth like sunshine after rain,
  But lust's effect is tempest after sun ;
  Love's gentle spring does always fresh remain ;
  Lust's winter comes ere summer's heat be done ;
  Love surfeits not, lust like a glutton dies ;
  Love is all truth, lust full of forgèd lies."

CHRISTY CULKIN'S first care on the day after their arrival was to slip away down a path that led through the heart of the demesne, and beyond that through a hawthorny lane to where a cottage stood, just within the uttermost skirting of the wood close down by the lake.

It was a pretty cottage, and comfortably built by Sir Valentine Blake in the old days, for his foster mother and her husband, with flowering creepers on the walls and an orchard at the side, and well fenced fields of pasture land and tillage in front. For they held at an easy rent, and Mark Blake, knowing his father's feelings, had so far spared them.

It were vain to try to describe the surprise and rapture with which Christy was welcomed back by the old folk from " foreign parts." They could never see enough of him. His stories of his travels were listened to with open-mouthed delight. But on one topic his mouth was tight shut. He could not be got to speak one word about the old master or his fate. His mother appealed to him to tell her at least if her " darlint boy " was safe and well. Stimulated at once by affection and curiosity she tried all sorts of devices quite in vain.

" You might as well try to coax a weasel out of its hole as coax a secret out of Christy," she complained to her husband.

" Na boclish, mother," Christy replied composedly to all her teasing. " The secret is not mine to give or share. I have only the lend of the loan of it for safe keeping, and I 'll give it back, please God, as I got it. One word borrows another. If we wance got talking there 's no knowing where we would stop. It 's like taking the cork out of the poteen bottle just to taste it. Moryah! Troth it is not long afterwards till the last drop is gone down the red lane."

But Christy had a harder trial than even his mother's questioning.

When he first visited his father and mother he had noted a pretty girl of about twenty years, who moved about the place, not as a servant moves, but like a daughter of the house.

This young girl had kept shyly apart and busied

Christy Culkin.

herself, or seemed to busy herself, about simple household duties, while the old folk sat on either side of their returned prodigal, and questioned, and wondered, and rejoiced, and wept over him with many a "Glory be to God," "Think of that now," "Was the like ever heard."

Do what he would Christy's eyes would keep wandering to the pretty figure dusting the bright-coloured delft at the great dresser that filled one side of the kitchen. Small blame to him that eyes and mind turned in spite of himself to that animated picture, and the blood began to course quicker and warmer through his veins as he gazed on that fair face, which, flushed a little now with curiosity and excitement, was one to charm a severer critic than Christy.

A perfect type she was of Irish beauty. Blue-black hair, with a shine and wave like the deep lake's water when the light breeze curls it, framed a forehead low and white. Eyes as blue as the sky that mirrors itself in the summer lake glanced side-long looks under their long lashes at the group by the fire. The merry sparkle in those eyes, the saucy dimples lurking round the ripe red mouth, spoke a spirit as frolicsome as a kitten's. A kitten could scarcely be lighter or more graceful in its movements than that dainty figure. A plaided kerchief was pinned modestly over her swelling bosom, and the pretty bare ankles and feet glanced white under the short scarlet petticoat. Thackeray seems to have found such a beauty in his rambles through Ireland just fifty years afterwards, when he wrote—

> See her as she moves,
> Scarce the ground she touches,
> Airy as a fay,
> Graceful as a duchess.
> Bare her rounded arm,
> Bare her little leg is ;
> Vestris never showed
> Ankles like to Peggy's.
> Braided is her hair,
> Soft her look and modest,
> Thin her little waist,
> Comfortably bodiced.

Christy's mother, when her first excitement was passed, caught his eye returning from one of its frequent excursions, and answered its question in words.

"It's Peggy," she said. "Peggy Heffernan. Don't you know Peggy? But it's a wool-gathering I am. How could you know the baby that was born five years after you left for foreign parts. But you mind Con Heffernan, a near friend of your father's? He was a tenant under Lord Clearanstown, worse luck ! Well, my dear, it is better nor fifteen years since Con was down with the slow fever, very weak, and dying by inches. Things went from bad to worse wid him, and when he died late in the autumn there was near hand a half-year's rent due, not counting the hanging gale, a thing that never happened him before.

"In Christmas week the widow and her little colleen were put out on the street, and between the sorrow and the hardships the poor woman's heart was bruck entirely, and she died in the bed within, calling out constantly, 'I'm coming, Mike, I'm coming. I was lonely without you.' But her wits came back clear and steady before she died, and the only word she had in her mouth was to be good to the poor little colleen she was leaving behind her. Troth that was the blessed gift she left us. It's she that is the joy of our heart and the light of our eyes, and sad and lonely the house would be without her.

"Come here, Peggy acuschla," she went on; "come over here at wanst. What are you afeared of? It's only our own boy Christy. Sure, you often hear tell of Christy. Well, he's come home to us at last."

Peggy came when she was called, smiling her welcome with a flash of white teeth and of blue eyes that shot out a look half saucy, half shy, as she stretched a plump, dimpled hand to Christy.

"Kiss him, asthore," said the mother; "kiss him, child, can't ye, and him so long away. Is it a stranger ye'd make of the boy in his father's and mother's house?"

Peggy pouted her red lips demurely for the salute like an obedient child, yet with a comical tantalising look in the mischievous blue eyes.

The young country girl, who had never been twenty miles from home in her short life, was cool as a cucumber. The seasoned old warrior, who had travelled half-way round the world, was overwhelmed with confusion.

A belated blush strove to find its long-forgotten way to his face, and turned the brown of his sun-burned cheek to rich mahogany colour. He fidgetted with his hat and blackthorn, and dropped both on the floor.

"Where's your manners, Christy?" said his mother reprovingly. "Troth, I'm ashamed of you."

Thus encouraged, he touched with his own the sweet lips that were raised to him invitingly.

That kiss sealed his fate. Thenceforward he was Peggy Heffernan's slave. Mischievous Cupid had wrought another of his madcap miracles. He had drawn fresh water from the hard, dry rock. He had made the withered, old, weather-beaten bough bud and bear sweet-smelling blossoms.

Poor Christy had a hard time of it with the sprightly young girl, to whom the whole world and all things in it was matter for lighthearted merriment. That tough old campaigner, silent and stern of nature, was never meant for a young girl's plaything. Yet there was an interest in the game, too, in which strength and beauty played their respective parts. The flowering creeper never shows more beautifully than when it makes mirth of the gnarled oak, or the sturdy grey tower.

At times Christy's quiet humour was more than a match for Peggy's lively playfulness. But for the most, he was mocked into glum silence.

Christy had enforced secrecy on his father. But it

was impossible to keep such a secret as Christy's
return from "the neighbours." The news soaked
through and through the little community till all
minds were saturated with it. Then it began to
break out in little rivulets of talk.

When the neighbours, men and women, girls and
boys, were "giving a day to his honour wid the hay"
gossip buzzed about this exciting topic.

"Christy Culkin's home again, that was off with the
ould Master on his travels?"

"Musha now, do you tell me so. And what news
has he of the ould Master at all, at all?"

"Divil a word, good or bad, is there out of his
mouth."

"Then sure it's bad work that was in it or he
wouldn't be so close. Maybe it's et by them blacks
he was," hazarded a lean, blear-eyed, hungry-looking
man who was known in the village as Greedy Pether,
and was popularly supposed to have a "wolf" in his
interior.

"Or married a score of wives and has them hould-
ing him," suggested a gay young fellow, one of the
sprightliest "bachelors" of the district.

"It's truth I'm telling you," he went on in reply to
a chorus of "Musha, be aisey now wid yer jokin',"
from the women.

"It's Gospel truth I'm telling ye. Larry Lanni-
gan, the sailor man that was over from Galway, says
there is such a sight of women in them parts that
they're to be had for the picking and choosing, an'

many a man there has as many wives as he has fingers an' toes on him."

"Bad cess to them, the haythens, anyhow," said a meek young giant, who had the reputation of being kept in particularly good order by his own sprightly little helpmate. "Troth, wan wife is enough, and lavings, for any dacent Christian. But sure a Blake of the ould stock and the ould religion would never demane himself to do the like."

"Maybe it's turned Protestan' he did," chimed in a sheepish-looking youth, who had listened open-mouthed to the discussion.

But this terrible suggestion was received with such a storm of obloquy that the unfortunate offender felt that he might as well have turned Protestant himself from the treatment he got.

The notion of the ould master a "jumper" was too much for their feelings, and the tossing and trampling of the hay was resumed with a will, as if the horror of this last suggestion could only be worked off in active physical exertion.

But tongues kept wagging about Christy all the same, at fair and wake and pattern. Maurice Blake's likeness to the family did not escape the quick eyes of those shrewd peasants, and a thousand conjectures, each more fantastical than the other, were afloat about them both.

The echo of their gossip reached the ear of Mark Blake, and he in his turn did not fail to detect something of the singular resemblance which Maurice bore

to Sir Miles. Something he had heard in a vague
way about the departure of his uncle, Sir Valentine.
But ever since he was of an age to think intelligently
of the subject he had assumed his death as a matter
of course. In the coming of Maurice Blake and the
foster-brother of his uncle (for so he quickly discovered Christy to be) there was a mystery which
he did not like. Some scheme was afoot, he half
suspected, " to rob him of his rights," and he resolved
to probe it to the bottom.

For this reason he vigorously opposed all the
efforts of Maurice to bring his lengthened visit to a
close. He had always some new reason to urge for
delay; some new scheme of amusement to propose;
and as his efforts were heartily seconded by Sir Miles,
who found in his guest's society a pleasant companionship which his son's never afforded, Maurice yielded
again and again. The life was very pleasant to him,
and the kindliness of his hosts—father and son—
made departure more difficult.

Between Mark Blake and Christy Culkin, however,
there was no love lost. Mark had tried to pump him
with masterly dexterity, but he might as well have
tried to pump one of the grey stone family tiger cats
over the entrance gate, for any information he got.
Christy's answers to all questions were stolidly and
impenetrably stupid. Mark had a shrewd suspicion
that the stupidity was assumed, but there was no
getting behind the utter blankness of Christy's face
and words.

Another cause of feud there was between them.

The "young master" had cast an eye of favour on Peggy Heffernan. It was amazing how often his way from the hunting-field or stubble-field with horse or gun lay round by Culkin's cottage; how often he slipped in for a draught of new milk or a light for his cigar. It was still more curious how often they met by accident when Peggy was going to the milking or returning, and how invariably Mark found her path was his whichever way hers led.

Jealousy has keen eyes. Sometimes when Mark came down the long lane that led to Christy's cottage, looking wonderfully handsome in the bright pink hunting toggery or green shooting-coat, he found the old campaigner and the fresh young beauty return-ing from the pasture together. Then he would pass with a good humoured " good evening," which Peggy would repay with a flashing smile of red lips, white teeth, and blue eyes, but he would mutter impatient curses when he passed.

Sometimes it was Christy who found the other two in the lane before him, walking slowly, with the gentleman's lips, as he thought, too near the tempting beauty of the young girl's face, while he whispered gay nothings in her ear, and she listened, and blushed, and smiled. Then it was Christy's time to pass, with face as stolid as grey stone, and as hard to read as an Egyptian inscription, but with hot wrath in his heart.

Mark Blake had an impatient contempt for the

hard-featured veteran who crossed his pleasure, and who, as he guessed, was silly enough to hanker after the gay young beauty on whom his lordly self had deigned to smile.

Christy had fierce hatred, the fiercer because it smouldered suppressed by his strong will, for the wanton libertine who coldly plotted ruin for this pure young creature, blithe as a bird, and so innocent, that went, thinking no evil, straight into the net of the snarer.

It chanced on a fair evening in the late autumn, Christy carried the young girl's full milk pail home from the pasturage, walking by her side with those long strides he had learned on the prairies, which needed three of her pretty short steps to keep pace with. He was what she called "sermonising." He found it hard work, for he was as shy in her presence—this middle-aged man—as a hobbledehoy in the rapturous misery of his first calf love. He could not hint the nature of the peril from which he would fain warn her. A word or two he dropped ever so cautiously; but the look of frank childlike surprise in her pure blue eyes closed his lips.

Her surprise dissolved in merry laughter, that rang out in the still air like a bird's song, as merry and as sweet.

"Oh! you foolish, foolish Christy," she cried, when she got breath. "Man alive, is there no sense at all left in ye. Is it a gomeril ye are out and out? To warn me against falling in love with the young master. Don't ye see it's yerself I love like "— another burst of laughter broke the words short off at her lips.

Christy was dumbfounded. His heart with one great effort sent the hot blood surging to his face, and then stopped beating altogether.

"Love me," he faltered out at last. "Ye don't mean it?"

"Mean it," she said ; "of course I mean it. I love ye like a father." The merry laughter broke out again, but how much merriment there was in it, and how much mockery, let those skilled in woman's ways decide.

To Christy it seemed all mockery. He was wounded to the quick. Without a word he set the pail of milk he carried down beside her, and turned on his heel, and was off with long strides back the way they had come.

Peg's laugh broke off in the middle. She looked after him with a look of comical surprise. Then she lifted the pail on to her head, where it sat like a queen's crown.

Christy had not gone a hundred yards, when at a slight bend in the lane his eye caught the flash of pink through the sparse leaves and thick branches of the hedge. Instinctively he stepped aside into the shade, and without seeing him Mark Blake went by, whistling a gay air and beating time with his gold-mounted riding whip on the polished leather of his boots. Almost in spite of himself Christy turned back. He saw Mark quicken his step as he caught sight of the lithe figure in front, and with step as light as when he stalked deer in the western woods, Christy followed him.

Mark touched Peggy's cheek with the silken tip of his riding whip, and with a smile and blush she turned to greet him. He tried to take the pail from her head, but she would not allow it.

"It will be quite safe here in the lane," he said, "for an hour or so, and that greyhound of yours, old Christy, will carry it home as he comes by."

The old greyhound heard him, and clinched his teeth tight as he followed stealthily.

He would have been comforted a little if he had seen the quick flash of anger in Peggy's blue eyes.

"You're right to misname him behind his back," she said saucily—"it's safer."

"What! angry, my pretty one, and all the prettier for your anger. Love me, love my dog, is it? Well, for your love the hound shall escape the whip. What is there I would not do for you?" he went on in a lower and more passionate tone. "Was it the Devil made you so beautiful, Peggy, to buy souls with your beauty?"

Something in his tone brought Christy's warning to mind, filling her with vague fear.

She walked on more quickly, but Mark kept close beside, leaning towards her.

Though her eyes were cast down she felt his hot gaze on her face. Her cheek flushed and burned under it. He spoke hurriedly yet falteringly, running his words into each other like one in wine.

"Look at me," he cried passionately, catching her hand as he spoke. "Look at me straight in the eyes, and read love there."

She looked up timidly, and dropped her lids again, frightened, she knew not why, by what she read in those dark eyes, all aflame with passion.

Again she quickened her step, but he kept his hold of her hand and his place beside her, drawing her towards himself.

"You are too good," he said, "for the life you lead; too good and too beautiful. You are out of place amongst those dull coarse creatures, whose lives are scarcely one degree removed from the brutes. I will raise you from amongst them, my darling. I will take you away with me to the gay city. You shall be robed like a queen, with a crown of diamonds. You shall have all your heart's desires. I will give you myself, body and soul, and in return for all I only ask your love."

His voice and words frightened her more and more. She blushed even to her neck at the way that word "love" was spoken.

"Why don't you answer me, sweetheart?" he said, gazing on her ripe charms hungrily.

"I don't know what to answer," she said. "I don't

"The pail of milk tottered and fell right on the head of the falling man."

know what you mean. You frighten me. Let me go. I am stayed for at home."

"Let them wait," he said contemptuously: "let them wait. You are too good to tend those boors. You are mine, Peggy, henceforward and for ever. I am impatient to take full possession of my treasure. One kiss at least I must have as earnest of the future."

His arm clasped her round the pliant waist, and drew her close to him. He bent down over her burning face, his own flushed with the fierce excitement of overmastering passion.

Christy, wild with anger, sprang forward, but the ready-witted girl needed no help.

"Look! look!" she cried, in tones of such unaffected terror that Mark turned his head aside for a moment.

In that moment she flung him from her with a strength that none could have dreamed of in those slim, rounded arms of hers.

He staggered backwards with the unexpected vigour of the push. The girl herself was slightly thrown off her balance. The pail of milk tottered and fell right on the head of the falling man, blinding him with the white cataract. Crash back he went into the quickset hedge with the pail still bonneted over his head, while Peggy fled like a frightened bird down the lane.

There was a grim smile on Christy's face as he looked at his gay young rival struggling in the ditch, his gay clothes saturated in the white stream from head to foot, and his head hidden in the wooden extinguisher.

But Christy's face was stolid and expressionless as an owl's when he lifted the pail from Mark's head—lifted him from the ditch and set him on his feet. Not a trace of surprise, not a hint of curiosity, not a gleam of amusement at the comical figure. To judge from Christy's face it was quite a matter of course to find a young gentleman in a ditch with a milk pail jammed tight on his head.

Very sulkily Mark Blake availed himself of his help, eyeing him closely the while, with the riding whip nervously clenched in his hand. The slightest hint of a smile on Christy's part would have been answered by a cut of the whip across the face—but his features remained stone blank to the end. Mark shook himself like a sulky dog, scattering the white drops into the air, and without a word of thanks or greeting strode hastily away.

Then Christy's glum face again relaxed slowly into a smile, and he followed leisurely the path Peggy had taken.

Just as Mark arrived, chilled and dishevelled, at the broad stone steps, a horseman, on a handsome thoroughbred steed, came pacing slowly up the avenue.

A glance was sufficient. That graceful figure, prim in spite of its perfect proportions, the trim appointments of horse and man, proclaimed Lord Dulwich a hundred yards off.

Mark waited on the steps for him. His hunting costume, he knew, would account for his bedraggled state.

Lord Dulwich touched his horse's sides ever so lightly with the rowels. The spirited animal sprang forward, and in a moment was at the steps.

"So glad to see you, Mark," cried out his lordship, more warmly than was his wont. "My visit is to you. I have been priest-hunting in this district for some weeks back, and have had good sport, though the best of the game is not yet bagged. You, I know, have no silly scruples in such matters, but I had my doubts how your father might receive me, though duty compelled me to come. You will introduce me to the master of the house."

Mark was in the mood when men find matter of offence in everything.

"I am the master of the house," he answered sharply. "But," he added in a moment, more gently, "come in. I will introduce you with pleasure to my father."

They passed together through the square hall to the library, where Maurice Blake and Sir Miles were reading, with an occasional lapse into talk as they read.

Both rose as Mark and his companion entered. Standing thus side by side, the likeness between Maurice and Sir Miles was very striking.

Sir Miles bowed coldly as Lord Dulwich was presented. At the same moment his lordship took the opportunity of whispering in Mark Blake's ear—

"Was there ever so wonderful a resemblance? He might almost be your elder brother."

Mark started as though a wasp had stung him, but his manner that evening was more cordial than ever to Maurice.

CHAPTER XV.

"AN EXCELLENT STRATAGEM."

Henry IV. Part II.

"He seemed in running to devour the wind."—*Henry IV.* Part II.

"Priests in holy vestments bleeding."—*Timon of Athens.*

"Abhorrèd slave,
Which any print of goodness wilt not take,
Being capable of all ill."—*The Tempest.*

"At last I left them
I' the filthy-mantled pool beyond your cell,
There dancing up to the chins."—*The Tempest.*

"I am old, I am old.
I love thee better than e'er a boy of them all."

Henry IV. Part II.

THE coming of Lord Dulwich cast a gloom over the party at Cloonlara. His lordship was of the class who cannot unbend unless they condescend, and it was hard to say which of his manners was more objectionable—his stiff formality with his equals, or his patronizing condescension. He cared nothing for literature, and little for field sports; his time between meals was for the most part occupied in riding to and from the small barrack, some seven miles distant, which was the kennel where his bloodhounds were quartered. The evenings up to midnight, and often after it, he and Mark Blake spent alone in a snuggery that abutted from the picture gallery, absorbed in heavy play at dice or cards. The superior skill of Mark in all games of skill was a poor counterpoise to the superior coolness of his opponent, who gradually accumulated quite a collection of Mark's signatures (in all stages of shakiness) on promises to pay.

From the first, Sir Miles Blake treated Lord Dulwich with a chilling courtesy that, to a sensitive man, would have been harder to bear than rudeness. Never before was guest so treated at Cloonlara. For Sir Miles was troubled with the suspicion that this priest-hunter had come to trap his friend, Father O'Carroll, even under his roof, and his blood tingled at the thought of such social perfidy.

Fortunately, Father O'Carroll was not at Cloonlara at the time, though there was no saying when he might arrive. He never gave warning of his coming. It was possible he might at any moment walk straight into the cruel clutches of Lord Dulwich.

Christy Culkin shared the suspicion, and resolved at the very first chance to put it to the proof.

The chance came soon enough.

The fourth night after Lord Dulwich arrived, he and Mark Blake retired with half-a-dozen of claret and a dozen packs of cards to spend the night in the fashion they loved best. They locked the door, stirred the fire, snuffed the candles, and began. Soon they were absorbed in the gambler's delirium, lost to all thought on earth in heaven or hell, except the coins on the table and the cards in their hands.

Half-an-hour later Christy stole into the picture gallery. His boots were off, and his thick woollen socks made no sound on the soft carpet. He held the light a little over his head, and glanced cautiously round at the pictures.

He stopped before the portrait of a beautiful young woman in the robes of an abbess, who was gently lifting from the ground a supplicant that knelt at her feet.

The frame of the picture was heavy and richly carved with religious devices. Wreathed round it, in and out through the other emblems, were rosary beads of fifteen decades, cut in *bas relief* out of the hard wood.

"Here it is, sure enough," muttered Christy. "I have forgotten the number, but I 'll try them all round if the worst comes to the worst."

He held the light close to the beads, but could find no shade of difference. Then he pressed the beads one after the other with his finger-tip, muttering a prayer. The seventh he touched yielded to the pressure. At the same instant a panel in the polished oak wainscotting, just below the picture, slipped aside, leaving an open space through which a man's body might pass, and darkly showing an iron ladder in the recess.

"It works as it worked twenty-five years ago," muttered Christy, lowering his light to the opening ; "I was little more nor a gossoon when I last tried it."

The wood must have been cut with an edge like a

razor, for when it closed, the finger-nail could detect no joining.

The way was familiar to Christy. Many a time as a boy he had brought meat and drink to Father O'Carroll, as he lay hidden for days in this secure retreat, while the Castle bloodhounds hunted him in vain, ransacking the house from garret to cellar.

Christy noiselessly climbed the ladder, shielding his taper carefully from the draught, and pushing open a trap-door at the top, found himself in a curious lop-sided chamber, narrow and low, with no opening for light or entrance except that through which he had just crept.

He was now, as he knew, right over the snuggery where the gamblers were engaged. With the light close down to the floor he sought and found a small steel ring turned flat down upon the wood. Very carefully he brushed the dust from about it, lest any should fall through.

Then passing his fingers through the ring, with quiet but strong pull he lifted a piece two inches square out of the floor of the room where he stood, and the ceiling of the room below. The opening was artfully concealed in the midst of the elaborate carving of the ceiling. Up through it at once came light and the sound of voices. Lying flat on the floor Christy looked and listened with all his might.

He was almost right over the card table, where the two were engaged.

The faces of the cards and the players were plain

to him. They were seated at a small table close to the fire, and on a second table near them was the huge silver claret jug and glasses. Three bottles of the old wine "aired" themselves on the chimney-piece. The floor of the room was strewn with discarded packs of cards. They were both intent upon the game.

Mark Blake was clearly winning; he seemed flushed, excited, and exhilarated. Lord Dulwich was imperturbably cool as ever.

Just as Christy looked a game ended.

Mark Blake laughed exultingly, and stretched out his hand. Lord Dulwich took from his pocket-book and handed to him a crumpled bit of paper, which Mark at once lit in the candle, and held lighting till it burned down to his fingers. Then he dropped the ashes on the silver ash-tray. He was burning his own I O U's, as he rescued them from his opponent.

Christy noted there was quite a pile of ashes on the tray.

"You are in luck's way to-night, Mark," said Lord Dulwich with a touch of annoyance in his cold voice, "that makes twelve hundred in three hours. You have only lost a single game since we started."

"Twelve hundred out of three thousand," retorted Mark brusquely, "leaves eighteen hundred still on the wrong side of my book and the right side of yours. But you know the proverb, your bad luck to-night augurs good luck in to-morrow's expedition."

"How comes your luck, then, by both roads,"

sneered Lord Dulwich, "for you are keener on the priest's capture than I am."

"I am, I confess it," replied Mark Blake. "I hate the fellow, and have hated him any time this five years. Often and often when he was hiding here I felt tempted to put a bullet or a sword-point through his soutane. He is for ever skulking and spying. One cannot kiss a pretty wench, deal cards, or draw a trigger, but his reverence must needs come preaching. He takes on him to lecture me as if I were a schoolboy. But he has quite bewitched my father in his dotage, and I dare not raise hand or voice against him. How comes it though, Dulwich, that you are not with your hounds in to-morrow's hunt? I should not wonder if the reverend fox gets to earth after all."

"It was thought better I should be away," stammered Lord Dulwich, a little confused at the abrupt question. "That is to say, it is more politic, lest suspicion should be excited, that I should not be seen in the matter. Hempenstal," he went on more smoothly, "is a good huntsman of such vermin. If there be resistance he will know how to deal with it in my absence, don't you see."

"Oh, ay! I do see, I think," broke in the other, with a laugh that was an insult. "Those fellows fight hard sometimes. They will be furious as a hive of stinging-bees, if their priest is meddled with. If there is a hole or two to be made with pitchfork or pike, better through Hempenstal's hulking carcase than through the precious person of your lordship. But have you taken all precautions; is the game sure?"

"Perfectly," replied Lord Dulwich, ignoring the insult in the other's voice and manner. "We have certain tidings that Mass is to be said at daybreak in the district, though the exact spot is not known. But there are not so many coverts that will hold priest and congregation that we need trouble much about that. We hope to take them red-handed, so to speak. By this time Hempenstal and his men are on the move. They have orders not to hesitate to shoot at the least show of resistance or flight. Moreover, they have a private hint that your friend, the priest, will be, at least, as acceptable at head-quarters dead as alive."

"Right," cried Mark fiercely, "I drink to Father O'Carroll's speedy salvation," and he drained a bumper. "There's a pious toast for his reverence. I should not wonder, Dulwich, if another friend of mine, 'my elder brother,' as you are kind enough to call him, were also of the party, for he is a notorious head centre. If a stray bullet comes in his way, I, for one, shan't grudge him it. But I don't envy the man at whom he aims. Your lordship was right to keep out of range of his pistol barrel.

"But come," he went on, shuffling the cards rapidly, and letting two or three straggle out of his hands on the floor, "we waste time, and at to-night's rate time is worth ten pound a minute to me."

Before the first card of the new deal had fallen on the table, Christy was out in the picture-gallery, and the panel closed behind him. For a moment or two he was bewildered at the imminence of the danger. He knew right well where the Mass was to be said, and knew, too, that Maurice Blake had started two hours before to be present. After Mass there was to be a meeting, and Father O'Carroll had promised "the boys" that they should have news from Dublin to warm the veins of their heart. Worse still, if worse might be, Peggy Heffernan was also gone to bring the priest's blessing home to the old folk, who had grown too feeble of late for such perilous devotion.

No wonder Christy stood for a moment dumb-founded at the thought of those three whom he loved best in the world in such deadly danger, and he ten miles away, with no power to help.

But his wits had been trained in a hard school to do their work rapidly.

Setting his lamp upon the broad library table, across which it threw a widening path of yellow light, he hastily scribbled a few lines on a sheet of paper, tied it up, and sealed it with a wafer. The note was short and to the point.

"The 'Yeos' will be upon you at daybreak," it ran. "Pass the warning to Father O'Carroll and Master Maurice. I will be in a boat at the corner of Stony Island to take off his Reverence if he is hard pressed.

"CHRISTY."

He had already determined on his messenger. The distance was ten good miles by the nearest way from Cloonlara.

The path lay at parts over rough ground, at parts through thick woods impossible for a horseman.

There was but one man in all Ireland who could cover the distance in the time. Luckily, that man was, at that moment, fast asleep in the stable-yard at Cloonlara.

Christy knew where to find him. He made straight for the doghouse where the huge mastiff, whose office was a sinecure, slept.

At the sound of steps the great brute roused itself and gave a deep, muffled bark. But his eyes and nose recognised a friend, and he wagged his lazy tail, and dropped off to sleep again.

In the uncertain light Christy could make out the dark outline of a man's figure stretched cosily beside the dog's on the clean straw. Here was the messenger he needed.

Stooping down, he touched the sleeper with his hand, and, in an instant, Thady O'Flynn, whose slumber was as light as a weasel's, stood, wide-awake, before him.

Christy handed him the letter. It suddenly disappeared. For Thady had a hundred tricks of concealment, and many a missive he had carried to its destination after he had been searched thoroughly by the yeomen.

Not a word yet had been spoken on either side.

Thady stood still waiting his instructions, with cheeks pale as the moonlight, and restless blue eye scanning the other's face eagerly.

"Thady," said Christy, "it is a matter of life and death."

Thady nodded.

"Father O'Carroll, Master Maurice, the whole county side are depending on you now."

It was wonderful to see the eagerness on that thin, white face. It lit up when Father O'Carroll's name was mentioned, and kindled to a flame at the mention of Maurice Blake. The flashing eyes questioned Christy impatiently.

"Father O'Carroll says Mass at daybreak on the top of Cloonascre." Christy went on, slowly, in spite of his impatience to impress his meaning on the wandering mind of the other. "The Yeos have got the hard word from some black-hearted traitor. It's yourself that must give the warning, Thady. I'll be close at hand."

"But the letther?" broke in Thady. It was the first word he spoke.

"You know Peggy Heffernan?"

The other nodded—"Master Mark's sweetheart?"

Christy raised his hand angrily as if to strike him. "Your own, then," said Thady. The hand dropped by his side.

"There is no time for fooling, Thady," he said very earnestly. "You must give this letter into the colleen's own hand on the hill of Cloonascre, where the Mass is to be. The bloodhounds have a long start of you. Every minute is worth a man's life. You must race as if the devil was behind you and heaven in front. Now go."

Swift as a bird and as silently, Thady fled away, a quick gliding shadow in the moonlight.

Christy's face brightened as he watched him from the gate of the courtyard. A five-foot wall bounded the paddock. He leaped lightly to the top, throwing out his arms to balance himself, so he stood for one moment outlined against the white night, then plunged down and disappeared.

Then Christy turned to the house to make ready for his own part in the desperate effort to rob the bloodhounds of their victims.

For over an hour Thady flew as a bird flies, straight and tireless. Now down through by the water's brink, now through the dark recesses of the woods speckled with moonshine, now over rough and rocky ground, that even in the day-time demanded caution, he leaped lightly forward.

No sound broke the silence of the night save the hare that sprang from the covert at his feet, or the wild duck that bustled up from the bullrushes by the lake's edge, and vanished a dark speck in the still air that whistled to the beating of his stout wings.

The light was fading from the moon, a cold greyish glow began to dabble the edge of the eastern horizon, and the breath of the early morning blew faint and chill when Thady's quick ear caught the measured tramp of men in the woods in front of him. Then he knew that the first half of his task was accomplished. The first heat of this terrible race for life or death was won.

Peering cautiously through the brambles he could see the yeomen, fifty strong, marching steadily forward. The scarlet uniforms, indeed, looked black in the waning moonlight, but here and there the steel of their accoutrements glittered coldly.

Their officer was a man of colossal stature, whom Thady recognised with a choking sensation in his throat as Hempenstal, "the walking gallows." He moved like a moving pillar, taking but one step to every two his men took.

Thady slipped away to the right, and then headed again for the hill of Cloonascre as fast as before.

Two miles more and he reached the wood's edge. The sleepy birds were beginning to rustle in the branches, and call to each other with drowsy chirp, and the sun's upper edge, a flaming red crescent, just showed over the lake, when he leaped out still with the same even, steady speed, on the open space of smooth sod that now stretched between him and Cloonascre.

The space between, and the hill itself seemed quite deserted. A round low mound clad in close green turf, scarcely a hundred yards high, and double that in diameter at the top, the hill of Cloonascre had plainly been fashioned and used in distant days as a military encampment. A ridge six feet high thrown up around the outer edge, converted the entire table-land on the top to a shallow flat-bottomed basin where a thousand men might lie concealed.

Even now, while to the quick eye of the anxious runner who sped across the plain the hill stood out dark and lonely in the golden dawn, five hundred men and women were gathered on its summit, earnestly absorbed in the celebration of the great sacrifice which is the crowning glory of the Catholic faith.

It was a strange wild scene as ever eye looked on. An altar of stones and green sod, even such as that on which the Patriarch bound his son, stood at one end of the oval space, level and green as the billiard-table, which formed the summit of the hill.

At that simple shrine Father O'Carroll celebrated the august mystery, his youthful face all aglow with devotion.

He was clad in faded vestments which had served generations of persecuted priests. There was a dark stain over the left breast of the chasuble which tradition told had been dyed into the texture by the oozing life blood of a former wearer stabbed at the altar. The vestments were a relic hallowed by a hundred associations. What the torn and faded colours they have borne through the thick of many battles are to the hardy veterans of the regiment, that and a thousand times more were those faded vestments to the devoted priest, and the fervid congregation grouped round the altar. They added, if ought could add, to the intensity of their devotion. Never surely since the first parents knelt reverently in the fair garden of Paradise to praise and thank the giver of all good things, was purer or more self-forgetting homage offered to the Creator than now by those poor and persecuted peasants, ragged for the most part and starving, on the bleak summit of the lonely hill. The very peril which surrounded them, the shadow of death in which they prayed, brought their souls closer to the unseen world with which they so earnestly communed. Right well they knew that at any moment the Mass might be converted into a martyrdom.

Old men were there, white-haired and haggard, whose feeble limbs had toilfully carried them up the steep ascent to hear Mass again before they died. Children were there, round-eyed with reverence and wonder, to remember that day, standing out clear and vivid from the misty background of infamy, even to the end of their lives.

The men, however, who formed the congregation were for the most part, in the full prime of life, broad-chested and cleaned-limbed fellows, ready and eager when the hour called to carry a pike in defence of the land and faith they loved ; the women, bright-faced and virtuous, worthy to be the wives of such men.

Peggy Heffernan knelt at the outskirts of the

crowd, with her check shawl drawn modestly over the masses of her shiny hair, absorbed in her devotions, and little dreaming of the trial and the peril that approached so rapidly.

Thady came on apace, but even his endurance was beginning to yield at last under the the terrible strain. As the long shadow from the rising sun at his back glided in front, and began to climb the hill, his breath came thicker and faster; and a pain like an iron band gripped his chest.

Yet he boldly breasted the steep ascent, following in the track of his shadow. This final strain was terrible. The beads of perspiration stood out on his white face, he breathed in quick sobs that half choked him. But with head bent almost level with the sod he strained up and up till the outer edge of the embankment was won, and he slipped down quietly and unnoticed on the outskirts of the congregation.

The first Gospel was just over at the moment, and the standing groups about the altar were settling down again to their knees on the green sod. In the movement all around his movements were not heeded.

For a moment it seemed as if his mission would prove in vain. With rest, reaction came. His over-wrought frame shivered like a ship that has just struck; his brain was dizzy, and the scene spun round him, a wide circle of bright colour. His heart beat like a hammer against his side; a weight on his chest seemed to stifle him. If he had not leaned against the inner surface of the embankment he must have fallen. With a great effort he filled his labouring lungs with air; another deep breath, and another, then relief came.

His strength returned and his keen instinct with it.

A little distance off he saw Peggy Heffernan. He stepped lightly and softly as a cat to her side, and put the note in her hand without a word.

She looked up quickly. A single glance at the pale face and wild eyes told her of danger close at hand. Her heart ceased beating as she read the note.

"Where, Thady, where? she whispered trembling.

"There," he answered in the same tone, pointing towards the woods, "not a quarter of a mile from the edge now."

"So near! good God, so near! There is no hope at all, at all."

She glanced round at the women and children who were scattered so thickly amongst the congregation; her eyes went on to the priest at the altar. "They cannot escape," she thought. "They cannot escape; they will be slaughtered where they stand." She sought some plan in her quick mind with a fruitless eagerness that was an agony. The awful moment of the Consecration came, she bowed reverently to the earth and breathed a silent prayer for guidance from above. Her prayer was answered.

She rose up calm, but very pale. "Thady," she

said, "listen to me and attend, I'm going down to meet them. Here is the note back; don't let your mind go wool-gathering; watch over the edge of the bank; watch as ye never watched before, and the first red coat ye see stepping out of the wood give the note to Master Maurice. There are men wid him here to fight, if fight they must, and the hill is hard to climb. But I'm trusting to the good Lord that all will be well yet and no innocent blood spilt."

"Except my own, maybe," she uttered in a lower voice, as she drew her shawl closer about her head and blessed herself devoutly. Then she slipped over the embankment at the side furthest from that on which the yeomen were approaching, and ran like a goat to the bottom of the hill.

But no thought of fear or flight was in that brave young heart. She flitted round the base till she faced the point of the woods to which Thady had pointed. Stepping out bravely she walked swiftly and steadily right into the mouth of the enemy.

The brightly-dressed, rapidly-moving figure was conspicuous in the morning sun, shining clear on the lonely plain, with the lonely hill as a background.

The yeomen were now close to the edge of the woods. The moment his eyes lit on the approaching figure Hempenstal cried "Halt!" in a muffled voice.

"Down, boys!" he whispered excitedly; "lie close. Here comes our guide. We must catch our decoy duck before we go a-shooting. A dainty duck she is, by George," he added, with an ugly leer, as she came rapidly on.

Right into the midst of the enemy the unsuspecting Peggy plunged, humming a hymn as she walked, with face as bright as the sunshine and voice as sweet as the birds.

Hempenstal, suddenly emerging from behind the huge tree that sheltered his huge bulk, stooped and coiled his arm round her waist, holding her fast.

A growl of hoarse laughter went up from his exultant followers.

"Welcome, my beauty," said the giant, his huge mouth grinning close to hers. "Here are a lot of nice young men anxious to have a walk with you; but first come first served, and my turn is first."

He offered to kiss her as he spoke; but she struck him on the broad expanse of cheek sharply with her clenched fist. Then ducking her head, and leaving the shawl still under his arm, by a dexterous twist she freed herself, and fled back the way she had come.

At another time the nimble-footed Peggy could have outstripped the entire troop. Was it fear that ailed her now? Before she had gone ten paces, Hempenstal recaptured her.

"Fair and easy, sweetheart," he said, as his hand closed like a vice on her arm, "you must not run away from your friends. You're right about the kissing, though—business first, and pleasure after.

There will be time enough for that by-and-bye, and those red lips of yours won't fade. But religion goes first ; we 're all going to Mass, and we want you to take us there."

With flushed cheeks and flashing eyes, Peggy glanced round the rough group that circled her, and read their purpose in their savage looks.

"To Mass?" she faltered out, "the likes of ye goin' to Mass!"

"Ay, ay, by George," said Hempenstal, "to Mass, and to massacre," he added between his teeth, chuckling at his own grim joke.

"But I was not going to Mass myself, I——"

"What's this," he interrupted, brutally snatching the prayer-book she held with almost inviting carelessness. "A Mass book, by Jove. You were not going to read this to the birds, Miss, I suppose? It is a comfort now to know we are not taking you out of your way. Come, stir yourself, or we 'll be all late, and that 'll be a mortal sin on our souls, won't it ?"

Again his coarse followers laughed admiringly.

Half dizzy, as it seemed, Peggy took a few steps back the way she had come.

But he again caught her roughly, and held her. "Where are you going ?"

"Where the Mass is saying," she answered.

She pointed vaguely in the direction of the Cloonascre hill, which was just visible through the branches.

Hempenstal looked at the naked hill and plain, and said, with a coarse laugh—

" In heaven or hell," he asked, " for there is no sign of them on the earth's surface ?"

" Face about," he added, turning her sharp round, "and go right on the way you were going when you met us. We should be sorry to interrupt a pretty girl's pleasant walk."

Then Peggy found her tongue again in the midst of her terror.

" What is the likes of you going to Mass for ?" she asked.

" To say our prayers, in course," interrupted the sergeant, before Hempenstal could speak.

This was a red-headed, big-boned savage. He was a " jumper," too, and was the more hated on that account by the people, and hated them back freely in return.

" To say our prayers, in course," he said, " and maybe serve the Mass itself, and lend a hand with the music. Won't you help Father O'Carroll to a good congregation, miss ?"

" Hurry up," said Hempenstal, savagely, his innate brutality breaking out. " There is no time for further fooling. The Papish rebels may escape while we stand idling here."

Peggy said never a word, made never a move.

Hempenstal grew furious. " Give the jade a touch of the spur, sergeant," he said.

With the keen point of his bayonet the brute

prodded the wretched girl until the blood oozed through her clothes in patches of dull red. She writhed and groaned, but made no move, and said no word.

"He may be tempted to drive it clean through," growled Hempenstal, "if you don't speak out, and step out as well."

"If you were to cut me to pieces I'd never turn informer to please you," the brave girl sobbed defiantly.

"If the spur won't do, try the halter, Captain," said the sergeant, driving the point of his bayonet into the earth to clean the blood stain off it. "She may be led, though she won't be dhruv."

Hempenstal took the hint. He drew from his capacious coat-tail pocket the ominous cord, without which he never moved, and dangled the running noose in the girl's face.

She dropped on her knees before him.

"Mercy!" she faltered out. "Do not kill me."

"Faith, you kill yourself, my girl," he said, coolly, "when you won't save yourself. If other folks' necks are more precious to you than your own it is no affair of mine. You may take your choice. Speak or choke."

He dropped the noose over her bent head as he spoke, and tightened it till the rough cord rasped her neck.

She leaped to her feet, trembling.

"Come," she cried. "I'll lead you."

"I thought so," said the brute, complacently. "I thought when you felt the squeeze of the rope you would not want much more pressing. Lead on."

She turned her back on Cloonascre, and led the troop at a rapid pace through the woods—straight away from their intended victims.

They followed her confidingly. Her well-acted reluctance completely deceived them. Besides, she had been taught what to expect if she failed. They never doubted that she led them straight to the "nest of the cursed Papishes."

After a little time Peggy turned to the right, and soon the party emerged from the wood out on a wet moorland that skirted the lake.

Cloonascre was then visible in the distance, standing out clear and lonely against the sky line.

As she saw it Peggy quickened her pace till a sharp turn brought the wood again between the party and the hill, and shut it from view.

They were getting in on wet bog now, where a man *must* sink to his ankle and might sink to his neck if he were not careful.

Their way lay between the lake on the one hand and the wood on the other. In front about two miles distant at the wood's edge stood the old abbey, whose great grey walls and shattered windows broke the sky line rising amid the trees. Behind those vast walls five hundred Papishes might shelter. There Hempenstal and his party were sure the Papists were concealed, and thither Peggy was leading them straight through the strip of open bog between the wood and lake.

The ground was soft and wet as a sponge—wetter and softer it grew as they advanced.

Here and there little green pools showed in the quivering morass. The men had to leap from one trembling knob to another; and he whose eye or foot failed went down to his knees at least, sometimes to his waist in black slime.

Peggy sprang from point to point as lightly and as safely as a squirrel through the branches.

The brute Hempenstall had kept the rope still round her neck as a warning and as a restraint, holding her like a dog in leash.

But she loosened the strangling cord with her hand, and held it beyond the noose, and so felt no strain.

She felt no strain; but she made her persecutor feel it with a vengeance. Anyone who has seen a blind man follow a lively dog on a rough road can fancy what his state was. Peggy played him as lightly and as dexterously as an angler plays the salmon, that scarcely feels along the line the subtle force of pliant wrist which kills him.

As Hempenstal balanced himself on a tuft that tottered under his weight, a faint strain on the cord turned the scale, and forced him to step out into black slime, as fluid as honey and as tenacious.

Like Falstaff, he had a "kind of alacrity in sinking. If the bottom were as deep as hell he would down."

To say truth, he was more than once in danger of going prematurely to the devil, if theologians speak true as to the devil's headquarters in the earth's centre.

But each time his troop gathered round and drew him from his mud-bath, while the innocent Peggy looked on with demure regret in her soft eyes.

The rescued savage would glare at her then, yet found no excuse to vent his rising anger. But gazing on that fair face and trim figure, he swore in his own black heart that he would mingle pleasure and vengeance later on.

The men began at last to mutter and curse, as their way grew each moment more treacherous.

There was no escape. To the right towards the wood the bog grew wetter and softer, till it merged into an impassable morass. On the other hand, the deep lake, fringed with bulrushes at the edge, hemmed them in. Further out in the lake a steep, rocky island shut off the level rays of the rising sun, and enhanced the gloom.

Angry suspicion began to whisper amongst the priest hunters. It was not likely, they muttered, that a congregation had gone to Mass over this shaking bog, where no trace of footstep was to be seen.

There was no sign of life at all in this desolate place, only now and again the tall bulrushes, close to the lake's margin, rustled as if shaken as by wild fowl passing stealthily. They could even hear the splashing in the water, but no birds rose.

Suspicion begat fear, and fear begat rage.   The men began to point their bayonets and finger their triggers ominously.   It would go hard with the girl if their passions (as every moment threatened) escaped control.

But she moved forward lightly and jauntily, as if unconscious of the fierce storm that was brewing, though its low mutterings could be heard all round her.   She never so much as turned her head, but kept looking out steadily at the lake and the shaking bulrushes.

Even Hempenstal, infected with the general suspicion, tightened his grasp on the rope.   He was standing at the moment, both feet close together, on a wobbling little islet of sod in the centre of a quagmire.   There was bare foothold where he stood, and he had to keep a stiff perpendicular to balance himself.

Peggy jerked the cord—this time with a quick, palpable jerk there was no mistake about.

Hempenstal swayed like a pillar—as tall, as stiff, as straight.   He growled an angry curse, and leant back against the strain to steady himself.

Instantly Peggy flung the noose from over her neck, and loosed her hold on the cord.   Down he went, splash like a log, full length in the mud on the broad of his back.

At the same instant Peggy leaped forward like a hare, over the shaky surface of the bog, and, plunging into the lake amongst the swaying bulrushes, disappeared.

R

For a moment surprise and confusion stopped pursuit. Hempenstal's condition claimed the instant attention of his men. The slime was settling over his face, and he sank the quicker for his struggles.

They pulled him out, spluttering black mud, and foul from head to heel with slime.

"Curse the jade," he blurted out savagely; "she has drowned herself, and robbed the halter of a chance. No! no!" he shouted again more eagerly, "she's alive yet."

Pointing to where the bulrushes bent and swayed violently close to the water's edge, he drew a huge horse-pistol from his belt, levelled it steadily, and pulled the trigger. But flint and powder-pan were coated with the wet and mud, and not a spark came.

More and more the rushes bent and rustled by the lake's brim. Then they opened towards the outer edge, as a dense crowd clears a space with much struggling when a reckless horseman goes galloping through.

Out from the thick cover there shot, not fifty yards off, a light boat, with a tall, gaunt man in it, pulling as if a life was on each stroke.

A dozen muskets were levelled instantly, and a dozen bullets ripped the water all round the boat. Two struck the timbers of it, but high above the water-line, and one drilled a hole through the oar-blade.

The oarsman was not hit. He made the boat tear through the water.

A trick learned on the great Western lakes, when arrows fell like hailstones, served now in good stead. He pulled first one oar, then the other, with a quick jerk that almost lifted the prow from the water. The boat shot along zigzag, like a swallow in the air, or a trout in the stream, making sure aim impossible. Still, the bullets from the straggling fire pattered close round him.

One marksman, more skilful than his fellows, or more lucky, first grazed Christy Culkin's temple with a ball, and the blood began to trickle, first in big drops, then in a little stream down his face.

He never so much as winced. The oars still kept going quick and strong, as if a machine worked them, and the boat was lifted forward at every stroke.

But, with a cry of terror at the sight of blood, Peggy started up from the stern, and flung herself between the oarsman and the threatening muskets.

Then, for the first time, Christy's face changed colour, and the scarlet blood showed ghastly on its ashen hue.

"Lie down!" he cried hoarsely! "for God's sake, Peggy, lie close."

His muscles were strained, even to cracking, and the oars dipped and rose as swift as a bird's wings, and the boat flew as swift.

The girl, wild with excitement, never heeded his cry, but turned and faced her foes, who were scattered along the lake's edge, with smoking or levelled guns, and waved her hand defiantly. At the sight of her a hoarse cry of rage went up from them. Guns were pointed, and triggers pulled ; but rage spoiled their aim, and the bullets pattered harmlessly in the water.

The next moment the boat shot round the projecting nose of Stoney Island, from shadow into sunshine. A huge rocky shield was stretched between it and the bullets.

The fugitives were safe !

Christy shipped his oars. But the boat still glided forward, smoothly and swiftly, from the tremendous impetus she had received.

His iron nerves were unshaken by the terrible strain. There was a grim smile on his face at the danger, over past. But Peggy, who had been a heroine while the danger lasted, was a weak woman now that it was over.

Tremblingly she began to wipe away the blood that still trickled, though more slowly, from the bullet-graze on Christy's forehead.

"Quiet, my girl," he said stoically, "let be. The bullet has only brushed away a bit of the skin. A half-inch nearer, though, and Christy would never have troubled you again. If you were not left in the lurch, colleen, I dunno but it would be better if the fellow held his gun straighter, and sent the bullet home."

He spoke sadly, for the bitterness of disappointed love was rankling in his heart like a poisoned arrow.

She had drawn herself close to his side, and was looking earnestly in his face.

All of a sudden she burst into a wild peal of laughter, that startled the morning air. Then, as suddenly, she fell to bitter weeping, her whole body shaking with her sobs. The poor girl's nerves were shattered by the terrible ordeal through which she had passed so bravely. Christy, surprised and frightened by the outburst, drew her close to him until the flushed, tear-stained cheek rested like a child's on his broad chest.

"Don't cry, acushla machree," he said very tenderly, very pityingly. "It's glad and proud ye ought to be this minute. It's the priest and people that will be proud of you. There is not another girl in Connaught would do the job ye did this morning. For many a long day it will be told at fair and pattern how Peggy Heffernan saved the priest and the boys from the 'Walking Gallows' and his gang, and left the priest-hunters up to their necks in a bog-hole.

"Cheer up, asthore, the danger is over now. Don't mind what an old fool like me says when the love fit is on him. Troth; I will never trouble you with the like again." She raised her head and looked at him with tearful eyes, half laughing, half angry.

"Ould fool, indeed," she said, "and truer word ye never spoke. Christy, can you look me in the face, and not see that I love ye?"

Her head sank again on his breast as she said the last words, very softly.

"Like a grandfather?" asked Christy bitterly, remembering the old taunt.

"Like a sweetheart," retorted Peggy, saucily. Then, with a sudden change of manner, "Oh, Christy, I knew that I loved you when I saw the bullets splashing all round, and you pulling away so quick and steady as if it was rowing a race you were. When I saw the blood streaming down your face I felt as if it was my own heart's blood. I came between you and the bullets because I must have died if they kilt you."

Christy sat silent and dazed. The sudden delight took sense and speech from him.

Peggy raised her head and flashed an angry look from her dark blue eyes.

"Is it a man ye are at all?" she cried, petulantly drawing herself away from his encircling arm, "that ye let a colleen do all the courtin'?"

Then he caught her in his arms, and held her close and pressed kiss after kiss on her lips. His temperate blood, that had flowed calmly in his veins in the moment of extreme peril, was all aflame with the fierce delight of love.

Blushing and breathless she struggled to release herself.

He noticed blood on his hand that had clasped her to him; he noticed blood on her dress. He saw the purple mark where the rope had tightened on her slender throat. He realised for the first time the sufferings she had endured. His face changed as the summer sky when the thunder clouds cover it. The rage of his heart burned in his eyes.

"The beasts," he muttered, "the brute beasts. But I wrong the beasts to compare them. The red Indians were Christians to them. The devils themselves would be ashamed of this work."

A quick stroke turned the boat's head, and shot it in towards the island.

"Where are ye going now?" cried Peggy, frightened at the change she saw in his face.

"Back," said Christy grimly, "to land ye, darlint, first, then back. I'll give them a lesson in shooting they'll carry to their graves, an' a short journey it will be for some of them." He stooped for the long brown rifle that lay at the bottom of the boat. "I'll send a few devils home to hell before I'm done with them."

"No! no!" cried Peggy, snatching the gun out of his hands. "If you go I swear I'll go with you, and I have had enough of blood and shootin' for wan day. Troth, I hadn't such a pleasant time over there, Christy, asthore, that I'd be in a great hurry back to it. Is it tired of me ye are already?" She went on looking up mischievously in his face, for he still held the gun. "I have a dale to say to you, and the long day, and broad lake shining before us. The cuts don't hurt no more than the scratch of me shawl pin. Troth, the mane omadawns are bad enough in the bog hole, and lave them there. We've won, Christy, asthore. Let us go off with our winnings."

There was no resisting such an appeal. The grim lines of anger relaxed. His whole face softened and warmed with a great tenderness and pity that well became it.

"My poor colleen," he said, "my brave colleen," and he caught her again in his strong, sheltering arms.

Out over the shiny surface of the lake they glided, where never a cloud rested nor wave rose, with happy hearts that harmonised with the bright sunshine and sparkling water.

Like the sun, love shines on the high and lowly, and it may be the lowly feel his light and warmth most. The wild woods have heard whispers as soft as were ever breathed in the perfumed air of the palace.

It was a long row that, and a slow one, and the sun had done three-fourths of his day's work when Christy sauntered slowly up the lane that led from his father's cottage to Cloonlara, the happiest man that walked that day upon Irish ground.

An hour later the gigantic figure of Hempenstal loomed into view, bedraggled and ferocious. He was speedily closeted with Lord Dulwich. Then Mark Blake was called into the conclave, and the muffled sound of voices in anger could be heard through the thick walls of the room where they sat.

CHAPTER XVI.

" O LOYAL FATHER OF A TREACHEROUS SON."
King Richard II.

" Ingratitude, more strong than traitors' arms,
Quite vanquished him."—*Julius Cæsar.*

"The Devil shall have his bargain."—*Henry IV.*, Part I.

" So did this horse excel a common one
In shape and courage, colour, pace, and bone."
Venus and Adonis.

" I WON'T have the girl meddled with, Dulwich," said Mark Blake, quietly. "If that great hulking savage of yours had hurt her I would have sent a bullet in search of brains through his thick skull."

Lord Dulwich had just proposed to hang Polly Heffernan.

The two were seated at a late breakfast in the room they had made their own in Cloonlara, still angrily discussing the events of the previous day.

Lord Dulwich seemed restless and feverish, as he crumbled and nibbled a morsel of dry toast, and wet his dry lips with brandy and water.

He could not keep pace with Mark Blake, who pressed him constantly to high play, late hours, and hard drinking.

"I cannot understand you, Mark," muttered his lordship, "you were keener in this business than I was, you were more savage at our failure, yet you grudge a halter to the treacherous jade that balked us."

"I cannot understand you, Dulwich," said Mark, slightly mimicking the other's manner. "Do you think there is no better use to which a pretty girl can be put than hanging? Have you seen her?"

Lord Dulwich nodded.

"Your blood must be ice water when you talk so coldly of spoiling that pretty piece of woman's flesh with a halter. Yet they say you married the handsomest woman in Dublin without a penny fortune. Was that love or revenge?"

Lord Dulwich's pale face flushed scarlet. Mark Blake's random shot had struck home. He remembered how it was in truth for revenge, not love, he married the imperious beauty, who, from the first hour of their wedded life, tortured him with her cold contempt.

He answered, sullenly—

"Of all follies in the world, the folly that pursues the pretty face of an artful woman is the most foolish. But this gaunt hound, Culkin, have you any special tenderness for him? Do you grudge him to the gallows?"

"No," growled Mark fiercely. "I would willingly fix the rope round his neck with my own hands. But——"

"But what? Afraid?" asked Lord Dulwich, with something of a sneer.

"There is no proof against him. Not one of your intelligent troop can swear to him. It is suspicion merely, though I confess I have no doubt myself it was his cunning set the fool's trap for your big booby and caught him. Yet it might be dangerous to touch him without proof. He stands well with my father and my mysterious namesake, his master. My father has still much influence, and Maurice Blake, you know, has a quick eye along a pistol barrel, and a ready finger on a hair trigger."

"There is nothing to be done, then," said Lord Dulwich sullenly, "but grin and bear it. We must, like good Christians, turn the other cheek to the smiter."

"I'm no more Christian than yourself," retorted the other hotly, as if resenting an insult: "and I at least answer a blow with my hand, not my cheek. Yes, I mean to have revenge, but not in your clumsy fashion. I'll catch, I'll hit, that grim phantom that haunts her in a sorer spot than bullet or bayonet can reach, if I don't mistake the man. Perhaps bullet and bayonet may get a chance, too, later on."

"How?—how?" eagerly demanded Lord Dulwich.

"Evict the old couple that harbours them," said Mark Blake with a look of triumphant malignity. "Peggy Heffernan will then have to take refuge in Cloonlara, where I hope to provide her with a warm welcome. Father O'Carroll himself exhorts us to comfort the afflicted. Culkin can easily be tempted to resist the law when the law turns his father and mother out of doors. Even your fellows can hardly miss him at a musket length, and so save the hangman a job."

"But the time," objected Lord Dulwich. "All this will take a long time. Meanwhile——"

Mark broke in upon him with a laugh. "You fancy you are in England, my dear fellow," he said, when he had found breath, "where they still plod on at the same old pace, on the same old road, through the ruts that precedent and prejudice have made. Here in Ireland, we do not stickle about the nice formalities of the law. We have learned to put a spoke in the wheel of the legal machine, and stop it or push it forward, as the case may be. Old Culkin owes, I do not know how many years' rent. The sheriff will send the bailiffs at a word from me. Your men will be on the spot at a word from you. Some of them, I know, can wield a crowbar better than a musket. A crowbar is about the most effective legal instrument I know. Culkin is bound to give your fellows a good excuse for shooting him. And Peggy—— Well, I fancy I 'll be able to find a protector for Peggy in her trouble. The only trouble is my father. But I 'll find a way with him or make it."

"And Culkin's master?" asked Lord Dulwich.

"My father's honest friend, and my own 'elder brother,' as you kindly call him. It would be terrible if anything should happen to him. He is liable to accidents down here, and yet I cannot persuade myself to let him go away, I am so fond of him. If he should break his neck or get shot by some awkward fellow of yours, I should be inconsolable. Yet such things might happen, you know."

Even as he spoke the figure of the man of whom he spoke passed the window, with a gun on his shoulder. An Irish red setter, whose silky coat glistened in the sunshine, wheeled round him in short circles, tossing up the gravel with his scampering feet, as eager for the sport as her master.

Mark, leaping up from the table, unclasped the window, which opened from the ground, and met "his friend" on the terrace with a cordial greeting.

"Off for a few partridges?" he said. "I know where there are three big coveys with only a brace out of each. They will be on the headlands in the thick cover, and get up in twos and threes. Just wait one moment and I'll join you."

As Lord Dulwich watched them striding away like brothers, under the light blue cloud their cigars made in the still air, his admiration for his friend's versatility and vitality was unbounded. "A wonderful fellow, Mark," he muttered, "he is bound to be a great man —or get hanged. Nothing can stop him except death —his own death. I am glad I am not a life in his way. I should not wonder if there were something else shot besides partridges this afternoon."

But Lord Dulwich's foreboding or anticipation, whichever it may be called, proved false. There was nothing shot except partridges, and of these a goodly quantity. All the evening Mark was loud in praise of the marvellous skill of his companion.

The next week passed pleasantly and quietly at Cloonlara.

Maurice Blake had ridden over for a few days to Galway, which he had never seen, carrying no luggage with him but his saddle-bags.

Christy, for the first time in their companionship, stayed when he went, no need to ask why.

When Mark had bidden his guest a cordial God-speed, he went straight from the door to broach the Culkin eviction project to his father. He was full of plausible argument, but found his father less pliant than he had hoped. The interview was a long one. The young man left the room at last, slamming the door angrily behind him, with a lowering look on his face and an evil purpose in his eye.

Sir Miles was utterly exhausted by that stormy interview. His face was as pale as marble and as cold. But something in his manner and face told that the spirit that underlay the affectionate gentleness of his nature was roused at last. The master trait in his character had asserted itself, and Mark Blake's wild reign over the Cloonlara domains was at an end.

Sir Miles retired early to his room, Christy helping his feeble steps up the broad marble staircase.

Mark had gone straight to the stable yard, flung himself on a fast horse, and rode away in the direction of the Yeomen barracks.

Lord Dulwich returned with him, and after a late dinner the two retired, with cards.

Again Christy came softly to the picture gallery, crept through the secret panel, and from his vantage ground above heard by what foul means Mark Blake was to suddenly become master of Cloonlara, and Lord Dulwich was to help and share.

When Christy returned to the library there was a grim look on his face that boded ill for the conspirators.

For half-an-hour he paced the great room with swift, noiseless strides. Then, sitting down to the table, he wrote all through the night laboriously.

The grey dawn began to flicker in the east, shining coldly through the great windows, when he tied the packet up and sealed and directed it—" United States, America," were the last words.

Before night had yet merged into morning he had saddled the fastest horse in the stable, and, riding as if for his life, he caught the American mail at Ballinasloe, with a quarter of an hour to spare.

Next morning early, with no word of leave-taking for his father, Mark Blake left Cloonlara, in company with Lord Dulwich, for Dublin. In the afternoon Maurice Blake arrived from Galway.

He found Sir Miles much broken in health and spirits, and could not resist his entreaty to remain. So he staid on, one day slipping quietly after another.

Of Mark Blake his father never spoke but once "He is wroth with me," he said, "because facts have come to my knowledge, demanding a great sacrifice on both our parts, and I am resolved at any cost to myself or to him that our duty must be done. He has used to me such words as are seldom used by son to a father. God forgive me if I have deserved them. God forgive him if I have not. Let us speak no more on the subject, I entreat you."

Daily the intimacy gave closer and kindlier between the two men. Mark, when he left, had entirely abandoned his control of the great estate. Sir Miles took up the tangled reins of management, and strove hard to make things run smoothly again and pleasantly.

Winter came unawares upon the autumn and killed it. The frost arrived before the leaves had fallen, and shrivelled up the last of them with the cold. It caught, and chained, and choked the streams, stilling their restless murmurings, and paved the broad lake with clear crystal.

It was a fine, clear chill morning—that fatal morning when the blow fell. Maurice Blake had been up and out on the lake from early dawn, skimming over the frozen surface swiftly and smoothly as a swallow—gliding like a shadow in and out and round about the distant islands, with great white trees on them. Sir Miles was breakfasting in the library, where a bright fire, half peat and half sycamore logs, roared cheerily in the grate.

"There is a man outside in the hall," the butler said, "with a message from Master Mark, which he'll give to no one, he says, except into your honour's own hand."

"Let him in at once," cried Sir Miles eagerly, and he had scarcely spoken when a tall thin man with red hair, who had apparently been waiting at the door, walked into the room, straight up to where Sir Miles sat at the head of the table, and put a thick, formal-looking document into his hand.

"From your son," he said with a leer—"a kind remembrance. Excuse me," he went on, rapidly drawing a second document from his pocket, "that is the copy and this is the original, and I don't think I ever done a neater service."

He was gone from the room like a flash, but not before the experienced eye and ear of the butler took in the situation.

Natural instinct in the Irish follower proved stronger than acquired propriety. The staid butler sprang after the bailiff like hound after fox, and a coat tail came away in his grip as the other fled through the open door.

But the butler's cry of "Bailiff! bailiff!" brought half a dozen men who were working about the grounds on the track. In a minute, the red-headed man was flying down the avenue with the *posse comitatus* in full chase after him, Thady leading the van, yelling with delight.

If the King's writ did not always run in the

West of Ireland in those days, the man that served it did.

But no sound of the shrill shouting reached the dull, cold ear of the owner of that stately mansion and wide demesne.

Sir Miles Blake lay on his back on the thick carpet, with the overturned chair close beside, and the fire's ruddy glow fell on the cold, pale face, it could not lighten or warm. There was a slight foam on the blue, half-closed lips, and the glazed eyes stared blankly upwards. Clutched tight and crumpled in his right hand was the document that had slain him, as surely and swiftly as knife or poison.

Startled by the strange manner of the man, but not catching his words, Sir Miles had opened the paper anxiously, when the bailiff handed it to him, fearing bad news of his son. He saw at once that it was a legal document. The words " High Court of Chancery," " Bill for Discovery," " Mark Blake, plaintiff; Sir Miles Blake, Bart., defendant," caught his eye. He read on eagerly, not quite able to catch the drift of the legal jargon as he read. The phrase " Statutes for the prevention of the further growth of Popery " occurred half-a-dozen times in the body of the paper.

But he did not quite realise what it all meant until he came to the words—" *The said Mark Blake, the plaintiff, has duly conformed to the Protestant religion as by law established.*" Then it flashed upon him that his only son, whom he had so loved and trusted, had basely apostatised from the old faith, and claimed the estates of his Catholic father as the legal price of his apostacy.

The old man's mind reeled under the shock. A thousand thoughts and memories half formed themselves in his brain, then whirled together in maddening confusion. The blood surged through his veins. His forehead throbbed painfully. His heart, where death had so long lurked, beat tumultuously, as if it would burst his bosom; then its beating fell away to a feeble flutter—then ceased. Darkness was closing fast upon him. The bright, sunlit casement became a glimmering square. Swifter and swifter the shadow fell. With one last, convulsive struggle the soul fled from the feeble body out into the life that stretches dimly beyond Death's portal. The body fell back, overturning the chair in its fall, and lay with outstretched hands on the carpet—quite still.

Half an hour passed, and there was no sound in the room.

Thady, returning from the successful chase, and the ducking of the process-server in the pond, looked in at the window, his white face scarcely less white than the corpse at which he looked. But he turned away without word or sign.

The stillness of the room seemed to grow more intense and solemn from death's presence there.

An hour later Maurice Blake came striding up the

avenue in the sunlight, in the full joyous vitality of young manhood. His skates were thrown carelessly over his shoulder, his cheeks flushed, and his eyes bright with healthful exercise.

He seemed to bring fresh, breezy life with him into the silent chamber of death. But a cold chill struck at his heart as he entered. He heard no cheery word of greeting; he missed the kindly face of the man whom he had grown to love like a father. In an instant his quick eye caught the prone and pitiful figure, with ghastly face and dishevelled white hair. One glance was enough—he had seen death too often in all forms to mistake it now. He knew it was a corpse on which he gazed. He took the paper from the clenched right hand, and glanced at it, and read there that the son had slain the father.

It was a dismal day in Cloonlara. The news spread all over the estate that the old master was gone. The grief with which the news was heard was his highest praise.

" God be with him," " The heavens be his bed this night," " It's a long day till we see the likes of him again," " It's hard times that's coming on us now," " Glory be to God !" were the phrases heard on all sides, mingled with prayers, deep and fervent, for the repose of the dead man's soul.

Early next morning Maurice roused himself from the stupor into which the suddenness of the blow had thrown him. He remembered to have heard Sir Miles more than once express the wish that, when

" The prone and pitiful figure, with ghastly face and dishevelled white hair."

death came, Father O'Carroll might be present at his bedside and his grave. But he had no notion of the priest's whereabouts.

Christy Culkin was as ignorant on the subject as himself. Thady O'Flynn, the one person sure to know, was nowhere to be found. At length, by mere accident, Christy mentioned his perplexity to Peggy Heffernan, and from her learned the priest's whereabouts, at a village twelve Irish miles away.

Within a quarter of an hour the saddle was on Phooka, and Christy rode at a hand gallop down the avenue. An hour brought him to the village. He found the cottage where the priest lodged, ostensibly as servant to the farmer. Working cheerily in the fields with plough or reaping-hook, he baffled the keen scent of the priest-hunters.

With some trouble Christy got the farmer's wife to trust him, and tell him what she knew. Thady O'Flynn had been with the priest three hours before. She caught the words, the " old master," and " Cloonlara," spoken between them, and then his reverence had ordered the horse to be saddled and set off at full speed.

" He must have been at the gate of the big house ten minutes after you left it," she said to Christy.

Pleased that his task was fulfilled, yet half vexed that he had his journey for nothing, Christy only waited to give a drink of " white water " to Phooka, and then turned him for home.

The gallant horse had not a hair turned by the

twelve miles quick journey. His skin shone like black satin. He was fresher than when he started, and arched his neck and tossed his head with sprightly impatience, and danced along the road when Christy, tightening the reins, forced him to a slower pace on their return ; for Christy had learned in a hard school in which life was the premium and death the punishment, that horse power should never be wasted, because one can never tell when it may be needed.

Another lesson, too, Christy had learned in that same school—that eyes and ears should be sentinels for ever on duty, which lesson he now unfortunately neglected. He rode with bowed head, buried in thought.

He was suddenly and harshly roused from his reverie. A short turn of the road brought him plump into the centre of a troop of yeomen.

Strong hands held the horses' reins on either side. A dozen muskets covered his body. A hoarse voice commanded him with a savage curse to dismount.

Christy's presence of mind came back to him in an instant. Instinctively his hand had gone down to his sword-hilt. But the first conscious thought rebuked his folly, and told him that resistance meant death.

He noted with a single look that both Hempenstal and Lord Dulwich were of the party.

Lord Dulwich stood a little behind his men. But Hempenstal pressed eagerly forward with a huge horse pistol levelled, delighted at the capture of his old enemy, eager for his death.

"Will you come down," he shouted fiercely, "or must I send a leaden messenger to fetch you down!"

Christy eyed him contemptuously. "I want a word with your master," he said, as quietly as if death were not peering at him out of the muzzles of a score of muskets and pistols on full cock.

Coolness conquered truculence, as it always does.

"My lord, the prisoner would speak with you," growled Hempenstal.

"Let him first throw down his arms," answered Lord Dulwich without moving.

Christy plucked his sword from his sheath and his pistols from the holsters, and flung them all down, clashing together on the strip of sward by the road ride.

"Well," demanded Lord Dulwich, now for the first time approaching.

"By what authority am I stopped upon the high road," demanded Christy, meeting the supercilious glance firmly.

"By mine," retorted Lord Dulwich. "My will, as you will find, is warrant sufficient. You must be searched. Dismount and submit. Insolence will not serve you here."

With a meekness very curious to any one who knew the man, Christy leaped from his horse, and submitted himself to be searched. Nothing was found.

He made a motion as if to remount. But Hempenstal laid a heavy hand on his shoulder.

"Not quite," said the giant jeeringly. "You and the horse part company. We won't have his morals corrupted."

"The horse is not mine," pleaded Christy, still very meekly, but with a curious twinkle in his shrewd grey eye.

"No, faith," said the other roughly, "he's the captain's now, and I could not wish him a prettier mount"—with an admiring glance at the superb charger. "He is too good for traitors. Oh, we know you," he went on with a savage leer, "we know where you have been, and where you are going, and what you are about. There are loyal little birds that tell us your secrets. We want to have a word or two ourselves with his reverence. But we would sooner speak with him in private. We would not have him disturbed for the world. We don't want any messenger going before to make ready for our reception. We are going to take pot luck at Cloonlara. As for the man whom you call master—"

"Silence," shouted Lord Dulwich sharply. "Hempenstal, you will still be prating. You, fellow," he added, turning scornfully to Christy, " be grateful that you are let off with a whole skin. We go on the King's business to Cloonlara and want no rebel warning there before us. If the power of the king is resisted, on the traitor's own head be it."

"But the horse?" persisted Christy.

"The horse is mine," said Lord Dulwich.

He dismounted as he spoke, and sprang into Phooka's empty saddle.

"You may be trudging on foot. But take my advice and keep clear of Cloonlara. Stay!" he cried, for Christy, as if in humble compliance with his command, was moving submissively back the road he had come. "Stay! you are a stickler for the law; we may as well have all legal formalities complied with. The horse is worth paying for. You are a Papist?"

"I am a Catholic," said Christy, firmly, and the troop laughed uproariously, Hempenstal leading the chorus.

"Call it what you will," retorted Lord Dulwich, "the thing is the same. You know the law. Five pounds is the price of the best horse a Papist can ride. There's your money, my good man, and the horse is mine."

He took five sovereigns from his pocket and flung them in the dust of the road at Christy's feet.

Without a word the other stooped, picked the gold up out of the dust, and quietly put it in his pocket. There was still the curious half smile on his face which it had worn from the moment Lord Dulwich took possession of his horse.

"Any message for Cloonlara, my lord?" he asked, with perfect coolness.

"I'll be my own messenger," said Lord Dulwich, "and I doubt if the message I bring is likely to

please your master. I 'll take his opinion on my last
bargain of horse-flesh."

"Perhaps," muttered Christy between his teeth.
He said no more, but turning at right angles to
the road he climbed a five-foot coped and dashed
wall that bounded it, and fled quickly across the
fields, in a direction almost straight away from
Cloonlara.

"There goes a coward," cried Lord Dulwich,
pointing after him the finger of scorn ; "there goes
a mean and cowardly dog, Hempenstal. Did you
notice how eagerly he picked the gold out of the
dirt? See how eagerly he makes off with his life
and his booty. Yet his master would swear to his
courage and fidelity."

Lord Dulwich was plainly delighted. The thought
that a man believed to be brave, proved a dastard in
an emergency, was specially pleasant to him.

"I wish you would let me send a messenger to
stop him," grumbled the surly giant. "I 'd have
paid him for the horse in lead, not gold, if I had my
way. He 's within range yet," he added, glancing at
the swiftly-retreating figure and shouldering his
musket.

"No, Hempenstal, no, I say," cried Lord Dulwich.
"The dog 's not worth powder and ball. We have
other game to hunt. We 've caught the priest and
the rebel this time in the same trap. If they struggle
it is their own look-out, not ours. We have them
safe, dead or alive. Quick, get your men into motion."

The whole party swept forward at a hand gallop straight for Cloonlara.

They had not been five minutes in motion when a wild shrill cry pierced the air, heard clear over the clang of horses' hoofs and the jangle of men's accoutrements.

Lord Dulwich stopped short in the road, and his men halted with him.

Again the same keen sound rang out like the cry of some wild beast or bird. Suddenly Phooka, with Lord Dulwich on his back, turned sharp at right angles to the road, took three strides at the solid built five foot wall that fenced it, and was over like a bird.

The troopers could just see the two polished shoes on his hind feet shining for a second at the top of the wall as he cleared it almost in a standing leap. Then horse and rider disappeared.

The suddenness of the thing took away Lord Dulwich's breath and nerve.

Practised horseman as he was, the deep drop on the far side of the wall flung him forward half out of the saddle.

As the horse tossed back his head it struck the rider in the face and stunned him. His nose and mouth spurted blood with the blow. He lost one stirrup.

For a moment it seemed he must have fallen, but with a desperate effort he regained his seat in the saddle and clung on.

The horse held his course straight forward as the crow flies.

Lord Dulwich was conscious of nothing but a wild rush. Now they flew over a wall; now they dashed through a quickset hedge, where the branches almost tore him from the saddle. The blood streamed from his face. His eyes were blinded with tears, partly from the sharp blow he had got; partly from the quick rush of the keen air. He was conscious of the horse stretching himself out quite straight and shooting through space. He just caught a glimpse of water below. Horse and rider alighted on the far side of a deep stream, twenty feet from bank to bank.

Fifty paces further Phooka checked his wild speed so sharply that Lord Dulwich lost his balance at last, and tumbled in a heap to the ground.

The horse had stopped as suddenly as he had started, under shelter of a hedgerow, close beside a tall, gaunt man, who stretched his hand to him and patted him caressingly.

Lord Dulwich was not left long in doubt who the man was.

"Get up," said Christy Culkin, pushing the prostrate body with his foot. At the same time stooping over, he quickly and quietly divested him of his silver-mounted pistol and sword.

"I left mine by the road side at your lordship's request," he explained; "exchange is no robbery."

"You are not going to murder me?" faltered Lord

Dulwich. His face, streaked with blood like an Indian in his war paint, wore a look of such comical terror that Christy laughed outright.

The laughter reassured Lord Dulwich, and restored his insolence.

"You will smart for this, fellow," he broke out furiously.

But Christy stopped him with a look. "You had best remember it is my turn now, my lord, and my temper is not always the best."

His lordship's mood changed again in an instant.

"If it is money you want," he began.

"It is not money I want," broke in Christy sharply. "Five pounds you gave me for the horse and I mean to keep it. If you got tired of your bargain and brought him back it is no affair of mine. I will turn your gold to steel, my lord. It will comfort you to know that it will pay for three score pikes."

"So he would buy you for five pounds, my beauty," he broke off, addressing the horse, which had dropped its nose into his hand, insisting on notice. "Pity he could not buy that true heart, and that quick ear of yours that hears a friend's cry miles away and brings you straight to him."

He sprang into the saddle, patting the arched neck of the horse, which turned its head round playfully as if to bite his fingers.

Lord Dulwich still stood stock still, a pitiable spectacle.

"Any message to my master?" inquired Christy

smiling grimly. "You see I am likely to meet him first after all, and you will not have a chance of showing off your bargain in horseflesh. Anyhow, I will have a welcome ready for your lordship."

Lord Dulwich strangled a curse between his teeth, only a hoarse mutter came from his pale lips.

"Good bye, my lord," cried Christy gaily, for Phooka grew impatient.

He leaned slightly forward, gripped the saddle with his knees, and with a light shake of the reins gave the impatient horse leave to be off. In a swift swinging gallop they swept across the field, flew over the ditch and gripe that bounded it, and disappeared.

Slowly and sulkily Lord Dulwich set out on his return journey. It took him a full half hour to retrace the distance it had taken him five minutes to come. He found his men awaiting impatiently on the road, cooped in between the two high walls, where he had left them. Their amazement and curiosity can scarcely be well imagined when they saw the bedraggled and mud-spattered figure of their captain, scrambling across the wall over which he had flown so jauntily half an hour before.

But he gave their curiosity no fair play. Something he muttered about being set upon by a party of rebels, and robbed of his horse and weapons. That was all.

"We waste time here," he broke in abruptly, when

Hempenstal hazarded further questions. "Get the men in motion at once."

"For Cloonlara?" said Hempenstal.

"No," answered Lord Dulwich shortly, "for barracks."

So the baffled bloodhounds trotted home disconsolately to their kennels.

The morning after the funeral Maurice Blake bade a cordial good-bye to Father O'Carroll, and scarcely less cordial to the old steward who had taken over the sole management on Sir Miles's death, with gloomy forbodings of dismal changes when the new master should arrive.

Christy had gone by himself to Ballinasloe to catch the "Fly Boat," that plied to Dublin, so-called because it "flew" along the canal at the rate of five and a-half miles an hour.

As Maurice rode down the avenue he reined his horse again on the rising ground, as he had reined him on entering it, and looked back on the fair wide landscape, white in the winter sunshine, that changed the hoar frost on the trees to diamonds and gleamed cold and bright on wood, and lake, and pasturage, and stately mansion gracing the centre of the picture. The thought came to him that all this fair inheritance had passed to the renegade and parricide, that the poor people, tender and faithful, whose clustering homes, scattered over the wide landscape, shone white in the sunlight, had changed masters, the best for worst. They were dependent for their very lives on the pity of him who had shown no pity to the white hairs of his own broken-hearted father.

For the first time Maurice Blake's heart rebelled hotly against his father's wanton exile as he turned his back, he believed for ever, on his father's ancestral home, now passed to such unworthy hands.

He looked round no more until the swift, free stride of his steed had carried him many miles from the place, and an interposing hill shut it from his view.

CHAPTER XVII.

"SAVES THE THIEF."

Cymbeline.

" I owe thee much.   Within this wall of flesh
There is a soul counts thee her creditor,
And with advantage means to pay."—*King John.*

O N the afternoon of the second day, as he rode
forward at an easy canter on the grassy margin
of the roadside, he heard, at some little distance in
front, the sounds of a fierce struggle, shouts, and
the clang of weapons.   Then a pistol shot, then
a volley, and then the clatter of hoofs apparently
in swift flight and pursuit.   He just tickled with
the spur the sides of his horse, who in an instant
leaped forward with a bound like a deer.   At a
turn of the road he came upon a horse lying dead,
and a yeoman, with many curses, dragging himself
out from under the carcase.   A glance told Maurice
that the man was unhurt.   In front, some hundred
yards off, he saw a dozen of his fellows lumbering
forward, their heavy horses in an awkward gallop.
Further still, there was a single horseman apparently
in full flight.   The thought flashed through his mind
that here doubtless was some wretched Papist whom
the law had given over to the tender mercies of these

T

true Christians, to be converted by pitchcap and halter, bullet or sword.

He resolved to lend a helping hand, if need be, to their victim.

Shaking Phooka's bridle rein, and keeping still on the strip of sward, he flew forward noiselessly, and was safely through the hunting troop of yeomen before they were aware.

It was no such easy matter to overtake the fugitive in front, who had increased his lead to a quarter of a mile. Even Phooka, at full stretch, gained on him at first only by inches. So they sped along for a couple of miles, and the space between seemed scarcely lessened. His blood began to tingle with the excitement of this strange race. While the air through which he rushed whistled past his ears in a hurricane of his own creation, he leant forward over Phooka's neck, and with caressing hand urged him to redoubled speed.

It was not needed. The pace had told. The gallant horse in front began to slacken in his stride. The pursuer was gaining rapidly.

A hundred yards, ninety, eighty, seventy, sixty, only fifty yards off now; as he closed in, Maurice noted the horse in front was a dapple grey, of splendid symmetry. A broad streak of red down its flank told the secret of the slackening speed. The red stream still oozing from the bullet wound drained the poor brute's life away.

The rider was a tall, strong man, but his right arm

hung limp and useless by his side, and slung back-wards and forwards like a pendulum with the swift motion of the horse. His left hand held the reins.

He heard the sound of quick hoofs behind him, and turning, shouted some words which Maurice Blake could not catch.

Maurice shouted back "a friend." But his voice, too, was lost in the clatter of the galloping horses.

The race was nearly over. The grey still struggled forward gallantly, but one of the hind legs began to drag a little in the stride. With swift, easy stretches the black crept closer and closer. They are scarce twenty yards apart now, and that narrow space is closing rapidly.

The man in front flung the reins on his horse's neck. His left hand went down to his holster. He wheeled half round in his saddle. Maurice Blake saw the gleam of a pistol-barrel levelled at his head. There was a crack and flash, and a bullet hustled by so close that he felt the rush of the air as it almost brushed his cheek.

At the same moment the gallant grey, wounded, exhausted, and no longer sustained by a strong hand on the bridle, stumbled, staggered for a moment, and then came heavily down, flinging its rider forward on the road half stunned by the fall.

Maurice Blake was going too fast to stop. Right in his way the fallen man and horse lay together, a struggling heap, to be tumbled or trampled under his horse's hoofs. But he lifted Phooka with the rein.

The gallant steed rose lightly as a bird and lit as lightly.

Maurice turned him in his length, and was beside the fallen man and horse in a moment.

The grey horse lay quite motionless where he had fallen. The rider's leg was caught under its body. and he struggled with his left arm to free himself. The right arm Maurice could see was broken above the elbow, and the sleeve drenched with blood.

The wretch's condition quenched at once the quick anger of Maurice at the murderous pistol-shot aimed at his own life. He was eager to help and save.

The fallen man's struggle grew fiercer as he saw him approach. He writhed like a beast caught in a trap that sees the trapper coming through the woods.

" I 'll not be taken alive," he growled out. " You are not one of those hellhounds. Have some pity in you. Shoot me right off and have done with it. If I could only reach my own pistol I——"

With a violent effort he moved the wounded limb, and then lay quite still, groaning with the agony of it.

Maurice Blake was full of pity. His guess, then, was right. Here was a hunted and persecuted Papist ; he must save him at any cost.

" I am a friend," he said gently.

The other seemed more startled with the gentle tone of his voice, than if a pistol shot had been fired off close to his ear.

He looked quickly in Maurice's face to find the meaning of it. He seemed satisfied with what he saw there. His wan face brightened. Maurice noted that it was a wild but hardly an evil face. One restless eye alone lit its pale expanse. But the tangle of bright red hair and beard gave it a kind of light of their own.

Without another word Maurice drew him from under the horse's body and set him on his feet on the road, when he shook himself like a dog, testing the soundness of his limbs.

"Hurt?" asked Maurice.

"Only this," replied the other, touching his disabled right arm with his left hand.

At that instant the trained ear of Maurice, which rivalled that of the wild beasts or the Indians in its acuteness, caught the sound of the hoofs of the yeomanry horses clattering over the road, afar off; no louder yet than the feet of mice in the wainscotting.

There was no time to be lost.

"Can you ride?" he asked the stranger abruptly.

"If I had a horse," was the reply, "but this one never again. In all Ireland there was not a better an hour ago. Confound the cowards who killed him." He bent over the motionless body of the grey, as he spoke, and touched the shapely head quietly with his left hand.

"You shall ride with me," said Maurice hastily; "if you can hold on. It is not the first time that

Phooka has carried double weight. He will get us to Mullingar yet—it is but a few miles off—before those bloodhounds can catch us. If not—well, we have our pistols. You have shown me you can shoot with the left hand. I can shoot with both, and use a sword, too, at a pinch."

"Not to Mullingar," groaned the other, his helpless right arm slinging loose while Maurice lifted him to the horse. "Not to Mullingar. If you will carry me to that clump of trees yonder," pointing to a clump a mile farther on the road, "I will be quite safe, and need not burden you nor your horse further."

Gallantly Phooka stretched forward with his double load, and the sound of the horses' hoofs, which had grown more distinct behind them, again died away. A mile farther on, Maurice drew rein at the clump of larch stretching up the side of a steep hill.

The stranger slipped quickly to the road.

"You have saved me," he said abruptly, "from death, and worse than death. If my thanks were worth having you should have them. They are not worth having. But I may sometimes get the chance——"

Here he broke off—"You must tell me your name and where you live," he added very earnestly.

"Maurice Blake is my name. At present I am bound for Dublin. Now tell me yours."

"No," returned the other, "You will know my

name too soon, if you ever know it. You have saved a man who, bad as he is, is not ungrateful. Pray God you may never know more of me: or else, know me only when you need my help."

He climbed the high wall with an agility that was almost miraculous remembering his disabled arm, and plunged in amongst the trees. The ground was rough and rocky. Maurice saw him spring from boulder to boulder, until he had reached more than half-way up the ascent. Then suddenly, as if the ground devoured him, he disappeared.

Even Phooka was a bit blown with that last burst under double weight, so Maurice dropped the reins on his neck, and let him walk, while nearer and nearer came the tramp of the galloping yeomen behind.

They came up to him at last, men and horses completely blown.

"Hallo, you fellow!" shouted their officer; but something in Maurice's appearance checked his insolence in full career. "Your pardon, sir," he went on, awkwardly. "Have you seen a man on the road —a tall fellow, with one eye and red hair? You could not mistake him."

"Certainly," replied Maurice, with a quiet smile. "He introduced himself with a pistol shot."

"The very man," cried the officer; "well?"

"He missed his aim and his footing, and I, or rather he," patting his horse's neck, "leaped over both, as they lay sprawling on the road together, that's all."

" It 's a pity," said the other, "you did not waste a
bullet on him when he was down and at your mercy.
You would have been well paid in good gold for that
ounce of lead.   There is a big price on that fellow's
head.   We found the dead horse by the roadside ;
but the fox had stolen away.   He must have got to
earth close at hand.   They say he has one of his
caves somewhere hereabouts."

" Back !" he shouted to his men, "we will try close
round where the horse lies, he cannot have gone
far from the spot on foot."

" Stay," cried Maurice, as the officer was whirling
round to follow his party, who went clattering back
the way they had come.   "Who is the man you hunt
so hard."

" Freeny," replied the other, "the notorious robber,
Freeny.   You have not travelled much in Ireland,
sir, or you would know Freeny when you saw
him."

CHAPTER XVIII.

"LOVE'S LABOUR LOST."

> "The venom whispers of a jealous woman
> Poison more deadly than a mad dog's tooth."
>
> *Comedy of Errors.*
>
> "Father: and in that name doth Nature speak."
>
> *Timon of Athens.*

MANY startling things Maurice Blake heard on his return to Dublin. The playful prophecy which he had uttered to Lord Edward Fitzgerald when they had last met and parted had come true. His heart had been caught on the rebound by a fair maiden of France, whose beauty was the theme of the gay Irish capital, and in whose veins it was rumoured coursed the royal blood of the Bourbons.

Pamela, Lord Edward's fair young wife, was at Carton, the ancestral seat of the Leinster family, when Maurice arrived, but her husband welcomed his friend back with bright eyes and beaming smile, which told that happiness had found him out at last, and that his bitter love trials of the old days were dead and buried deeper than ever plummet sounded.

The organisation of the United Irishmen meanwhile went bravely on. The Government were already beginning to respect its power; they would soon learn to fear it. It was even hoped that all the patriots sought for might be effected by fear without fighting, and reform, not revolution, give Ireland her liberty.

In return for this good news Maurice Blake had to tell his friend of a widespread revival of spirit in the West, and of tens of thousands determined men maddened with misery, and eager to strike a brave blow for freedom when the call to arms should sound. But Maurice Blake had not lost his old hatred for war, and he prayed heartily that the battle might be won without slaughter.

Lord Edward, though a little dazzled at the glorious prospect of leading the forces of Irish patriotism to victory against the arms of Great Britain, shared the gentler hope.

In truth, Maurice Blake's thoughts were at this time turned quite away from war and slaughter. It may be that the sight of his friend's happiness softened his own heart with a kindred hope, of which he was but vaguely conscious. Certain it is that desire ever carried him gaily to Dr. Denver's door, and duty—even duty to Ireland—carried him reluctantly away.

So Norah Denver and Maurice Blake lived in a blissful dream. Only they two in all the world were real to each other; all else seemed vague and far off. Every thought, look, or word, however slight or playful, which love touched, became a delight. Only once to man or woman (and not to all) comes the rapture of true love, that joy to which all others life holds are weak and colourless. Better be born blind than miss that ecstacy.

They floated pleasantly together, those two, down the shining stream, with no thought or care where it should lead. They lived in the present only, and never wearied of its delights. Love, to be perfect, must be unconscious, and theirs was perfect.

A fortnight had flown like a day. Earth and water were still locked in hard frost. To them pure air made mere living a delight. To Maurice it was a pleasant reminder of Canadian winters. He taxed the skill of Dublin artizans for a Canadian sleigh.

Very sweet and beautiful Norah looked as she sat beside him in the sleigh, cosily muffled in a suit of sables (of his providing), which closely wrapped slim figure and slender throat, and nestled softly to the soft, rounded cheek, bright with health and happiness.

Merrily the ponies pranced along, jangling their silver bells as the sleigh sped over the frozen ground, and merriest of all was the sweet music Love sang in their hearts.

The time flew swifter than the sleigh, and, with a start of surprise, they found their journey done. They had reached the broad lake, seven miles from Dublin, where skaters in those days did most resort, and found the youth and fashion of Dublin gathered on its shores or scattered over its frozen water.

In a few moments they, too, joined the flying skaters on the shining surface of the lake. The gentle confiding pressure of those little hands he held so softly in his own, sent the blood leaping through his veins with a wild rapture that was akin to pain. Like birds on the wing, they flew over the lake, whirling and circling as birds do in sheer delight of the smooth and easy motion.

The grace and swiftness of their movements challenged the admiration of the crowd. A low buzz of admiration followed as they swept past, lightly as the wind, and as swift. Norah noticed it with a blush that deepened the roses the keen air had made to bloom in her cheeks.

"We will go in, Maurice," she said. "How strangely those people stare as we pass."

Swiftly and smoothly they wheeled round on the outer edge, and glided in, hand-in-hand, to where a seat stood invitingly vacant, a little on the outskirts of the gay crowd.

Again the thought came to Maurice with a thrill, half excitement, half fear, that here was his chance to bring his wooing to a close; to whisper, as he hoped, in willing ears, the question on whose answer the happiness or misery of his life depended.

His earnestness made him awkward. He could not find the words he wanted, nor the time to speak them.

Norah, by the look in his eyes, or the trembling in his voice, or by that subtle power by which souls that love speak to each other without word or look, guessed what was coming.

Her heart was all in a tumult at the thought; with joy or fear she could not tell, so wild the whirl of emotion. Overmastering all else, came the womanly instinct of flight.

All her faculties were on the alert to escape, for the time, from the avowal of love which she longed for, yet feared. She was a true woman. She trembled inwardly, but her voice was calm as she smiled and chatted more gaily than her wont.

With delicate tact she made their talk play upon light and lively topics. A dozen times Maurice tried to lead it, a dozen times it slipped from his clumsy control under her deft control.

He had seated himself dangerously close to her, leaving an empty space on the seat.

"How kind you are," she said artlessly. "You have left room for another. I should never have thought of that; and there are many people who must be tired."

He moved back on the vacant space, with a glance that certainly was not an invitation to passers-by.

Then there was a silence; almost the first they had known when they were alone together. Norah broke it before it grew dangerous.

"How beautifully the soft, rosy light of the sunset plays upon the shining lake and moving figures. Look, Maurice! see how the rich glow settles upon the summit of the hill yonder. Have you ever seen anything more beautiful?"

"Yes," he answered, "far more beautiful." His eyes were upon her own fair face, and the colour deepened upon her cheek under the passionate intensity of his gaze. But she kept her eyes resolutely away from his.

"Oh, I see," she cried lightly, glancing aside, "you, too, are an adorer of Lady Dulwich; even the sunset is less brilliant."

Maurice followed her gaze, and saw Lady Dulwich approaching in all the glory of her resplendent beauty. A young, soft-eyed, dark-haired girl was beside her. It seemed as if her ladyship was coming straight up to speak to Norah. Her lips wore a welcoming smile that had a touch of patronage in it. Her hand was half extended. But there was no answering sign in Norah's face. Their eyes met, questioned and answered each other, then, with a scornful movement of her lovely head, which was half a salute, half defiance, Lady Dulwich swept by with her companion and seated herself some little distance away.

"You know her?" Norah whispered to Maurice, delighted to find any topic foreign to themselves. "Poor Lord Edward has told you, I am sure. I have not seen her since until to-day. How he suffered, poor fellow, for a lovely face and a hard heart, and now he has forgotten all about her. What a foolish thing is love!"

Not very encouraging this to a man that wanted to speak of love, and nothing but love.

There was no help for it. He felt he must dash straight to the subject. He was conscious that he was talking like a stage hero; but he could not help it.

"Norah," he said faltering, "can you love?"

"What?" she asked, looking him innocently in the face with such childlike simplicity that he could not for the life of him say "Me."

"Anything," he answered foolishly.

"Almost everything. There never yet was anyone more given to love. But why do you ask?"

There was a mocking light in her eye, the humour of the situation had conquered her fear.

The longing was strong on him to catch her in his arms and answer her with a shower of kisses. Perhaps she guessed this new danger, for she spoke again quickly.

"Look, look," she cried, "how beautiful! how graceful!

It was not all artifice, there was genuine admiration in her voice. Looking where she pointed, right out over the lake, Maurice shared her admiration. A beautiful boy was flying over the ice in bend and whirl and curve with inimitable grace, while all eyes watched him from lake and shore.

With a boy's love of peril he sought the corner of the lake where alone it was possible to meet it. A pole and board with the ominous word "dangerous" on it stuck up from the ice. Round and round this pole he circled with whirls and turns as fantastic and as graceful as a tumbler pigeon in mid air.

The murmur of admiration changed to a cry of warning. Norah's face grew pale, her lips parted, and her heart beat quickly with the excitement and fear of it.

" Is there any danger, Maurice ? " she whispered.

" Throth, an' there is that, ma'am," said one of the keepers of the ground, who came up at the moment ; "great danger, intirely. The ducks and the swans have been boring holes in the ice out there with their bussums, just fornint the place where he is sliding. The frost has put a skin over the holes, but it is no thicker in parts than an egg shell. If he were weightier than a bird, bedad, he'd be through long ago. Glory be to God ! it is dancing poulkas he is on it now."

The keeper's cry was echoed by the crowd. The reckless boy was figure-skating on the thin shell of ice that stretched between him and forty feet of black water with chill death lurking there.

Heretofore the speed he went at saved him. Though the ice might creak and crack, it had not time to break as he flew over it. Now with a short quick rush on the outer edge he leaped clean into the air, spun like a ballet dancer, and lit again on the sharp edge of a single skate. He struck right over one of the death traps the birds had made. Crash through the thin ice the skate went, and the skater after it.

There was a cry of horror from the gazing crowd as he disappeared.

But in a moment the blue cloth cap and the yellow curls showed over the level surface. The brave boy held fast to the thick edges of the hole through which he had fallen, and so kept himself afloat. A shout went up for ropes and ladders and lifebuoys, and the crowd surged and scattered wildly in noisy excitement, but none ventured down to the treacherous hole, where the chill water was freezing warm young life out. A keen eye could see the small hands, blue and red with the cold, on the slippery ice's edge—could see the agony of intense cold on the pitiful face.

The boy had uttered no cry from the first. But there was a lady in black on the ice, screaming and struggling violently, with half-a-dozen people holding her. It was the boy's mother, straining to fly to him and perish with him.

"It cannot last long unless help comes," whispered Maurice to Norah, who was looking out over the lake with pale face and wide open eyes. "The cold is enough to freeze the very blood in his veins. He cannot hold out. Great God! it is too horrible. There is one chance, a narrow one, but I 'll risk it.

"Good-bye, my darling," he whispered so softly she did not hear the last words. "If so be we meet no more, good-bye for ever."

Then he stumbled awkwardly, but rapidly, with his steel-bound feet to the lake's edge, and shot out like lightning over its surface. The crowd parted as he came.   Like a hawk on the wing he swooped straight for the boy.   It seemed that he was going crash into the same trap.   But as he neared it he swerved a little and planted both feet firmly on the ice.   Then as he swept by with lightning speed at the very verge of the death trap, he stooped, grasped the golden hair that floated like a spreading weed on the surface, and, with one tremendous effort of his strength, lifted the light body clean from the water, and so held his course, with the two small feet trailing after him on the ice.   The ice cracked with a loud report under the sudden strain and the double weight.   The hole from which the body was snatched spouted and bubbled, as if greedy for life.   But the wild speed saved both.   Before the great shout of applause had time to break from the lips of the excited crowd, Maurice had flashed outside the circle of danger, and sped along securely where the ice was firm as a granite pavement under his skates.

Very gently he gathered the limp body of the poor child into his arms and carried him, half insensible, to his mother, who kissed, and fondled, and laughed, and cried over him.

When Norah Denver saw Maurice shoot out across the ice, straight, as it seemed, to inevitable death, her heart beat quicker than his feet flew.   When she saw him wheel back safe, triumphant, its beating suddenly ceased, her limbs lost strength, her eyes light, and her brain thought, in the same instant. The whole scene swam wildly round and vanished in thick darkness. With a faint cry she fell forward upon her hands and face.

At once there was a crowd of women round her. She was lifted gently to a seat with much slapping of hands and little tender cries of pity.

Some offered smelling salts, some stood idly by and gossiped and wondered, as compassion or curiosity prevailed. All talked and wondered.

Norah's consciousness returned almost as quickly as it had fled. A faint pink tint showed in the pure white of her cheeks, like the wavering flush on the pearly lip of the sea-shell.

There was a buzzing in her ears; then the murmur of voices.

"Poor thing!" she heard a quiet voice say, "I saw him beside her just the moment before. It was the fright of it overcame her. I suppose she is his sweetheart."

"Rather wants to be his sweetheart," answered the cold, clear voice of Lady Dulwich. "It is the talk of the town how she has angled for him. This judicious faint ought to complete the capture."

"Hush," cried half-a-dozen voices together, for the flush deepened on Norah's cheek, and a quiver ran through her body. "Hush; she is coming to." At the same moment the dark lashes lifted from the white cheek, and the brave blue eyes looked straight in Lady Dulwich's face, who knew then that her poisoned arrow had gone straight home.

Bravely did Norah strive to hide the sudden pain planted in her heart. But her pale cheek and quivering lip told their own tale. The world, then, had meddled with her fair name. So ran the bitter thought that tortured her. She was censured for lack of maiden modesty. The bitter truth was the more bitter from the lips of an enemy. Besides, the world was right. Unwooed, she had given her love. Oh! how she loved him. She never knew how she loved him till now. Every nerve in her body quivered, and the blood burned in her cheek and forehead. Perhaps he had seen her love and pitied it. This then was what his kindness meant. The thought thrilled her through with shame. How weak she had been, and how foolish. But she would conquer her love, and hide it till she could conquer it. Never, never, would he guess her heart's secret.

She nerved herself for the first brave effort, as her quick eyes caught sight of the form she loved so well, pressing eagerly through the throng with an anxious fear on his face, which brightened with delight as he saw her.

"So you fainted, Norah," he said, when he came close up.

"Tell me," he went on more softly, "was it for my sake or the boy's?"

He could not have hit upon a more unhappy question. Lady Dulwich's cruel words seemed to sound again in her ears. Her fainting was taken as a public profession of her love.

" For both," she said very sweetly and softly.

What was in the words or tone that chilled the heart of Maurice Blake—a moment before warm with triumph and love.   Her words were not unkind, they were gently and even kindly spoken.

He had come to her full of joy and love and pardonable pride in a brave deed, done bravely in her sight.   He had hoped for a warm welcome.   He had resolved that now was his time to speak and make her his own for ever.

Two words of hers—only two—sweetly spoken and with a smiling face, and he felt he might as soon strike her in the face as ask her to be his wife.

No change in voice or manner was there that ear or eye could find.   But every pulse of his heart felt the chilling change.   Soft word or sweet smile brought him no comfort.   The sunshine cannot warm, nor blue sky cheer, when the chill of the cold, dry east wind is in the air.

What a change was the drive home from the morning's drive, when the jingling of the silver bells in the clear frosty air was less joyous than the beating of their own hearts.   The subtle flow of sympathy which seemed to reach from mind and mind, and heart and heart, without the aid of words, suddenly ceased.   No fits of tender musing broke the even tenour of their talk.   Norah was bright, beautiful, and kind as ever.   But the something which had so thrilled his heart was gone from the smile in her blue eyes and the tones of her gentle voice.

His whole soul rebelled against the vague, chill barrier interposed between him and the hope and happiness of his life. But it rebelled in vain, as the impatient bird beats out his life against the clear glass, which keeps it back from summer air and sunshine.

With a dull, aching sense of something lost and wanting, Maurice took his leave, and pressed the little white hand that frankly returned the pressure, and looked into the blue eyes that answered his own with open courtesy.

Norah went straight from him to her own room, and throwing herself upon her face wept tears that hurt, not eased, her bursting heart—tears of passion and despair. But with every choking sob her resolution grew stronger. " He must never know."

If he loved her, she told her troubled heart again and again, he would have spoken his love. It was his right to speak. If he guessed her secret now he would pity her—a hot flush of shame covered face and neck at the thought—and offer her his pity in mistake for love.

So those two drifted slowly apart, each chilled by the other's coldness, and the few frank words that would have made both happy were unspoken. So much the poisoned words of an angry woman could effect—

> Alas ! how light a word can move
> Dissension between souls that love.

Day by day the gulf between them grew wider. Maurice could not stem the impalpable and mysterious current that carried them apart. He could not understand, nor resist, nor resent the change. He had no cold look or word to complain of, yet by slow but sure degrees he slipped down to mere acquaintanceship.

He felt no anger at all, only an aching pain. He would trouble her peace no longer with his unwelcome love. He groaned in secret, and she wept ; but they saw each other no more.

All the more eagerly Maurice Blake now flung himself into the torrent of political excitement that then rushed, seethed, and boiled under the surface of Dublin society, making the solid-seeming and stately institutions of the Government shake, and frightening the ears of the wary with the hollow, threatening murmur of impending change. Here all the impetus of his suppressed passion found a vent, and he worked with an untiring industry, a feverish zeal, that surpassed and surprised the most devoted of his comrades. Lord Edward alone could keep pace with his enthusiasm.

It was a fair morning in the early spring. Maurice sat alone by a table at the open window of his room, through which the sunshine and cool air entered to tell of the green world without, and woo him in vain to healthful exercise. He bent resolutely over his papers, and put all the energy of his pent-up passion into his work.

Christy entered without knocking. He seemed curiously excited, and stumbled as he crossed the room. His hand shook so that a letter which he silently offered to Maurice slipped from his fingers to the floor. Maurice stooped to pick it up, and in that instant, still without a word, Christy disappeared.

The letter was in Dr. Denver's handwriting. It was very short. "Dear Maurice—I have desired this while back to see you, to break some news which must now come to you as a surprise—but a pleasant surprise. Come to me at once on receipt of this, and bring your manhood with you. I have that to tell and show which will test your stoicism."

Without a moment's delay Maurice was out of doors and striding towards Dr. Denver's house, which was close at hand.

His mind was in a whirl. In some vague way he associated the sudden summons with Norah and hope.

Up the stone steps of the doctor's house he went three at a time; but before his hand could touch the knocker the door was opened by the doctor himself.

"Come in," he said, cordially pressing Maurice's hand and walking with him to the parlour. It was a large dim room, with a rich red, velvety paper on the walls that made a kind of rosy twilight in it. Standing a little away from the door by which they entered was a tall, gaunt man, dressed quietly in black velvet, with the deep lace ruffles and cuffs that the fashion of the day prescribed. His was a face and figure to catch and rivet attention. The large features were finely formed, but his forehead was seamed with innumerable wrinkles, so deep and clearly cut that they seemed carved, with a chisel's edge, on stone. His hair and beard were iron grey, and his keen blue eyes looked out with an eager longing look from under his grey eyebrows. There was dead silence in the room—silence so profound that Maurice could hear his own heart beat.

Dr. Denver spoke at last, in a voice that quivered with excitement.

"Maurice," he said abruptly, "this is your father. Sir Valentine, my old friend, I can honestly congratulate you on your son."

Maurice was surprised that he felt no surprise. Rather with the speaking of the words came the thought that he had known the secret all along, as he eagerly clasped his father's hand.

So those two met for the first time in silence. They looked into each other's honest eyes with joy and love; the aching yearning of their hearts at rest.

CHAPTER XIX.

" TELL TRUTH AND SHAME THE DEVIL."
Henry IV. Part I.

" Scorn and defiance ; slight regard, contempt."—*Henry V.*

" Is this proceeding just and honourable?
Is your assembly so ?"—*Henry IV.* Part II.

C HRISTY'S letter told the hideous plot which
Mark Blake had concocted with Lord Dulwich,
and the startling news had given Sir Valentine
power to break the galling links of habit which
bound him to savage life, and against which he had
so long chafed in vain. He determined that an
apostate should never be heir at Cloonlara, and with
him to determine was to do. When he set foot in
Ireland, he learned from his old retainer that his
brother was dead, and that his nephew was a
parricide as well as an apostate.

An action in trespass was promptly begun for the
recovery from Mark Blake, who entered into possession on his father's death, of all the lands, tenements,
and hereditaments of Cloonlara, on Sir Valentine's
arrival. The famous Philpot Curran and Leonard
M'Nally, the leading senior and junior counsel of the
bar, were engaged for the plaintiff ; and in compliance

with the quaint legal fictions of the day "John Doe" and "Richard Roe" were called into court to do forensic battle for the respective claimants. Of the result no doubt was possible. Sir Valentine was recognised by all his former friends. The decision was merely a question of time. But Mark Blake's advisers exhausted every subtle technical objection, which the stupid and cumbersome procedure of the courts so plentifully afforded itself, to stave off the evil hour.

Sir Valentine pursued his course steadily, but with stoical calmness. Nothing deterred him and nothing disturbed him. He took his place in society and held it with stately ease, as if those long years in the wilderness had been no more than a fantastic dream. Silent, reserved, apparently emotionless—he made the manner of the woods and wigwams seem the perfection of high-born grace in what was then the most courtly capital of Europe.

His tenderness for his son was most touching, by reason of a certain humility that mingled with it. It seemed to ask pardon for the stubborn wilfulness which sundered them so long, and robbed the son of a father's love and care. With every look of his eyes, every tone of his voice, the younger man paid back the long arrears of duty and affection.

Against Mark Sir Valentine's resentment was silent, deep, implacable. He refused all overtures of meeting or compromise. His wrath found vent in resolutely pushing forward the suit which would drive the apostate from Cloonlara.

But it was with Norah Denver that the real character of the man most showed itself. The womanly tenderness of soul which had dominated his life, making at once its delight and its misery, still lay soft and warm under the sternness with which grief and misfortune had overlaid his character.

In Norah's presence the cold and stately dignity of his manner softened to a gracious old-fashioned courtesy wonderful to see. They grew to be close companions: those two. He humoured her fancies; he anticipated her wishes. It may be that the keen instinct of a father's heart hinted at how matters stood between her and his son, and that he set himself to clear away the obstacles that sundered their lives. If it were so he watched and waited with quiet patience, biding his time, and said no word.

Norah met his affection with unaffected delight. He seemed to take his place almost at once beside her father in the daughter's heart. She lavished on him all the little tender tokens of thoughtful affection that only a woman can bestow. The strain of her secret love for Maurice hurt her sorely, though she hid her suffering with smiling lips or cheerful words. To her woman's heart it was relief to give her love for the son free scope in her tenderness for the father.

Sir Valentine entered heart and soul into the "United Irishmen" organization, with his son and his son's bosom friend. There was good hope, then, of a peaceful victory; for the power of the Castle quailed before the power of the people.

The Government, however, still played a game of brag, and pressed forward in their course of bigotry and oppression, though they were walking with concious fear, on the thin crust of a volcano.

The more moderate party, of which Grattan was leader, bided its time, and made no sign.

But Lord Edward believed that the hour had come for a bold stroke in the House of Commons itself, which would teach the Government that the power of the United Irishmen must no longer be trifled with.

Maurice Blake and his father strongly seconded his views. It was resolved that by Lord Edward himself, who typified their organization alike to the country and the Castle, the challenge should be made.

The occasion was not long wanting. Under the auspices of the United Irishmen the policy by which the Irish Volunteers had succeeded in wresting something of Ireland's right from England's reluctant grasp was revived. An armed association had been organised, calling themselves The First National Battalion, and having for device an Irish harp, surmounted, not by the customary crown, but by a cap of liberty. Its meetings had been proclaimed and suppressed by the Government. As usual the coercion proclamation bred new trouble for its authors. A body of delegates of the old Volunteer corps of Dublin retaliated by announcing their intention of holding a meeting to celebrate the successes of the French Republic.

The Irish Government, in desperation, resolved that this meeting should also be suppressed. It was thought advisable by the bigots to strengthen the hands of the Lord Lieutenant, by an address from Parliament approving of the proclamation. Lord Edward went down to the house on the day the address was to be moved, with a number of friends he could trust. Maurice Blake and his father were, of course, of the party.

These and others of the United Irishmen waited in the Strangers' Gallery, while Lord Edward, his lips compressed and his bright eyes blazing with restrained excitement, walked up the floor to his place. It was a full house. The beautiful amphitheatre in which the money changers now rustle paper and chink coin, was then crowded with the wealth, the intellect, and the beauty of the gay capital. Grattan was there, eagle-eyed and eagle-beaked, resolute for liberty, but biding his time, and, as the United Irishmen thought, too patient of oppression. Curran was there, his ugly features luminous with the genius that shone through as light through a transparency.

On the over-crowded benches of the Government Lord Castlereagh was the most prominent figure, sleek, graceful, cold, and false. A few seats off sat Flood, dark-eyed, cadaverous-looking, awkward, and uneasy in the Ministerial chains in which he had fettered his genius and patriotism.

As Lord Edward passed to his place he received kindly greeting on all hands. From the Ladies' Gallery especially bright glances were showered on the handsome and noble young patriot. In that gay throng were many by whom the beautiful Pamela was envied.

But Lord Castlereagh frowned and bit his lips as he saw him, and Mark Blake, who had been "brought into Parliament" by a noble patron, after his apostacy, rose quietly and slipped out.

The obnoxious address was being read as Lord Edward entered. It was couched in the language of undiluted coercion. There was a ruthless trampling down of popular rights in every sentence of it.

The speech in which it was moved was boisterous and truculent. The seconder was as savage as the mover. "The Papists" were denounced as "crawling slaves for whom life was an excess of toleration." The United Irishmen were "disloyal traitors, the flame of whose vile conspiracy must be quenched in blood." The Lord Lieutenant was exhorted "to stamp with armed heel on the poisonous snake which mistaken mercy had engendered." Each furious sentence was followed by a furious burst of applause from the Ministerial benches. But a quaver as of fear seemed to run through those wild cheers. There was a touch of terror in the desperation of their defiance, and many an eye wandered uneasily to where the gallant young leader of the United Irishmen sat, with face pale and resolute, only the flashing eyes to tell the fierce scorn that consumed him. The debate was short as it was violent. Only the Government hacks and partisans took part in it. As taunt and insult were repeated without reply, their spirits rose, and their triumphant jibes and scornful laughter rang through the house.

At length the time came to put the question, and a momentary silence fell on the assembly.

As the Speaker rose, Lord Edward rose with him. Before a word could issue from the Speaker's lips his fresh, young voice rang out boldly through the hushed assembly, in words that have lived to our own day.

"Sir, I give my most hearty disapprobation to this address, for I do think that the Lord Lieutenant and the majority of this house are the worst subjects the King has."

All eyes were upon him. For a moment after he had spoken the silence seemed to grow even more profound than before. Then the storm burst loud and furious round the daring young patriot, who stood there facing them smiling and defiant. At first it was an inarticulate roar of rage; swords were half drawn and seats overleaped by the howling throng, and it seemed as if the Government partisans would attack him even in the sacred precincts of the house itself; but the more cautious of the placemen noticed that in the strangers' galleries were those whose hands were on their sword hilts, and whose eyes waited only a signal from Lord Edward; and held back their furious friends.

Prudence prevailed. Men were pulled by main force to their seats, swords were pushed back in their scabbards, the wild cry of rage took articulate sound at last.

"To the bar, to the bar." "Take down his words," resounded from the Government benches.

The house was cleared. At first there seemed to be a movement as of resistance from the galleries : but at a slight gesture from Lord Edward it subsided.

For three hours the private session lasted. Lord Edward faced the full house of the Government, smooth and smiling as the summer sea, resolute as the rocks and as hard to be stirred. Threats and entreaties were alike wasted on him. His words had been taken down. He was called upon for an explanation.

"I am accused," he replied, and the low clear tones of his voice reached to the furthest verge of the spacious hall, distinct as they issued from his lips. "I am accused of having declared that the Lord Lieutenant and the majority of this house are the worst subjects the King has. I said so, 't is true, I 'm sorry for it."

The angry murmur with which this contemptuous explanation was heard was slightly dashed with laughter. His friends took heart from his coolness. But it kindled anew the anger of the Government party.

A resolution was promptly moved and carried without division—"That the excuse offered by the Right Hon. Edward Fitzgerald, commonly called Lord Edward, for the words so spoken, is unsatisfactory and insufficient."

But the Government seemed more troubled by their own hostile resolution, when they got it, than the man against whom it was directed.

When the hoarse chorus of ayes that carried it died away, their passion died with it, and fear followed. Lord Edward's look of unaffected unconcern more and more disconcerted his truculent opponents.

Lord Castlereagh hesitated a little as to the next step, but at the moment there was no chance of retreating. With a very visible faltering, he moved —"That it be ordered that the said Right Hon. Lord Edward Fitzgerald, commonly called Lord Edward Fitzgerald, do attend to-morrow at the bar of the house."

This resolution, too, was carried without division ; but the applause that greeted it was feeble and faint-hearted.

Men had cooled down by this time, and were beginning to ask themselves what next, and found no answer to please them.

When the public were again admitted, no stranger

could have guessed that the smiling and fearless young fellow, who stepped out gay and *débonnaire* from the excited meeting, was the arraigned, and that the group of scowling and shame-faced men yonder were his arraigners. Uninformed conjecture would simply have reversed their places.

"We shall win," said Lord Edward, as they walked home together in the order they had come.

"Those fellows are cowed. They feel there is a power behind us stronger than their own, which corruption cannot tempt nor force intimidate. They will be in no hurry to tackle us. To-morrow will tell."

"They have professed duellists in their ranks," said Maurice, "and professed bullies in their pay. They may try to pick you off by assassination, licensed or unlicensed."

"I will keep my temper quiet and my sword ready," replied Lord Edward, laughing. "But talking of—do you see those two muffled figures there—there in the dusk? By heavens! they are shadowing us. They have followed us the whole way from the house."

"I have noticed them before," said Maurice, quietly. "My father and myself scarcely stir from the door that we are not honoured by their company, always in the shadow. But one gets a quick eye and a keen ear in the backwoods. We have kept, as you say, our tempers cool and our weapons ready, and so far the spies have kept their distance. If I mistake not the taller figure of the two is my worthy cousin."

"And, by heaven!" cried Lord Edward, glancing keenly over his shoulder at their shadowy attendants, "the other is his most worthy friend, Lord Dulwich. Hatred has good eyes, and I hate the fellow. What does it mean?"

"I think I can guess," replied Sir Valentine, gloomily, for the shadow of a black presentiment was on his soul. "My nephew has shown scant scruple in clearing obstacles from his path."

Next day, attended as before, Lord Edward returned to the house.

He walked as blythely to the bar as ever accepted lover to his rendezvous. Again, in reply to the solemn questioning of the Speaker, he flung in the face of the majority of place-holders, place-hunters, and bigots, the scornful words of the previous day.

But time had brought reflection, and reflection fear, to the dastard majority. The angry murmur with which his defiance was received was slight and brief; silence came quickly, and remained.

At length a shamefaced man from the Government side got on his feet and proceeded to move, amid an angry murmur behind and scornful laughter in front, "That the explanation of the Right Hon. Edward Fitzgerald, commonly called Lord Edward Fitzgerald, be accepted as satisfactory by this house."

He stumbled awkwardly through a few sentences, and sat down. The motion was silently seconded

from the same bench. Then silence. The motion
was put from the chair. A triumphant chorus of
"Ayes" thundered out from the Opposition benches,
whose spirit revived with the discomfiture of their
opponents. A few venomous "Noes" were shouted
by the Orange gang, whose bigotry surpassed their
prudence. The division was taken, and the motion
carried by an overwhelming majority. In a crowded
house only fifty-five members ventured to record
their votes against it. The triumph of revolt was
complete.

In the person of their leader, Lord Edward, the
United Irishmen had defied the intolerant and corrupt
majority of the house, and the majority had meekly
swallowed the insult.

When Lord Edward showed himself on the steps
fronting College Green a great cheer went up from
the exultant crowd with which the broad space was
filled. They would have caught and chaired him.
But he slipped down into the throng, and forced
his way through. With Maurice and his father on
either side he came swiftly down the quay.

"Victory! victory!" he cried joyously to Maurice,
when at last they had got clear of the crush of the
crowd and the din of the cheering; "that victory
without bloodshed for which you always longed.
We have taught them to-day to respect our power;
the next lesson is to obey it. We will speak pikes
but use none. By the way, I did not see your
worthy cousin in the house."

"You may see him now if your eyes are keen enough," replied Maurice, pointing to an archway, where the gathering shades of twilight thickened into darkness, and common eyesight could catch only the bare outline of muffled figures lurking. But Maurice Blake's was no common sight. It pierced and searched the darkness like a cat's.

"My cousin and Lord Dulwich," he said, "are hiding yonder like a brace of pickpockets. By heavens!" he went on, "there is that great brute Hempenstal half crouched behind them. There is mischief brewing. We must be on our guard. Those three are not there together for nothing. Three to three, however," he added, with a smile; "we are more than their match."

His right hand, as he spoke, dropped down to his side, where his sword hilt ought to be, and he uttered a low cry of surprise.

His sword belt had been cut in the crowd—belt and weapon were gone. His father had been similarly despoiled. Some silver chasing on Lord Edward's belt had stopped the knife half way through the leather, and left him still armed.

"The cowardly assassins," growled Maurice between his teeth. "But they must win us before they wear us." He grasped and shook his stout blackthorn ominously. "Step out, Lord Edward," he whispered; "let us get to shelter in Dominick Street as soon as may be. My father is unarmed, and it is on his life, if I mistake not, the attack is to be made."

The excitement in the House of Commons had proved contagious. Torches began to dance about hither and thither in the twilight. The whole city seemed astir. From Cork Hill came yells of anger or triumph, interspersed with fierce bursts of laughter. There the butchers of Ormond quay and the tabinet weavers of the Liberties were engaged in one of their senseless faction fights.

High over this noisy tumult there broke occasionally, on the evening air, from Lord Beresford's "Riding School" the wild, long shriek of agony, followed by laughter such as the devils might laugh in hell. Right well Edward and his companions knew these sounds and their gruesome meaning.

To the pillar of that ill-famed establishment of Beresford's someone in ghastly jest had pinned the legend "Mangling done here." It justified the description. Torture was the recreation of the noble proprietor which it pleased him to call loyalty. Men were half hanged till their eyes and tongues protruded, then cut down to struggle back as painfully to life again. Caps of brown paper or sheep skin lined with boiling pitch were clapped on the bare heads of the wretched victims, where they stuck and scorched, and the frantic hands that tore them away in fragments tore hair and bleeding skin with them.

Another yell, wilder and keener than any they had yet heard, cut the air like a knife ; another, and yet another. The cries come nearer and nearer. A victim had escaped the torturers. There was the quick clatter of hurrying feet on the pavement behind. A man with the torturing pitchcap steaming on his head rushed wildly past them, and mad and blind with pain, plunged over the low wall into the quick current of the Liffey, swollen with the high tide.

Quick as a well-trained retriever Lord Edward was over after him, splash into the dark water.

He caught him before he sank. The cool current eased the wretch's pain. He was a brave fellow. With ease of his agony his courage came back. He could swim a little, and Lord Edward helping, they reached together the iron ladder that rose out of the water close to' Essex Bridge, and climbed back to the quay.

Maurice and Sir Valentine lent a hand as they mounted. All three recognised the rescued man as Dan Corbett, a brave and prominent member of their society. But there was no time to question him, for quick upon his track the bloodhound yeomen came, yelling out fierce curses—a score of them— Lord Beresford and Major Stirr at their head.

"You will not desert me," the poor wretch faltered.

The kindly grasp of Lord Edward, and Sir Valentine's friendly hand upon his shoulder, answered him without a word.

"Quick!" whispered Maurice; "quick! for the bridge; with our backs to the balustrades we will keep those bullies at bay. There is a chance those foolish fellows yonder on Cork Hill will be drawn down by the sound of the fight, glad to join forces against the Castle."

They had scarcely gained their vantage point on the crown of the bridge, when the yeomen, flustered with drink, stumbling and shouting in their eagerness of the attack, were upon them.

Maurice was nearest. Again his hand went down instinctively to his side, and he remembered, with a pang, his good blade was gone. Next moment his thick, blackthorn stick whistled over his head. It caught the raised sword of his first assailant, and dashed it from his hand. The second stroke fell on the man's head, and sent him down like a nine-pin. Quick as light the rescued man, Corbett, picked up the blade of the fallen foe, caught an incoming yeoman on its point, ran him clean through the body, regained his weapon, and stood on guard again.

Lord Edward was less fortunate. Always impetuous, his eagerness was heightened now by the feeling that he was the one armed man of his party. He did not wait for the assault, but rushed right into the midst of the advancing yeomen. He parried a shrewd thrust at his breast, and spitted the man who made it on the point of his sword. But before he could regain his weapon his arms were seized from behind, and pinned to his sides; a coarse hand was pressed to his mouth, and he was half-carried, half-dragged away up Parliament Street by a dozen of the party, to take the place of the man whom he had rescued from the torturers.

Maurice was too hard pressed to note his capture, much less attempt a rescue. He kept his ground bravely in front of his father. Timber against steel, he beat down the points and beat in the heads of his opponents. The half-drunken fellows in the first close rush impeded each other's weapons. A couple tumbling back amongst the throng heightened the confusion. They had begun to give way. Each hung back himself; each urged his neighbours to the assault. The fight seemed almost at an end. But at this moment three muffled figures that had from the first hovered on the outskirts of the tumult pressed into the centre and renewed the attack. These men were masked. All three were strong and active. One was a giant.

Without a word of warning one of the three delivered a point-blank thrust at the breast of Maurice Blake, whose quick eye caught the cold glint of the steel only just in time. So sudden was the thrust and so quick, that the keen point tore the lace ruffles on his bosom as he dashed the weapon aside. Quick as lightning another lunge followed, and another. Here was no child's play. His assailant was a deadly swordsman. The rapier was sheathed, but four inches of bright steel protruded from the extremity of the scabbard, and darted hither and thither like a serpent's tongue, searching for his opponent's life through every opening in his defence. Maurice Blake's stout parries fell on leather, not steel. In vain he sought by sheer strength to break the weapon, or wrest or dash it from the hand of his skilful assailant. The sword point pressed him closer and closer, glancing everywhere. He was forced to give ground a little to avoid those pitiless thrusts.

His father was now opposed with empty hands against the gang of armed ruffians.

The masked giant made at him with huge sword uplifted.

But before the blow could fall Sir Valentine leaped forward, caught his wrist in a grasp of iron, and so wrenched it, that with a cry of rage and pain the brute dropped his great weapon, clashing on the pavement. Then they closed in a fierce death-struggle, bulk against bulk, strength against strength. It was a tussle of giants. Though Sir Valentine was a man of splendid physique, Hempenstal was a full head taller, and half again his weight. But from head to foot Sir Valentine's gaunt figure was bone and muscles, made tough as whalebone by a life of incessant exercise. His hug was that of a grizzly bear. As they spun round in their fierce struggle, Hempenstal felt the strain of those strong arms crushing his ribs like a closing band of steel. He put forth all the strength in his huge sluggish frame to save himself. Straining up over his enemy, he strove to force his clenched hands into his back, and so bending him down fall on him, and crush

him with his weight. The device seemed to succeed.
Sir Valentine bent under the pressure. Hempenstal
threw all his cumbrous weight forward on him.

Suddenly, with a supreme effort of strength, Sir
Valentine straightened himself under this vast load
of brawn and bone, lifting it sheer into the air.
Then, with a sudden whirl, he slung the giant's
dangling limbs clear of the low parapet of the
bridge, and, straining to the uttermost, raised and
hurled him down into the swift, full current of the
river, to sink or swim.

Turning, he caught up the great sword from the
pavement, and faced the affrighted foe.

Well might they shrink back in dismay from that
threatening figure. With grey head uncovered, keen
blue eyes blazing with the light of battle, and huge
brand uplifted and quivering to fall, he stood for a
moment terrible as the Angel of Destruction.

The next moment a pistol report rang out. The
pellet of lead struck full on his forehead, and went
crashing through his brain. The stately figure fell
prone on the pavement, quivered, and lay quite still
—a ghastly heap of ruined humanity.

Maurice Blake half turned at the sharp report,
and saw his father's fall. For a moment he was
thrown completely off his guard. At that moment,
his treacherous opponent, watching his chance, drove
the keen steel into his side.

He faced round instinctively, galled by the sharp
sting of the steel. The mask had fallen from his

"With a supreme effort, Sir Valentine hurled him down into the swift, full current of the river."

enemy. He saw the white face of Lord Dulwich, a smile of cowardly triumph on it. Then, with a last fierce effort, Maurice struck out wildly. He felt the tingling sensation in his arm; he heard the dull smash as the heavy stick struck the white hand-some face with horrible force, burying the rugged nobs in the quivering flesh. He saw the blood squirt out and the man go down. A wild shout seemed to peal in his ear; then darkness came upon him. He reeled and fell.

The shout that filled his ears as he fell was the cry of a swift-coming rescue.

When Lord Edward was hauled up Parliament Street he heard, hotter and fiercer as he approached, the din of the faction fight of the Ormond quay butchers, who stormed Cork Hill, and the Liberty tabinet weavers, who stubbornly defended it, with no other meaning in their deadly conflict save the love of fighting for its own sake.

Just at the entrance of the Castle Yard he wrenched himself free of the yeoman who held him on the left. His right hand went into his bosom, and came out clutching a poignard. At the mere flash of the steel the fellow on the right hand let go his hold. Lord Edward flew away like a pigeon from an opened trap; a score of swift strides, and he was half-way up the steep ascent of Cork Hill, in the very thick of the struggling faction-fighters.

Half-a-dozen of them recognised him in a moment —staunch United Irishmen every one.

The cry, "Lord Edward for ever!" was instantly raised, and caught up by both factions. The conflict ceased as if by magic. The men close beside him were shame-faced and silent under his angry gaze.

His voice rang out clear over their cheers, with scorn and anger in its tones.

"You fools!" he cried ; "you besotted fools! Have you no enemies, that you must need waste your strength and courage on each other, while your brethren are tortured and butchered with impunity? Come! If you would fight foes, not friends, follow me."

He pointed to the yeomen at the Castle gate. With a shout they ranged themselves behind him, dashed like a torrent down the steep ascent, and sent the enemy shrieking and flying before them up Dame Street.

"On!" shouted Lord Edward; and, with unchecked speed, they poured after him down Parliament Street to the bridge. The fight was over there.

Maurice Blake lay where he had fallen, prone on his father's corpse.

Lord Dulwich, helped off by his companion, had disappeared. The yeomen closed in on their first victim, Corbett, who had defended himself with desperate courage, but was now overwhelmed by numbers. With shouts of triumph they were hauling him away, when the live torrent from Cork Hill swept down, and scattered them. "Liberty boys" and butchers vied with each other in the chase. They seized upon the flying yeomen with shouts of fierce laughter, and slung them over the low river wall into the water, like the blind puppies of a litter of curs.

But Lord Edward, frantic with fear for his missing friends, took no part in the pursuit.

In the gathering twilight his eyes missed for a moment the bodies lying so still under the shadow of the bridge's parapet.

"Maurice! Maurice!" he shouted wildly, "a rescue! a rescue! Answer but a word."

Still shouting and rushing wildly to and fro, he almost stumbled over the bodies that lay, as it seemed, embraced in death.

He stooped and touched them, and his hand came up wet and clammy with blood.

Trembling, he knelt beside them on the blood-stained pavement.

Maurice and his father both bleeding, both senseless. "Both," so his first thought ran, "dead."

But Lord Edward had been in battle, and the soldier's instincts were keen in him. Sharp as was the pang he felt, it did not rob him of quick, cool judgment. He found the blood was still oozing in a little stream from Maurice Blake's wound. There was life still in his veins. He tore open coat and shirt, and pressed his ear to the naked side. He rather felt than heard the feeble flutter of his heart.

The small round hole in the centre of Sir Valentine's forehead told his fate only too plainly.

Hastily, but skilfully too, Lord Edward staunched the oozing blood, and bound up the deep wound in Maurice Blake's side with two tattered strips of cambric, while his followers, tearing down a gaily-painted barber's pole that stretched half across the quay, managed under his direction to construct a litter, of which the covering was the coats stripped from their own shoulders.

As softly and smoothly as calm water bears a boat upon its bosom, they bore him through rough, dark streets, until they laid the litter, with the still body on it, down at the door of Dr. Denver's house in Jervis Street.

CHAPTER XX.

"A KEEPER BACK OF DEATH."
                                        Richard II.

"Some Cupid kills with arrows, some with traps."
                            Much Ado About Nothing.
        "Hang there like fruit, my soul,
Till the tree die."—*Cymbeline.*

SILENT, pale, with lips shut tight, and quick-beating hearts, Norah and Lord Edward waited for Dr. Denver's verdict of life or death.

He paced the room impatiently, never ceasing for a moment. She sat apart, in a darkened corner, quite still, with strained eyes fixed on the door through which the news must come.

At the first sound of many feet and whispering voices in the hall, a strange instinct had told her what had happened. As clearly as if she looked upon his ghastly face, she knew the man she loved was wounded nigh to death.

For a moment she had reeled under the blow, which drove the frightened blood to her faltering heart, leaving cheek and lips ghastly pale. But that nobler instinct of woman's nature—the instinct that commands to aid and soothe—conquered grief and fear.

Y

Quietly, calmly, as though it were some customary household duty, she had directed the men to lift their senseless burthen to her father's commodious bed-room on the ground floor. With her own hands, which never trembled, she set the pillows softly under his head, wiped the blood-stained foam from the poor cold lips of his which she longed to kiss and dare not. With deft skill she helped and tended her father, who marvelled at her calmness, while he examined the wound. It were hard to say if the practised surgeon, whose nerves had been strengthened by sad experience of grief and agony at a thousand bedsides, or the young girl, whose very heartstrings were breaking in her first sharp misery, seemed the more composed.

When the wound was skilfully bound, and the bleeding stopped, Dr. Denver administered a strong cordial through the tightly-closed teeth. Then, with eyes on his patient's face and finger on his wrist, watched and waited. Only trained eye and hand could see life in that ghastly face, or could find the faint quiver of the thread-like pulse that told the heart still beat.

For five minutes—for ten, the doctor watched and made no sign. Looking up, he saw his daughter's pale face, pitied the silent anguish in it, and motioned her from the room.

Quietly she left—quietly and without a word she found Lord Edward waiting silently for the verdict, and waited with him. Each knew and shared the terror in the other's heart, each feared to speak their common thought—the message would be death.

The minutes dragged on slowly; the solemn ticking of the marble clock on the mantelpiece made the dead silence in the house more silent. To Norah's strained fancy it seemed to tell of the life she loved so, ebbing slowly away. She found herself half-unconsciously counting the seconds he had got to live.

She had reached to ninety-eight, when the door opened noiselessly, and her father entered.

Their eyes questioned him eagerly.

"Neither despair nor hope," he said in answer to their questioning look. "The wound is deep and dangerous. I fear the sword's point has grazed the heart. Another half an inch death had been certain. With any man but him death were certain now. His body had been quite drained of blood. But he has a wonderful reserve of vitality hoarded up by free air, health, and exercise, and never yet drawn upon."

Norah hid her face in her hands while he spoke, and hot tears—tears of joy swelled through her white fingers. The revulsion from despair was complete. She had had no hope. She had no fear now. He would live. He must live. If her feeling might be traced to its source it would be found to be a trusting confidence in Maurice. He was so strong and brave he would conquer death itself.

Yet, mingling with her joy, a sad whisper at the bottom of her heart kept repeating, though she strove to stifle it. "Oh! how I love him. How I love him, unasked, unloved! how shall I hide my love."

For days and weeks death and life fought at close quarters, over Maurice Blake's prostrate body, and the victory was still doubtful.

Norah Denver was life's best ally in that silent struggle.

Fever followed lassitude, and the body, drained of the vital blood, struggled, at fearful odds, against this fierce invader.

The distracted soul forgot itself. As Norah watched by his couch night after night "like Patience smiling at grief," she found that his body only was subject to her ministrations. His soul, for the time driven out by the hot fire of the fever, wandered at large through the scenes his youth had known, and visited the hunting-grounds, battlefields, and encampments of the byegone days in the wild, free forests of the New World.

As she listened to his rambling words that told of the sport and danger his youth had known, or the more recent trials of his manhood, ever and again her own name would drop from his unconscious lips in accents of such plaintive tenderness that, for a moment, her heart would thrill with vague, delicious hope; and she blushed and trembled, sitting there alone, till cooler reason came to kill her hopes, and whispered that it was pity only spoke. Then maiden modesty would fight and conquer love, and lead it captive, and strive to hide it even from herself.

Yet through all this weary time, when even the doctor was tempted to despair, she never doubted he would live, and the event justified her confidence. Five anxious weeks she watched and tended very patiently, grudging Christy Culkin every hour of his share of that long vigil.

Sir Valentine was more than a month in his grave, resting peaceably in Irish ground after his sore troubles and long wanderings; and the spring daisies were beginning to blossom on the green sod that covered him, when the fever that threatened his son's life was at last driven out, and banished reason returned to its domain.

Very faint and feeble was the conquerer in that desperate strife. His eyelids had scarce strength to open, his lips had barely power to falter a single word, when, returning from his long, painful wanderings in the vague region between life and death, he found himself, with faint surprise, lying between white sheets in the cheerful best bedroom of Dr. Denver, with spring flowers in the vases, and spring sunshine streaming through the open windows to the lightsome room.

Slowly, very slowly, he crept from death to life, often faltering and turning back upon the road. Norah no longer kept her place at his bedside, only now and again she peeped in at the door when he was in deep slumber, and heard the countersign "All's well" from the faithful sentinel Christy, who had relieved her guard. Yet her spirit seemed to hover about the place, amid the sweet spring buds that made the city room smell as fresh and sweet as a country flower garden. It may be that Christy, with that quickness which love lends to all eyes, had surprised her precious secret. But he made no sign and said no word.

It is certain she surprised his. How or when neither he or she could tell; for a woman's mind gathers a love secret as the conductor gathers lightning from the air. Christy, nothing loth, told her of his sweetheart, Peggy Heffernan, the truest, hearted colleen in all Ireland, and how she saved the priest's life and Master Maurice's, God bless her, when the priest-hunters were on the track. If he sometimes mingled the praises of "the young master" with his sweetheart's, Norah listened none the less eagerly, be sure.

When Maurice Blake, still very white and feeble, made his way to the drawing-room, Norah welcomed him to her own domain with sisterly joy, clasped his thin hand warmly, and looked frankly in his pale face. But he, searching those clear eyes of hers with a longing look, could find no love there.

For women can hide their wounds patiently as the Spartan boy, and smile when the pain is most.

Thenceforward they were much together. But the

same impalpable barrier was still between them—impalpable, impenetrable, separating their souls as completely as if they lived in different worlds. Maurice had hoped something from his wound—had hoped that sympathy might help to open a way for love, and in a curious way rejoiced in pain and danger for the hope they gave. But at their first meeting the hope died.

So they lived apart, though together, for neither could quite forego the pleasing pain of the other's company. Their talk, when they talked, was for the most part civil and strange, a little awkward, too, and nervous, as conscious how thin the ice and how deep the gulf below.

But for the most part he read in silence, stealing a stray glance at her fair face, and she sketched or painted, silent also.

Sketching was no mere school-girl art with Norah. The artistic taste was born with her. Nature and training equally befriended.

As a child, her pictures on slate and paper were not as other children's, mere black or white dots and lines. Hers had a meaning. Her horses galloped, and her birds flew. Her houses looked as if they might be lived in, and her people were live people, with character in their faces.

She was fortunate to find a master, eager to guide, not cripple, her taste. So she learned to make Nature's beauties, animate or inanimate, her own. She most delighted and most excelled in quick, slight snatches from art or Nature. Her sketching book was a treasury of all things living or dead that pleased her fancy. It seemed as if she caught up a scene or face with the point of pencil or paint brush, and lifted it right on to the paper. Here was a tall, slim spire piercing the blue air with one white bird flying close to it; there was a ragged street cherub, with fluttering rags, and a yard of rough pavement for him to stand on; a cluster of wild flowers, primroses and violets intermixed, sprinkled through the live green moss; a flash of a summer stream, with meadow-sweet by its brim and an overhanging willow dipping in its waters; all fair sights and fancies were transplanted to the white pages of her book for eye and memory to rejoice in.

She sketched patiently, while Maurice read silently, the pain of his heart eased by her silent presence. He pleased himself by bright pictures of what might have been, to make sad atonement afterwards in the bitter thought of what could never be. The narcotic that numbed his pain brought its punishment in reaction. But he was powerless to abandon it. Sometimes he had a curious feeling that her gaze was on him, while he sat reading in the deep arm-chair, close to the window that looked into the street, and she sketched, standing for the most part at her easel in the far end of the room. Though his eyes were on his book, he seemed to feel her glances search his face. But looking up, however suddenly, he found her intent upon her work, and so dismissed the idle fancy for the moment, to recur to it again and again.

But his life was not all love and idleness. Lord Edward Fitzgerald visited him frequently, full of life and spirit, and told the fresh, wholesome news of the outer world. The hopes inspired on that eventful day on which he braved the wrath of the hostile majority in Parliament had not deceived him. The combined terrors of the prospect of a war with France, and of armed revolution at home, had sobered the Government and rendered them meek and amenable to reason. The moral effect of the great Catholic Convention, and the rapidly cemented alliance between the Presbyterians, victims of the Established Church, and the Catholics, victims alike of Church and State—all these motives pressing together had, at the beginning of the Parliamentary Session of 1792, produced a sudden accession of conciliation on the part of the Government for the people, which greatly surprised alike its officials in the Castle and its hirelings in the House.

But those servile instruments of tyranny did not allow surprise or disgust for one instant to block the way of self-interest. They endeavoured at the word of command to promote justice and conciliation, as they had up to the week before laboured to promote bigotry and oppression. They wheeled right round and came up to heel with a whining servility that brought discredit alike upon authority and its supporters, and rendered them hardly more respectable in the right than in the wrong.

In the course of the summer months violent declarations had been issued by most of the Grand Juries and Corporations, denouncing fiercely not only the religious, but the moral and political tenets of the Catholics, and proffering prodigally the aid of their own lives and fortunes in excluding them from all liberty. At more than one of these inflammatory meetings persons high in official trust assisted ; and the greater number of them, it was supposed, had received sanction and impulse from the ruling powers.

Almost in the very face of this movement, with that blind recklessness of character by which such a Government forfeits the confidence of its friends, without in the least degree conciliating the good-will of its opponents, the present sessions opened with a recommendation to Parliament to take into its " wise and liberal" consideration the condition of His Majesty's Catholic subjects. The measure of grace was, in this instance, represented as originating in the bounty of the Crown ; and a deputation from that lately execrated body, the Catholic Convention, was now seen, day after day, amicably closeted with the Minister, negotiating for their admission to power on a far wider basis than that from which, but a few months before, the same Minister had so con- temptuously dislodged them.

While thus on one of the two great questions that

agitated the country, symptoms of a more just and liberal policy were manifested, on the other no less vital subject of Parliamentary Reform an admission had been, for the first time, made on the part of the ruling powers of the principle and practicability of such a measure, by their consenting to the appointment of a committee to inquire into the state of the representation.

Lord Edward rejoiced in the reform, regardless of the motives which compelled the Government to adopt it.

Maurice Blake, who, unlike Lord Edward, regarded war or slavery only as a choice of evils of which slavery was the greater, rejoiced still more keenly in the prospect of a peaceful revolution.

But deep grief for his father, so suddenly found and lost, combined with the bitterness of hopeless love, gave a sober tinge even to his rejoicing.

His troubled mind reacted on his feeble body.

Halfway up the gentle slope of convalescence stealing back to health, he stuck fast and got no further. He seemed to have lost purpose and interest in life, and pined and moped, languid and listless. The Doctor, who found convalescence at a standstill at the point where it ought to be most rapid, could make nothing of his symptoms.

In vain Lord Edward Fitzgerald tried to rally him out of his despondency, painting the future in glowing colours.

Love is blind, and Lord Edward, though now

nearly a year married, was still as much in love as ever with his sweet girl-wife Pamela. He did not see—he could not see—that the raptures of his love made Maurice Blake's hopeless longing harder to bear.

He raved about Pamela, lamenting always that her delicate health, to which he alluded very shyly, prevented her from coming up from Carton to visit his friend. He had no doubt that the sunshine of her presence would revive Maurice Blake. There was nobody, there was nothing, that could resist her witchery.

"Why, the very flowers look brighter and smell sweeter, and the birds' song grows more joyful when she walks abroad amongst them," cried the enthusiastic one-year-old husband.

"You have never seen Pamela," he went on, in reply to a few words of kindly curiosity and regret from Maurice Blake. "Never seen Pamela!" this in a tone of the most intense pity. "But surely you have seen the portrait of her that Norah sketched. It comes as near to doing her justice as a picture can, still a long way off, of course. You 'll forgive me, Norah ; but next to my darling herself—and the artist, of course—that picture is the prettiest object in the world. And Maurice has not seen it?"

"It is not worth his looking at," said Norah quickly in a startled voice, from the corner of the room where she sat sketching. "It is a libel on Pamela. It is only your good nature, Edward, that—"

"Do you think my good nature would make me acknowledge a libel on Pamela to be a likeness?" interrupted Lord Edward. "Maurice will judge for himself."

"May I, Norah?" asked Maurice, for in the coldness that had grown so imperceptibly between them, the familiarity of Christian name had not been lost, only the tone in which it was spoken was different.

"Certainly," said Norah, "if you think it worth while, I will be most happy to show you the sketch. Only I warn you against the cold shock of disappointment after Lord Edward's too warm praise."

Lord Edward sprang up at the challenge, "I will accept his judgment," he cried. "Against all the world, I'll maintain it; the face is the fairest face, and the picture the prettiest picture, in the world. There is no time like the present to decide. Is that her portrait you have upon the easel, Norah? It looks about the same size."

Quick as lightning Norah snatched the portrait from the easel as he approached, thrust it into her portfolio, and snapped the spring lock defiantly before he could lay his hand on it.

She laughed at his disappointment, but Maurice, whose eyes love made keen, noticed that her hand trembled and her cheek was flushed, that her breath came quicker than its wont, and that the laughter sounded a little strained.

"Not fair, my lord," she cried; "not fair. In justice

to Pamela, if not to me; let us at least have daylight for our exhibition."

She was deaf to all entreaties to open the portfolio, and seemed so nervous about it that Maurice came to her relief at once, with a request that she would give them a little music.

"All right!" cried Lord Edward; "I will leave off teasing if she will. I hardly know whether I like her playing or her painting better. Something old and Irish, Norah, please. You might give us that quaint old Irish air you played when I was last here. I have got words to it, which I think will fit it."

"Willingly," said Norah, apparently much relieved to get them away from the portfolio.

She sat down at the great gilt high-shouldered harp, and struck from its strings with flying fingers those low, sweet plaintive strains, which the chatter of the modern piano can never hope to rival.

Standing a little behind her, Lord Edward, with the full light of the setting sun on his handsome face, sang in a fresh, manly voice, with sweetness and vigour in it, while Maurice sat apart in the shade, choosing a seat where he could watch the fair face of the player.

Lord Edward sang—

> "A knight dwelt in the West Countrie
> Whose arm was stout, whose heart was free;
> And foes went down before his spear—
> This knight who knew no fear.
> But love-lit eyes of beauteous dame
> Could kindle in his heart no flame.

"The knight was stricken on battle plain
   With grievous wound and almost slain,
   His heart was weak, his eyes were dim,
   A maiden tended him.
   With gentle power to soothe and save
   His love repaid the life she gave.

"She pitied her good Knight's sore distress
   From heart replete with gentleness,
   But love for love she could not give
   Nor he unloved would live.
   So 'scaped the wrath of foeman's sword
   To die for lack of one sweet word."

How often it happens! If a man have bruise or wound upon him, a friend's hand, in careless friendly greeting, will press upon the wounded place. If his heart is wounded, a careless look or word will ever strike where the hurt is sorest.

Lord Edward's song was torture to Maurice Blake. He searched Norah's face with anxious looks, as words and music combined in plaintive strain to tell his story of hopeless love.

The song went straight to Norah's heart. To her Maurice was its hero, brave, victorious, wounded, dying, saved. If all the rest might but be true! Her heart thrilled at the sudden hope, her cheeks paled, and her eyes half filled with tears. But quick came the cold answering thought, "He is not like me, he is not forbidden to speak of love. He loves me not, he loves me not, and he must never know my love."

So she forced her lips to smile, and there was no

touch of sadness in her voice, but only quiet pleasure as she thanked Lord Edward for his song.

From his seat in the shadow Maurice read the changes of her face, and read them wrongly, and was confirmed in his despair.

As he left that evening Lord Edward again urged his friend to see Pamela's portrait at the earliest opportunity, dwelling with lover-like raptures upon her beauty. So Maurice promised, caring but little, if the truth be told, about Pamela or her portrait, but rather with something of pity in his mind for the blindness or the folly of the man who could so rave about any woman's beauty but Norah Denver's.

But when he entered the drawing-room next day at noon and found Norah there alone, seated in the cool shade, sweet and fresh as the spring flowers in the vases, he remembered his promise to Lord Edward, and begged again to see the portrait.

She seemed fluttered by the request, but all the same smilingly assented. The portfolio was on the table beside her. She unlocked it with a small gold key that hung at her chatelaine, shuffled a little nervously amongst the heap of cardboards, and picked out one and handed it to him.

" They give you but a poor notion of Pamela," she said, "those paltry lines and shades of black and white. I cannot show the delicate rose tint of her cheek, or the flashing, laughing light in her beaming eyes."

'Yet, she must be very beautiful if she is at all

"It was his own face that smiled back on him from the picture on the floor."

like this," said Maurice, gazing on the portrait with unfeigned admiration, which made Norah feel a curious little twinge of jealousy of her own hand-work.

Norah's art had set not the face merely but the character, of Lord Edward's beautiful girl-wife before him. Vivacity, tenderness, the playful candour of a light-hearted child beamed out from that speaking picture, yet Maurice felt vaguely there was some want there. He sighed very softly as he laid it down. Norah heard the sigh and mistook its meaning, and was thrilled again with a little jealous pang.

" Have you ever seen a more beautiful face ? " she asked, smiling resolutely.

" I have never seen a more beautiful portrait," he replied, playing with her question, and stealing a glance at a face which he thought a thousand times more lovely.

He made a motion at the same time to replace the picture, but she snatched the portfolio from his hand so hastily and so nervously that some of the drawings slid out of it on to the carpet.

Norah uttered a little cry of dismay as she saw them fall.

Maurice stooped quickly to pick up the sketches, but started back in surprise from the first he laid hand on.

It was his own face that smiled back on him from the picture on the floor. Smiled as it almost seemed with hope and encouragement, as if the cardboard were a flattering mirror. His own face—and yet not his own. He was conscious that it was the face of a man, purer, nobler than himself. The features were indeed his, but illuminated and idealised by love.

Intense surprise was his first feeling, nothing more. But glancing at Norah to read the riddle, he saw that she had sunk down on a couch overcome with confusion. She strove to hide her face with her small white hands, through which her flushed cheeks glowed like the red leaves of the sweet monthly rose through the snow at Christmas tide. The white lace on her bosom heaved tumultuously with a billowy motion.

Then the full meaning of it flashed across him at once, sending the blood to his heart in a thrill of delirious joy.

"Is it true, my darling—can it be true," he asked, in a voice that quivered with eagerness.

No answer.

Stooping over her with gentle force he drew the clinging hands from her face.

The bright tears shone tangled in the silken lashes that lay on her flushed cheek, the sweet rosebud lips were quivering ; but not a word came.

"One word, Norah," he pleaded ; "only one little word—tell me if you love me ? "

" Have some pity," she murmured, pitifully. " Have pity, and leave me now, some other time I "——

Here her voice broke into a sob, and the two big bright tears breaking through the silken meshes rolled down her flushed cheeks.

But Maurice was pitiless: love made him so. "Only one word," he persisted, "one little word. It is not hard to speak."

Then her mood changed to anger, and she strove to break from him. "It is cruel," she cried passionately, "it is unmanly, it is not like you, Maurice—not like what I thought you. I have been weak and foolish, but you are cruel. If you have a man's heart in you, leave me."

But the sweet hope, rekindled now, and warm in his heart, rebelled against such banishment.

"One word," he pleaded still. "Only one word, and I will go or stay as you tell me. If you knew how I love you, you would forgive me. My darling! my life! my soul! I cannot live without you. I have tried, and I cannot. I feared to make avowal of my love lest I should forfeit the sight of you. But it has grown too strong for me—too strong to be suppressed. I must speak, and you must answer. Can you love me, Norah? Will you love me? Oh! do not kill the hope that is alive in my heart."

He pleaded as a coward on death's brink might plead for life.

Still no answer. But the little hands that had struggled to release themselves now lay soft and warm in his clasp, trembling a little. As he looked in her face the silken lashes were raised for an instant and the frank blue eyes flashed one look of love into his soul.

He asked no more. Stooping lower he clasped his affianced bride in his arms, and pressed a passionate kiss upon her sweet lips.

Then Norah first knew the sacred mystery of love's kiss, which thrilled through all her pulses with a delicious shame, and she lay still in his strong arms trembling, and fetching her breath short like a newly-taken bird.

Norah gently unclasped the strong arm that circled her slim waist, but left the little warm hand a willing captive. Never, surely, came purer pleasure to a woman's heart than glowed in her's while Maurice, in words to which rapture lent eloquence, poured out for her acceptance the rich treasure of his love.

Shyly and softly, compelled by much entreaty, she laid bare, in return, the precious secret of her virgin heart—all her fluttering hopes and joys, her doubts, her sorrows, her despair, and her delight. She told how the breath of a few venomous words had poisoned love's pure atmosphere, and, looking back together, they marvelled how so slight a cloud had power to dim the dawning sunshine of their lives.

Then those two went out together into the bright future, and peopled it with hopes and fancies, and ever and again Maurice, in lover's fashion, took assurance of his joy from those sweet lips, and

Norah tempted him the more by shy resistance. So the spring day went swiftly by. They took no heed of time, and were startled when, late in the afternoon, Dr. Denver came quietly into the room.

He, too, was startled at finding them seated there so close together, with clasped hands.

But Maurice rose and led his daughter to him, and Norah stood before him, blushing like a rose, with eyes downcast; for the first time in her life, fearing to meet her father's glance.

" I have come to rob you of your greatest treasure, sir," said Maurice. " Can you pardon me."

" I fear it is too late to resist or resent the theft," replied the Doctor, smiling, yet sadly as it seemed. " Anger won't help me. Where the treasure is there also the heart is. Is it not so, Norah?—no longer my Norah. You need not ask my blessing, Maurice, you have it when you have her."

He spoke playfully, patting his daughter lovingly on the bent head. But there was an undertone of sadness in his voice. He loved Maurice almost as a son, but even to him he half grudged the heart of his daughter, which had been heretofore all his own.

But Norah fled to him swiftly, even from Maurice, and kissed him, and fondled him, and wept in his arms, and told him over and over again that she was still his own Norah, his own little girl, still his own pet, and plague, and plaything, and that no crumb of her love for Maurice was stolen from his share.

There were tears in her father's eyes—tears half of sorrow and half gladness, as he fondled the little hand in his. Then he placed it gravely in her lover's clasp.

"She is your own now," he said. "Your own henceforward to love and cherish, and may God judge you as you guard her."

"Amen," Maurice said solemnly.

As quietly as he entered the father left the room, and the lovers were again alone with their love.

Smoothly and softly the course of this true love ran with light on its waters and music in its flow. First love! Earth has no joy like it. It was one remembrance of Paradise that stole out of the Garden with the poor fugitives, to comfort them and their children in the wilderness ; and the pitying angel lowered his flaming sword, and smiled as he let it pass.

Love only has power to give a foretaste of that exquisite, all-sufficing delight, which the devout dream of in heaven.

There was no longer langour in Maurice Blake's step, nor paleness in his cheek. For happy love brought health home with him as guest to his chosen abode. The very air he breathed was a delight, his food was ambrosia. His whole frame tingled with vigorous vitality ; his love mingled with his life, and transformed it to ecstacy.

He and Norah drove, and rode, and walked, and sat, and read together, and the fairest scene in nature took new beauty from her eyes, and the sweetest poetry took sweeter music from her gentle voice. The hopes of the future so mingled with the happiness of the present, that they seemed to live their whole lives through in each delicious moment.

CHAPTER XXI.

" FLAT BURGLARY AS EVER WAS COMMITTED."
Much Ado About Nothing.

" These nice sharp quillets of the law."—*Henry VI.* Part i.

" A plague upon it when thieves cannot be true one to another."
Henry IV. Part I.

" And in a word outfaced you from your prize ; yea, and can show it you here in the house."—*Henry IV.* Part I.

BUT love was not permitted to monopolise Maurice. Duty claimed her share of his attention, and was not to be denied. Law is the traditional enemy of love.

The ejectment action for the recovery of Cloonlara had, after his father's murder, been revived in his name, as heir-at-law, and was being pushed vigorously forward.

In his innermost heart Maurice suspected that his cousin's was the cowardly hand that fired the murderous pistol-shot at Essex Bridge. Even to himself he hated to confess that horrifying suspicion. Still, unconsciously, it had, no doubt, its influence in stimulating him to press forward the eviction.

As for Mark, he made no secret of his delight at the " accident " that had befallen his uncle, as he now confessed him to be—" in a drunken brawl." He professed himself quite confident of the result of the new action.

"The old war-whooper," he said, "might have given me some trouble, but as for this fellow who claims to be his son, there are, no doubt, scores of half-bloods running wild through the backwoods of America with as good a claim as his. We could find a drawing-room full of Lady Blakes among the Indian wigwams, if it were worth while looking them up."

The rumour was industriously put abroad that the first wife of Sir Valentine was alive and well, and would be produced as a witness for the defendant at the trial.

The audacity of the trick took Dr. Denver's breath away when he first heard it. He had seen the woman lying dead; he had followed her coffin to the grave. To resurrect her seemed impossible. But a little thought showed him the rumoured fraud was ingenious as it was audacious. There had been one real revival of Lady Blake. Why not a second sham? It would be easy to show that she had not died when it was said she did. It would be hard to show that she had died afterwards. There were, no doubt, innumerable abandoned women who could be hired to play the part.

"We must be all the more careful with our proofs," said Curran. "We must leave no point of attack or defence uncovered or unassailed."

They had met at consultation at the house of the

great orator and lawyer. They were seated in his study, whose walls on three sides were lined from floor to ceiling with law reports, text books bound in formal half calf. Two handsome glass-fronted cases beside the fire-place contained the culled treasures of English literature, and space was found for a handsome old Shakespearean proof engraving over the chimneypiece. Curran sat close to his writing table, in the centre of the room, lost in the depths of a great Russian-leather arm-chair. He held in his hands a huge brief, whose leaves he fluttered over with something very like impatience.

By a little straining of professional etiquette, and at the express desire of Curran himself, Dr. Denver and Christy Culkin, as two vitally-important witnesses, had, as well as Maurice, been admitted to the consultation.

"We must patch up every hole in our suit, Mr. Lawless," Curran went on, "if we are to keep out wind and weather. There is a stitch or two here and there to be put in yet before we are ready for trial."

Mr. Theophilus Lawless, the solicitor for the plaintiff, a stout, pompous little man, bridled indignantly at words that seemed to hint at something lacking in the preparation of the case.

"I assure you, sir," he said, swinging his heavy gold chain impressively while he spoke, as if to indicate that he also was a heavy, sterling, eighteen-carat gold solicitor, hall-marked in every limb. "I assure you, sir, all that human foresight or sagacity could do was done in this case. I have spared no pains or attention or expense. I understand it is a title case—well, I have briefed to you the entire title to the estate for three generations."

Curran smiled a little sardonically, as he turned over the leaves of the large brief, heavy with scores of irrelevant deeds which had been copied into it.

But Mr. Leonard M'Nally, the junior counsel, as in duty bound, came to the rescue of the solicitor.

"A most admirable brief, Mr. Lawless," he said; "most admirable. I found in it everything I wanted."

It might have been by accident that his eye dropped on the back sheet, on which was endorsed a fee heavy in proportion to the heaviness of the brief.

"I never," he went on, "in my professional experience, knew of a case more admirably put before counsel. It would seem to me nothing is wanting. We have fortified our whole line of defence, and are prepared to deliver an irresistible attack on the enemy. If anything——"

"Lawless," Curran broke in abruptly on Mr. M'Nally's smooth phrases, smoothly delivered, "there is a reference in my brief to a confession which Dr. Denver took down from the lips of Lady Blake, and a certificate of her death, but I can find no copy of any of these documents."

"I did not consider the documents relevant on a question of title," returned Mr. Lawless pompously.

"You are aware, of course, sir, that it is not part of our case that our client was the son of this particular Lady Blake. Our case is that he is Sir Valentine's son by a second marriage. It was by an oversight, for which I have to apologise, that such irrelevant documents were mentioned at all in your brief. My senior clerk is responsible."

"A lucky oversight," said Curran tartly, "which probably has saved the case. Did it never occur to you, Mr. Lawless, that the death of the first Lady Blake was necessary for the marriage of the second? Without a marriage there cannot be an heir-at-law. Our opponents are shrewder, if the rumour runs right, that they are about to resurrect the lady for the purpose of their case."

Leaving the discomfited solicitor to ruminate, with face of blank solemnity, over this new aspect of the situation, Curran turned with a smile to Dr. Denver.

"You have the documents safe, Doctor, I hope?"

"Certainly," said the Doctor, "quite safe, and at your immediate service. I keep them in a despatch-box in a bureau in my dressing-room. I asked Sir Valentine to take them when he returned, but he begged me to retain them in my custody."

While the doctor was speaking the junior counsel, Mr. M'Nally, idly scribbled the precise locality of the important despatch-box in the fold of his brief, in a way junior counsel have.

Then Curran turned quickly to the solicitor, who

was still ruminating. "We can do no more without these documents, Mr. Lawless. You will kindly get them from Dr. Denver and have copies made and briefed to us. Stay, there is no time for copying; bring the originals, and I will look them over. We must have another consultation here to-morrow with those papers before us. What say you, gentlemen, will twelve o'clock suit you all?"

There was a murmur of assent, and they trooped together out of the great lawyer's study. Maurice, the party chiefly concerned, was glad even for the brief interval to exchange law for love.

The rest departed to their several occupations, "for every man hath business and desire such as it is." What was the special business of Mr. Leonard M'Nally, junior counsel for the plaintiff, during that brief interval, may perhaps appear a little plainer in the sequel.

Two hours later a different consultation was in progress on behalf of the defendant. Mark Blake and Lord Dulwich were seated over their wine and dessert in the spendid dining-room of his lordship's splendid mansion in Merrion Square. They were silent and motionless, save the motion needed to move the heavy decanters of claret backwards and forwards, and to fill the rare old goblets of Waterford cut glass with the rare old wine. Mark looked angry and Lord Dulwich sulky. There had plainly been stormy words between them.

Lord Dulwich was no longer the man first

introduced to the reader. His lordship's handsome face had been disfigured by the terrific blow Maurice Blake dealt him as he fell wounded almost to death by that cowardly sword-thrust on Essex Bridge. The nose was broken, and now stood at an angle of forty-five degrees to his face, dragging the mouth a little askew with it. The rough knobs of the heavy stick, swung with such fearful force, had cut and bruised the flesh of his right cheek even to the bone, and the wounds had healed in ugly livid scars.

His lordship had got a trick of passing his white hand across his face, which only served to obtrude the ugliness he hoped to hide.

Neither had Mark Blake improved in appearance. His cheeks were redder and coarser, and his eyes a little bloodshot. Incessant drinking was beginning to tell even on his iron frame.

For a good ten minutes the two men sat silent and sulky in the dusk, for the candles were not lit. Lord Dulwich had taken a dislike to lights lately.

This silence was the brief sultry lull in the thunder storm.

Mark Blake broke out again with more determination than anger in his voice.

"It must be so," he said slowly and hardly. "I say 'must,' my lord. We are in the same boat now, and shall sink or swim together. If I go down you go down too, of that be quite sure; you must help to pull me out, or I'll help to pull you in.

Those papers, as I happen to know, are all-important to the case. Curran himself has expressly said so. I know where to get them and how, and I have the very man ready for the job. 'T is to-night or never."

"But what do you want of me in this business at all?" grumbled Lord Dulwich. "Cannot you and your friend"—this with a suspicion of a sneer in his voice, "manage the thing between you?"

"You are my partner in this game," said Mark sharply, "and I won't let you stand out until the last hand is dealt. There may be some fighting to be done, and that sword-point of yours will come in handy again. Only leave a couple of inches more of the blade out of the scabbard this time. You are to share the plunder, so you must share the risk. Is it any special affection for the man that left you those keepsakes that stays your hand?"

He pointed a scornful finger to the livid bruises on the other's face.

Lord Dulwich grew pale with wrath. The livid scars showed like clots of blood on his white face.

"Curse him! curse him!" he cried fiercely; "I would give my soul to perdition for one straight thrust at his heart. I hate him worse than you do; but "——

The other knew right well what that "but" and the pause after it meant. The coward's hot anger in its full tide had been frozen by fear. A sharp taunt was stayed on Mark's lips by the sudden opening of the door.

Lady Dulwich, queenly in her stately beauty, stood framed in the doorway, holding a wax taper in her hand. She was dressed in black tabinet, sprigged with rose buds, which threw out in startling relief the dazzling whiteness of her neck and arms. A great ruby pendant burned like a spark of red fire on her white bosom, rubies and diamonds blazed in her hair.

She was going out alone to the theatre, as was her habit, and had idly opened the dining-room door on her way, believing the room empty.

Just for a moment or so she glanced at its two occupants, with a look too cold and distant even to be called contempt. For, after all, contempt is a feeling with something of passion in it, and in her haughty, handsome face there was none. She glanced at them listlessly, as at repulsive animals in a cage ; then closed the door without word or gesture, and in a moment they heard the rattle of her carriage wheels down the street.

"Curse her ! curse her !" muttered Lord Dulwich fiercely, changing the gender of his execration, but bating nothing of its vigour. "She makes no secret of her scorn and loathing for me, even while she lavishes my wealth with both hands. I believe she has a hankering after that mongrel cousin of yours. She stormed so about his wound, and roundly rated me as a murderer, swearing that with her own hand

she would give me up to justice if he died. Curse
her!"

"Come," he went on abruptly, carried away by the
passion in him, "come, Mark, I am your man for
to-night's job. If the heir-at-law comes within
sword's length again, curse me as well as him if he
'scapes a second time."

Half-an-hour later the two sallied out together
into the dark street, wrapped in loose cloaks, and
armed to the teeth with sword and pistol.

They slipped like shadows, as swiftly and as
silently, through the murky streets, where only an
occasional oil lamp at long intervals served to make
darkness visible. At the corner of Jervis Street
they paused, and Mark whistled a thin, shrill whistle
through his clenched teeth that seemed to pierce the
air like an arrow. Out from a dark archway close at
hand came the figure of a man, looming gigantic
through the thick gloom, so swift and stealthily that
both Mark and his companion started guiltily when
they found him standing close beside.

The new comer chuckled hoarsely at their surprise.

"Be aisy, neighbour," he said to Lord Dulwich,
whose hand was on his sword-hilt. "Be aisy with
you, and give your carving-knife a holiday. Let us
get through our work first. If you want a fight in
peace and quietness, when the work is done, I am
not the man to baulk you."

Lord Dulwich could just discern through the
gloom that the stranger was a man of huge stature.

He had a flaming red head, on which a slouched hat was cocked, and his one eye blazed like a live coal out of the darkness. He, too, was armed to the teeth. By no means a pleasant midnight companion or opponent.

His lordship shook off the huge hand laid familiarly on his shoulder, and was about to make a contemptuous reply when Mark Blake whispered a few words in his ear that silenced him. The three then walked together down Jervis Street.

Right opposite Dr. Denver's house, Mark thought he noticed a line of darkness, stretching straight up through the dusk from the centre of the street to the eaves of the houses.

He walked to it cautiously, touched it with his hand, and found it firm.

"It is a ladder," said Freeny, shortly—needless to say, the newcomer was Freeny. "It is mighty inconvanient to meet the master of the house on the staircase when you are there without an invitation. So I thought I would like a staircase of my own, and I stole the ladder while I was waiting for you, to keep my hand in."

"You are a clever fellow, Freeny, and make robbery support robbery," said Mark, humouring him. "Make haste, now, and get this job through. There is five hundred pounds in gold waits you at the foot of the ladder when you come down."

"It's waiting for me at the foot of the ladder before I take the first step up," said Freeny, gruffly.

"Payment in advance was the bargain. Honour amongst—— gentlemen."

Mark cursed him between his teeth, but answered pleasantly.

"Here's the gold ready. I did not think you wanted to hawk this load up the ladder and down again." He produced from under his cloak a stout canvas sack, untied the mouth of it, and rattled the pieces with his hand.

Freeny drew the shade from the dark lantern he carried, and turned the strong stream of light down the throat of the bag on the yellow metal within.

Then he shook it in his huge hands, and listened approvingly to the clear metallic clink of the gold. "The yellowhammers sing true," he said. "There is no time to count, but by the weight it must be pretty nearly all right. I think I can take your word for the difference. I will go up lighter and come down quicker for having it with me."

He dropped the bag as he spoke into one of the huge leather-lined pockets that hung by his hips— "his honest receivers of stolen goods," as he jocularly called them—and went up the ladder, which quivered under his huge bulk, as swiftly and noiselessly as a cat. There was an iron balcony guarding the window. He caught it, and drew himself lightly over, and stood on the iron floor within, level with the window sill.

The sash-fastening yielded quickly and noiselessly to the skill of the robber, and he crept like a huge dog through the opening. Cautiously he took the shade from the bull's-eye, and made the restless stream of light play in turn on every object in the room. Each seemed to jump out of the darkness as the ray touched it, and jump back again when it left it.

Three things remained in Freeny's mind when this curious march-past was over—an old-fashioned watch on the dressing-table, a pair of silver-mounted pistols hanging by a couple of brass-headed nails on the wall, and an old-fashioned bureau in the corner. He put the watch in his pocket, the pistols in his belt, and then gave his attention to the bureau.

He looked at the lock under the searching light of his lantern, and uttered an exclamation of contempt, almost of disappointment.

" It is hardly worth the trouble of picking," he muttered, discontentedly. " They might as well bolt the door with a boiled carrot."

Then he drew a bit of wire from his pocket, shaped and bent it a little, thrust it into the keyhole, and drew back the bolt with perfect ease.

" The stupid thing does not know the difference between a bit of crooked wire and the key it is accustomed to all its life," he grumbled, with a grin, as he sent the searching ray of yellow light into the recesses of the bureau, where it quickly found the despatch-box he was in quest of.

He took it under his arm, shut the bureau, and locked it, crept out of the window, and closed and fastened it after him—"for fear of robbers," he muttered, as he stood on the iron balcony outside in the darkness. He climbed over the railing a little awkwardly, for he had the despatch-box in one hand, and the lantern in the other.

With dangling feet he felt about in the blackness below for the first rung of the ladder, and found it. It quivered under his weight. He was stooping cautiously to get his hands on the ladder, when he heard whispering far below, but could distinguish no words.

Then Mark Blake's cautious voice came up to him through the dark, still night—low, but clear—

" Have you got the box ? "

In the same tone he sent the one word, " Yes," down to the watchers below.

" Drop it." Mark's voice came up again out of the silence. " I will catch it in my cloak. Turn down the light."

Freeny turned the long gleam of the lantern towards the ground, and soon found Mark Blake at the end of it, with face ghastly in the yellow light, and the skirt of his cloak outstretched in both hands.

Nothing loth, Freeny dropped the incumbrance down through the beam of light, and heard the dull thud as it was caught below in the fold of stout cloth.

The next moment he felt the ladder quiver under him. Then, with one strong wrench from below, it was jerked from his feet, and went down with a crash, slinging him sideways into space as it fell.

One hand, thrown wildly out and up, caught the projecting edge of the window-sill under the iron balcony. There was room only for the ends of the fingers, but they held like grappling-irons. Down came the dead weight of his huge body with a sudden flop. The stout, crooked anchor of bone and muscle stood the strain. He hung suspended by one hand. But the stone to which he clung was smooth and worn, and he felt his fingers, or thought he felt them, begin to slip ever so slowly under the heavy strain. He stretched up his right hand, and found he could only just touch the iron of the balcony with the tips of his finger-nails. Far down below there was no sound but the quick tramp of his would-be murderers dying away in the distance. No hope of help. He dare not cry out. To be rescued was to be hanged. He knew that the iron spikes of the area-railings waited far below in the dark with fixed bayonets to impale him when he went whirling down through the night on the rusty points.

Yes; his fingers were slipping. He strained the muscles till the flesh seemed to grow to the stone. But they still moved slowly, slowly, along the smooth surface. The ghastly terror of it brought the big drops of perspiration out on his forehead. All the strength of his huge body was concentrated in his five finger-tips. But the muscular vice could not keep its place on the smooth shelving stone. His grasp was almost over the edge. One chance was left. With a last convulsive effort he jerked himself

"One hand, thrown wildly out and up, caught the projecting edge
of the window-sill."

breast high against the window sill. His left hand slipped clean off with the strain, but even as he fell, the right hand grasped the iron work of the balcony with a grip of iron, and he was safe.

Freeny had no nerves. Hanging there by one hand with fifty feet of vacancy under him, and under that sharp iron spikes, he was as cool as if he stood on firm earth or sat on his good steed's back. When the danger was over it was over. With his idle hand he drew a coil of stout rope from his bosom. " I thought you might come in handy as a deputy ladder," he said, "and, begorra, so you have."

Quickly and quietly he made it fast to the iron-work, and went down hand over hand like a huge spider on his trailing web. His feet touched the iron spikes of the area, and he leaped out into the street.

For a moment he stood stock still, with head bent a little forward, and strained his sharp ears to the uttermost, sending his consciousness out into the silence with an effort that was almost pain.

He could just catch the faint, far-off sound of hurrying footsteps away towards Carlisle Bridge, and he leaped forward in pursuit like a hound on its quarry.

As Freeny came racing down Bachelors' Walk, covering nine feet at least with each long stride, he caught a glimpse of two figures passing at a quick pace under the flickering oil lamp on the bridge, and his heart gave a bound of revengeful joy, for he knew he was on the track of his would-be murderers.

They turned, still walking rapidly, into D'Olier Street. Lord Dulwich carried the despatch box. Both men were laughing and talking excitedly as they went. They did not see the figure, vague, huge, threatening, that stealthily skulked along in the darkness behind.

"No suspicion can touch us," said Lord Dulwich, tapping the box, "when this is missed. Freeny's dead body will be our *alibi*. Yet I am not quite easy about the business, Mark. It looks remarkably like murder."

"Nonsense," retorted Mark, brusquely, "the fellow's life was due to the hangman. What matters it to him or anyone else whether he took his drop with a rope round his neck or without it. One road to hell is the same as another. But I grudge his corpse that five hundred guineas in good gold which the absolute knave dragged out of me. He has no use for it where he is gone. I wish the devil would let him bring it back to me."

A growling laugh behind, like a wild beast's, made both men look back suddenly.

For one moment Mark thought that his impious prayer had been granted. For there, towering over them, stood Freeny himself, with a face like a devil's, in the gleam of the flickering oil lamp. Mark had no time to speculate on the visitation. The huge fist rose and fell like a blacksmith's hammer flush on his forehead, and he went down in a heap, like a smitten ox, stunned and motionless.

With a cry of terror, Lord Dulwich started to run. But before he had taken three paces a grip, like a tiger's claw, was on his shoulder. The box was wrenched from his grasp, he was slung round and round with dizzying force, and loosed at last.

He staggered back wildly and blindly, tripped up and fell over the unconscious body of his friend in the kennel, and lay quite still, quivering with fear.

Freeny disappeared with the despatch-box.

CHAPTER XXII.

"O HEAVEN, O EARTH, BEAR WITNESS."
>
> *The Tempest.*

"Though I am not naturally honest, I am so sometimes by chance."
>
> *Winter's Tale.*

" It shall as level to your judgment 'pear
As day doth to your eye."—*Hamlet.*

"PERFECTLY inexplicable," said Mr. Lawless, with a solemn gravity that made even perplexity respectable. The ladder was found broken in the street, and from the window there was dangling down a long cord as if the robber had tried to hang himself.

Curran was pacing the room impatiently, too angry to speak or listen.

When the party had reassembled for consultation, the Doctor's story of the sudden disappearance of the despatch-box in which the papers were locked, had sent Curran fuming about his study like a bumble bee on a pane of glass.

Mr. Lawless further aggravated him by dinning into his ears inane platitudes about the motives and manner of the robbery. The rest of the party stood a little apart, silent and disturbed.

That bland and kind-hearted gentleman, Mr.

Leonard M'Nally, with tears in his eyes and his voice, mingled mild condolence with confident hopes that the missing documents would be immediately recovered.

"Nonsense," cried Curran, impatiently, in answer to a wise suggestion of Mr. Lawless that they should advertise for the documents and offer a reward for their recovery, "Nonsense, man, don't talk double-distilled nonsense like that. The other side have got them. Whether they took them themselves or hired a common robber is beside the question. The mystery is how they managed to find out where the papers were, and lay their hands on them at the very nick of time. You did not talk about the matter, I suppose, Dr. Denver?"

"Never mentioned it except here in consultation yesterday."

"Strange, very strange," muttered Curran, musingly, "some servant in your house guessed perhaps —and yet. But there is no use crying over spilt milk or puzzling how it came to be spilt, I much fear the thieves have carried off the broad acres and grand old mansion of Cloonlara in that despatch-box. Its loss leaves us naked of defence against fraud. We must trust to your memory for the dates, Doctor."

"I fear you are leaning on a broken reed," said the Doctor. "For some things my memory is strangely good, for others abominable. I have little or none for names, dates, or places."

This answer sent Curran pacing up and down again in a brown study.

There was a gloomy silence in the room. Outside could be heard the pattering footsteps and merry careless laughter of Curran's pretty little daughter, Sally, and her playfellow, Bobbie Emmet, who were sporting together in the hall.

Suddenly a thundering knock at the door seemed to shake the house. Then the bell was set fiercely ringing.

The two children rushed together to the door and opened it. There was the sound of a deep, rough voice mingled with the clear, shrill treble of the children.

Curran had his hand impatiently on the knob of the study door when the wee, solemn face of his pretty little daughter showed itself in the room.

" A gentleman for Mr. Maurice Blake, Pappy," she said, with great self-importance. " A big, grand gentleman with a beautiful large green lid to his eye. He is standing on one foot in the hall."

" Take him into the dining-room, Blake," said Curran, " if you think he has got anything to say worth listening to. Sarah and you, Robert, can run up to the schoolroom and play. I don't want you loose about the house."

In the hall Maurice found a tall and broad-shouldered personage richly, even extravagantly, dressed. His silks, and laces, and velvets were of the newest and the best, and set off his stalwart figure to advantage. But his hat was pulled down over his brows, and a green patch rested upon his right eye. His face, what could be seen of it, was florid, but his hair jet black. He wore a heavy cloak, which was trussed in a bundle over his right arm.

"You wished to see me," said Maurice, with a courteous bow. "I am Maurice Blake."

"I know it," said the other in a low voice. "I am not likely to forget you."

The words had a curious sound, as if some strong feeling forced itself into them in spite of the speaker's will. Something in the tone wakened a faint vibration in Maurice Blake's memory.

"You wish to speak to me?" he repeated. "Only a word or two, if you don't mind," replied the other, almost humbly. "I want to pay an old debt."

A little startled by voice and words, Maurice motioned him towards the dining-room door, and followed into the room, on his guard against attack or surprise.

As he closed the door the intruder turned and faced him. "Don't you know me, sir?" he said.

He had taken off his hat, and brushed the black hair from his face, and the strong light fell full on his strongly-marked face and powerful figure.

Maurice looked at him. The vague recognition grew stronger. His memory made a desperate effort to get hold of the man's identity, but it slipped from its grasp.

He shook his head, "I think I have seen you before," he said. "But where, or when, or how, I cannot say."

The other smiled. He put his hands up each side of his head and seemed to shake the whole covering of his skull.

Maurice looked at him in amazement.

The grin broadened on the stranger's broad face. "I can trust you," he muttered, "with such a trifle as my life." Then he pulled off the black wig, and showed a shock red head under it.

"Freeny!" cried Maurice with instant recognition.

"Aye, just," said the other, coolly, "Freeny, the highwayman and burglar, at your service. Freeny who never forgets a bad turn nor a good one. This may be of use to you."

From under his cloak he took the missing despatch box, and set it on the table. "Don't ask how I came by it," he went on. "I took a liberty with the lock when I had got it. I found the papers to be yours, and I brought them to you. I had reasons of my own for thinking they might be important."

"They are all-important," cried Maurice, excitedly. "They were stolen out of my friend's house. Did you——"

"Ask me no questions":—retorted Freeny, with a grin. "You know the rest. No man is bound to criminate himself, as the lawyers say. They kindly save him the trouble when they catch him."

"But what did you want with these?" Maurice began again.

Freeny cut him short.

"That's a trade secret," he said, "and in the way of business Freeny will keep faith with the devil. But this much I may say by way of warning. If you have any dealings with your affectionate cousin Mark, don't keep both eyes shut, or you may open them in Kingdom Come."

Then he fumbled for a moment in his pockets, and with something like reluctance, if not shame, he took out an old-fashioned gold watch, and a pair of handsome silver-mounted pistols. "You might give those to your friend, who had the box in keeping," he said. "I have reasons of my own for thinking he has a fancy for them.

"Now, good-bye, and good luck, sir," he added, turning to the door. "I don't feel aisy in a lawyer's house; it's the first stage to the scaffold. It's true I'm here on honest business, but it's more dangerous to be honest than otherwise in my profession."

Maurice impulsively stretched out his hand to him.

But Freeny put his huge paws behind his back. "No," he said, "once is enough. I am not worthy to touch an honest man's hand; I know what I am, sir, worse luck, and there are times in which I think I will buy a rope myself and save the hangman a job. When you hear tell what a bad boy Freeny is, think, if you can, that he is not all over bad. You owe me no thanks for what I have done. It is only the interest on a big debt. I owe you a life yet, and if ever I get the chance, I'll pay up as well as any honest man of them all, or lose my own in the endeavour."

He turned abruptly and left the room, and the street door banged after him.

Maurice carried the despatch box into the study and set it down on the table before Curran.

"Here's what you wanted," he said.

With a cry of delight the great lawyer pounced on the papers like a hungry dog on a bone.

One after the other he turned them rapidly, noting the contents on the fold of his brief.

"Perfect, perfect!" he cried delightedly. "I don't ask you where you got them, Mr. Blake—Sir Maurice, I should say. That will come later on. These papers fill up every crevice in our case, and make it air-tight and water-tight all over. There is not a mouse-hole for fraud to creep through. Of course, doctor, you can swear to the accuracy of the dates here, with the papers themselves in your hands to refresh your memory."

"Certainly," said the Doctor, "the dates are accurate."

"The confession itself is dated the 15th of June," said Curran. "You have not noted down the date of death, but I assume you can prove it was the same night."

"Oh, no," replied the Doctor smiling; "it was noon the next day. I did not think she had an hour to live when I was called away that night, and I was amazed to find her still living when I returned in the morning. But I am quite certain of the time. I remember that as she breathed her last the great church clock pealed out its twelve deep strokes, slow and solemn as a funeral bell, I thought."

He broke off abruptly, for something very like a curse came from Curran's lips, and he was fluttering over the sheets of his brief furiously.

The frown darkened on his face as he read two or three documents rapidly in succession, noting them as he read.

"There must be some mistake," he said anxiously; "some cursed mistake. I have here, Doctor Denver, a copy of your letter to Sir Valentine. You say not one word about her dying on the 16th. You write: 'Dear Friend, I have startling news to tell you. Your wife, whom you believed long since dead, survived up to a few days ago. On the night of the 15th of June instant, I was sent for to see her in hospital. I found her in a dying condition. She had just strength to dictate a confession of her sins against you and God, and utter an earnest prayer for your forgiveness.' Any man reading that would assume that the woman died on the 15th. Sir Valentine plainly so read it. He writes to you (I have his letter here) that, believing himself for years a free man, he had married the day after his first wife's death, and the certificate of his marriage is dated the 16th, the very day his first wife really died.

"I can understand your slip, Doctor," he went on more kindly, noting the agony of remorse and confusion on the other's face. "No one could guess when you wrote that, that a few hours would make such a difference. But it has become a question of hours, may be of minutes now. Who can tell the hour of Sir Valentine's second marriage?"

No answer. Dead silence in the room.

The doctor was very pale. And Maurice Blake had come close beside him and held his hand in a friendly grasp.

Mr. M'Nally was rapidly scribbling a note on his brief with a face of the deepest commiseration; Mr. Lawless looked on in blank and solemn amazement, while Christy Culkin had fallen quietly into the background close to the door.

Curran spoke again impatiently. "Am I to have no answer? Isn't there some one here from America who was present at the marriage?"

"Christy," cried Maurice, for Christy was slipping unobtrusively out of the room.

He turned, with his hand on the door-knob, and faced Curran's look of anger and amazement stolidly.

"Best leave me out of the business, Counsellor," he said, shortly. "You will settle it better yourselves without me."

"Sit down, sir," retorted Curran, "and tell me what

you know about the marriage. Mind, the whole truth, and nothing but the truth."

"Faith, I'm thinking a lie would serve your turn better in the present predicament, if I only had a good one handy."

"You were present at this marriage?" interrupted Curran, ignoring his reluctance to speak.

Christy nodded his head sulkily.

"At what hour did it take place?" demanded the lawyer, point blank.

"At eleven o'clock," the other gulped out. "You have it now, and much good may it do you. It was your business, I'm thinking, to try and row the leaky boat to the harbour, not help to scuttle her."

Christy's answer was like a thunder-clap to the party. It was felt to be the death-blow to the case. Maurice was too startled for the moment to rebuke his retainer's roughness.

Curran alone preserved his composure.

"Sure?" he said, laconically.

"Do you think I'd say the word if I weren't sure?" retorted Christy. "Do you think it's sport to me to rob Master Maurice of his father's place by the word of my mouth. It's sure enough, worse luck. The marriage was fixed for half-past ten, and the trap broke down that was taking us to the church, and the bride and party were kept half-an-hour waiting. Is that a thing a man is likely to forget? I could tell you every word the master spoke on the way. His language to the driver was a kind that impresses itself on the memory. It was driven in hard. We were not more than half-an-hour late; but the bride and her friends were leaving the church door when we drove up. Five minutes more and there had been no marriage that day."

"What luck," groaned the Doctor under his breath. "Five short minutes more would have saved all."

"The ceremony was over before twelve, then?" Curran went on, evenly.

"Well over," Christy replied; "Sir Valentine was not long pacifying the young lady, and the priest made up for lost time. They were away on their honeymoon, as man and wife, before the clock struck twelve."

"Not man and wife," Mr. M'Nally interposed lugubriously. "Not man and wife, my good friend, I'm afraid. Unfortunately, the real wife was alive here in Dublin at the time."

Curran said nothing. He was wrapped in a brown study. The whole strength and light of his mind was turned in on itself. His face was expressionless as a dead wall.

Mr. M'Nally went on in a plaintive voice, speaking half to his inattentive leader, half to the others. "It is very bad, though I don't think we need quite despair. We may stumble safely through the case even yet. A blot is never a blot, you know, until it is hit, and the other side do not know in what direction our danger lies. Perhaps the doctor need not be examined at all, nor our good friend here. Perhaps," he added, very slowly and meaningly, "his memory may chance not to be quite so clear in the witness-box as it is here."

"Nonsense, M'Nally," broke in Curran, brusquely rousing himself from his reverie. "We examine all our witnesses, and all our witnesses will tell all the truth. Our honest friend here"—he touched Christy on the shoulder—"will tell the jury just what he told me. But, as you say, M'Nally, we need not despair for all that. A case is never lost until it is over."

It seemed plain from the great lawyer's face and manner that he, at least, did not despair.

His junior looked at him with a face in which amazement was mingled with something very like anxiety.

"You have some plan in your head, Curran," he broke out eagerly. "What is it? I can see no way out of the tangle if our witnesses are examined. What's your plan?"

"I have no plan," Curran said shortly, "only a queer notion. There is no use telling it. This time you can neither help nor hinder." So saying, with a curious emphasis on the last word, he broke up the consultation.

Only three days intervened between the consultation and the trial. Maurice had absolutely no hope of a verdict. The assumed cheerfulness of Curran did not encourage him in the least. The point at issue was plain enough for a layman to understand. No man could marry a second wife while the first wife lived, that was the case in a nut-shell. Mark Blake was therefore his father's heir. In the eye of the law he, Maurice, was a ——. He did not like to finish the sentence in even his own mind—to think the word, much less speak it.

Doctor Denver also was in despair. "It was all my stupid blunder," he said over and over again. "If I had written the date correctly, if I had even written after the receipt of your father's letter, a second marriage in America would have been so easy. It is my stupid blunder, Maurice, that has robbed you of your name and heritage."

Norah alone took things cheerily, and comforted those two whom she loved most in the world. "We three have each other," she said, "what more do we want. If it were not for the sake of the poor people at Cloonlara, Maurice," she whispered to him, "I would be almost selfish enough to rejoice in a chance that seems to make you more than ever my own."

One thing Maurice resolved, in spite of certain sly insinuations of Mr. Leonard M' Nally, that every witness must be examined, and no fact, however fatal to his hopes, should be suppressed. In this Curran and himself were in complete accord.

But the other side saved him the trouble of thinking further on the point. For the day before the trial a *subpœna testificandum* was served upon Christy, and a *subpœna duces tecum* on the doctor, to appear and be examined on behalf of the defendant. Mark Blake had again mysteriously learned the weak point in his cousin's case. He had shot his arrow straight and hit the blot.

The court was crowded out to the doors and up to the ceiling. The trial awakened the keenest excitement in Dublin. It hit the line of cleavage in political matters so closely that the personal interest was lost in keen political excitement. Maurice Blake was respected by all who knew him; Mark Blake was hated. Yet were the Castle partisans eager for Mark's success as a triumph for bigotry and oppression. As an apostate from "Papacy" he had a special claim on their favour. The court was thronged with his partisans. The sympathisers of Maurice, United Irishmen for the most part, assembled in a vast crowd outside in the great hall, were refused admission to the court. The Right Hon. Arthur Wolfe, her Majesty's Attorney-General, led for the defendant. In the Lord Chief Justice of the Queen's Bench, the Earl of Clonmel, he had no unfavourable judge. The High Sheriff had obligingly provided a jury of sycophants, "by special appointment" to the Castle.

Mr. Leonard M'Nally opened the pleadings for the plaintiff. Then Curran laid a brief, clear summary of the facts before the judge and jury. Maurice Blake was not a little startled to hear him declare in calm, emphatic voice "that after the death of Sir

Valentine Blake's first wife, he married the mother of my client, and my client, as sole issue of that marriage, is indubitably heir-at-law to all the lands, tenements, and hereditaments of Cloonlara, for the recovery of which the present action is brought."

Maurice noted, too, that this calm statement provoked a short, scornful laugh from Mark, who was seated beside his solicitor in court, and the Right Honourable the Attorney-General himself smiled in quiet derision. But Mr. M'Nally nodded his assent and assurance to the judge and jury, till his wig, which was too small for him, tumbled off his head.

The evidence was got through quickly. Sir Valentine's letter from America was admitted on the other side without demur. " It is part of our case," said the Atorney-General blandly.

Dr. Denver was called for the plaintiff, and gave his evidence clearly and briefly in reply to Curran in direct examination. He proved the death of Sir Valentine Blake's first wife, the sending of his own letter, and the receipt of the reply in Sir Valentine's handwriting, and the certificate of death, all which documents were entered without objection, on the part of the defendant, in evidence for the plaintiff.

Dr. Denver was asked nothing, and he said nothing, in the direct examination about the day or the hour of her death.

But the Attorney-General speedily repaired that omission with half-a-dozen home questions. He struck straight at the weak spot of the plaintiff's case with singular directness. He wasted no time on any point but one.

"When did the woman die?"

"On the 16th of June, 1765," the doctor answered reluctantly.

Then the Attorney-General drew from the witness a vivid description of the striking incident by which the very moment of her death was fixed.

With that he dismissed the Doctor from the witness-box. His end was gained. So far the attention of the Jury was focussed on that single point of time.

It seemed almost a pity that Curran had not mitigated the dramatic directness of the discovery by a question or two in his examination-in-chief. But the blunder, if blunder it was, was repeated in the direct examination of Christy Culkin.

He, too, was taken shortly over the chief incidents of the case. He proved the marriage of Sir Valentine in America to the mother of the plaintiff. He proved the birth of the plaintiff. He had known him from his birth to the present hour. Not a question was he asked by Curran about the day or the hour of the second marriage. This strange omission struck the dullest man in court.

There was intense silence when the Attorney-General rose to cross-examine with a quiet, confident smile on his determined face. All felt the crisis of the case had come. Judge and jury strained their ears to catch each syllable. Again the Attorney-

General went straight to the point. "At what date did Sir Valentine Blake go through the ceremony of marriage with the plaintiff's mother?"

"On the 16th of June, 1765."

"You were present in court when Dr. Denver was examined?"

"Yes."

"You heard him fix the date of the death of Sir Valentine Blake's wife?"

"Yes."

"The 16th of June, 1765?"

"Yes."

"It was the same day you witnessed the second ceremony of marriage?"

"Yes."

"You heard him fix the hour of that death at twelve o'clock noon?"

"Yes."

"At what hour on that same day did the ceremony of marriage to the plaintiff's mother take place?"

A long pause; dead silence in court. The Attorney-General glanced significantly at the jury, who listened with open ears and mouths, and waited for the full meaning of the question to settle into their minds.

"Come, sir," he said at length, "answer on your oath."

"Answer," reiterated the judge, sternly.

Slowly and reluctantly the answer came.

"Eleven o'clock in the forenoon."

"Sure?"

"Sure."

"Go down, sir."

There was a low murmur in the crowded court—sensation made audible. The audience to this exciting drama had scarcely breathed while the issue hung in doubt. Now they seemed to draw one long, deep breath together of relief from suspense. Then silence, more profound than before, while they waited for the final *dénouement*.

In that silent, crowded court, all eyes were fixed on the faces of the two cousins, the plaintiff and defendant.

Mark Blake wore a smile of triumph, which he took no pains to hide. He looked straight at his opponent, exulting in his defeat.

Maurice answered his look with quiet contempt, that galled the other in the midst of his triumph; not the quiver of a muscle spoke his bitter disappointment.

The dead stillness was broken at last by the voice of Curran, cool and quiet as ever.

"I close for the plaintiff, my lord."

The Attorney - General rose, and spoke with manner and voice elaborately calm.

"I have respectfully to ask your lordship, on behalf of the defendant, for a nonsuit. I need not recapitulate the grounds on which I move. The plaintiff's own witnesses have put him out of court. We adopt every line of their evidence, and make it our own. They have conclusively shown that Sir Valentine

Blake, at the time he went through the empty ceremony of marriage with plaintiff's mother, had a legally-married wife still living. Out of the mouth of his own witnesses plaintiff has proved his own illegitimacy. With much confidence I ask your lordship to direct a non suit."

"Well, Mr. Curran," said the Lord Chief Justice, "what have you to say to this?"

There was a covert triumph in his tone, for there was no love lost between his lordship and the fearless Nationalist advocate.

To the amazement of the court, Curran came up smiling.

"I have respectfully, but confidently, to ask your lordship to direct a verdict for the plaintiff," he said. "His case is conclusively proved, and practically admitted by the other side. Shortly after the death of his first wife, Sir Valentine Blake married the plaintiff's mother, and the plaintiff is the sole issue of that marriage. This is our case as laid, proved, and acknowledged."

"Mr. Curran," broke in his lordship impatiently, when he recovered a little from his astonishment, "I fancy you take me for a fool."

"That, my lord," retorted Curran sweetly, "is an *obitur dictum* which, however creditable to your lordship's discrimination, has no bearing on the case before the court. As I was saying, the first wife was dead before the second wife was married."

"Don't talk nonsense," interrupted his lordship

rudely. "It has been conclusively proved by your own witnesses that the first wife was living when the second wife, as you call her, was married."

"Your lordship will pardon me."

"The first wife died at twelve o'clock noon," his lordship went on without heeding him—"the second marriage took place at eleven on the forenoon of the same day."

"Precisely," assented Curran, blandly.

"I am glad you have come to your senses," snarled his lordship. "A man cannot, legally at least, have two wives at the same time. You admit the first was living when he purported to marry the second. I therefore direct——"

"Not quite," broke in Curran again, "your lordship," he went on, while the Lord Chief Justice lay back on the bench speechless at his audacity. "Your lordship forgets to take judicial cognizance of the fact that the earth goes round the sun. This trifling circumstance has, as I will show you, a curious bearing on the case."

He drew his watch from his pocket as he spoke. "It is now a quarter to six by the correct Dublin time," he said, "but the correct time in New York is precisely thirty-five past one. The solar system has not altered since the date of Sir Valentine Blake's second marriage. When it was twelve in Dublin it was only twenty minutes past seven in New York. On the admitted evidence in the case his first wife was at least three hours and forty minutes dead when he married the mother of my client. I demand your lordship's direction for the plaintiff."

The judge could find no loophole of escape from the inexorable fact and argument. He looked piteously at the Attorney-General, who sat dumbfounded and powerless to help him.

"I demand your lordship's direction for the plaintiff," repeated Curran sternly.

There was no help for it.

"I direct a verdict for the plaintiff," his lordship stammered out.

"With costs?" said Curran.

"With costs," repeated the judge.

The issue paper was handed up to the jury, and handed down, signed, "Verdict for the plaintiff."

Maurice Blake was from that moment Sir Maurice, and unquestioned lord of the broad acres and stately mansion house of Cloonlara.

Those who cared to look might have noticed how curiously the face of Mr. M'Nally, the learned junior counsel for the plaintiff, fell when the verdict was directed in favour of his client. But the more prominent actors in the drama absorbed public attention—

Mark Blake's face was as the face of a demon—fierce, remorseless; his wrath shook him like a reed, and forced out a few hoarse words through his clenched teeth. "He's not safe yet," those close to him could hear him growl, as he elbowed his way through the crowded court and disappeared.

"' I demand your lordship's direction for the plaintiff,' repeated Curran, sternly. '"

"A good race, Sir Maurice, and a close finish," whispered Curran, with a beaming smile, as his client grasped his hand gratefully.

" How shall I try to thank you ?"

"Don't try. I kept my word; that's all. I promised, you may remember, from the very first, ' to move heaven and earth ' to win your case, and I did."

CHAPTER XXIII.

> "A contract of eternal bond of love,
> Confirmed by mutual jointure of your hands,
> Attested by the holy close of lips."—*Twelfth Night.*

> "Why, as a woodcock to my own springe,
> I am justly killed with mine own treachery."—*Hamlet.*

> "Yet again methinks,
> Some unborn sorrow, ripe in fortune's womb,
> Is coming towards me."—*Richard II.*

THE soft showers and mild sunshine of April had washed and warmed the world's fresh and green beauty. The May blossom in Phœnix Park was thick upon the hawthorn; the singing birds in the green leaves and the white were wild with the rapture of the spring. The mellow air that fanned the faces of the lovers was full of perfume and music. They sat close together, and the words of love were sweeter to the sense than the perfume of the May blossom or the clear song of the birds.

"Norah," he said, "I am called home, and I cannot go alone. I have had letters from Cloonlara that my presence is sorely needed there. Duty calls me thither; love chains me here. Join these powers, darling, and come with me. When?"

She was flushed and trembling; her heart consented to his prayer, but her lips could form no words.

"For their sake, if not for mine," he pleaded earnestly, "whisper the day that will make earth heaven to me?"

For your sake, my darling," she murmured so softly that her low whisper scarce stirred the warm air. "I have no will but yours. It's yours to command, and mine to obey. I am all yours, body and soul; take me to yourself when you choose."

"On May-day, then, be it, my May Queen," he said gaily, and sealed love's bargain.

Their wedding was to be simple and secret. Father O'Carroll had consented, at the earnest request of Maurice, to bind their lives together. A quiet little wooden chapel, half-a-dozen miles from the city, was selected for the marriage. Their honeymoon was to be spent in Cloonlara, and amid the fair scenes of their new home.

Lord Edward Fitzgerald, now a happy, excited, bewildered father, had pressed one request with so much earnestness that it was impossible to refuse it. They were to call at Carton for an hour or two on their flight westward. Maurice must make the acquaintance of little "Mother" Pamela, and his bride of the "baby."

"I, too, have a request to make, Maurice," said Norah. They were seated together in the drawing-room, where he had first told his love. "No, no; you must not have payment in advance, or at all.

It is to be a free gift.   But first tell me, have you guessed Christy Culkin's secret?"

"Secret?" said Maurice, lightly.   "He is all secrecy and silence.   But I know no one thing about him more secret than the rest."

"How blind you men are," laughed Norah.   "Have you never seen Peggy Heffernan?"

"What has that to do with Christy?   Oh, I believe he is her uncle, or something of that kind.   You will like her, Norah.   She is as sweet as a wild rose, and a regular rustic heroine to boot.   I have a story to tell you how she saved——"

"Save yourself the trouble.   I heard the story long ago from lips more devoted than yours."

"Not Christy's?"

"Yes, Christy's."

"You don't mean to say so, Norah?"

"But I do.   Now, if you look so dumbfounded, I may think you are jealous of his good fortune."

A fine was promptly exacted, and Peggy Heffernan and Christy were, for the moment, forgotten.

"But your request, Norah," he whispered at last his arm, as if forgetfully, still around her waist.

"I want Peggy Heffernan for my bridesmaid."

"Most gladly.   It is your right to choose."

"I want Christy Culkin to be your 'best man.'   I owe him many a kindness, and I can think of no reward he would value more."

"Why, Norah, you are a witch.   You beg me so prettily to please myself, and grant requests before they are asked, on pretence of making them. Christy has been my 'best man' since I was a boy. It is fitting he should hold his place still on the happiest day of my life. So that weighty business is settled —and now——"

But the lover's "now" belongs to themselves alone.

Brightly dawned the wedding day. Norah, very pale and quiet, and with happiness shining in her calm, clear eyes, drove down with her father to the church in the early morning.

In defiance of Mrs. Grundy, the bridegroom-elect was allowed a seat beside her in the phaeton. For the roads about Dublin were dangerous, and there were rumours of daring highwaymen at work at the very outskirts of the city.

An event occurred to justify this precaution. As the phaeton rapidly bowled along the road, about halfway from Dublin the galloping of swift hoofs was heard behind them. Their coachman whipped up his thoroughbreds. But nearer and nearer came the clatter behind. Looking back, Maurice could see a single horseman, on a powerful bay horse, thundering along the road. A tall and powerful man, dressed all in black, with his face covered with a black mask.

Norah grew pale, and her timid touch on his arm sent the blood coursing hotly through his veins. Very quietly he slipped out a double-barrelled pistol, and let it rest hidden on the seat beside him, with his grasp on the stock, and his finger on the trigger.

Woe betide the man who stood before the muzzle when the trigger was pulled.

Nearer and nearer the horseman behind came thundering along. He slackened his speed a little as he drew level with the phaeton. But one glance at Maurice, with the pistol half raised and ready, seemed sufficient. The robber's hand came out of the bosom of his coat empty. He raised his hat with a flourish, bowed to his horse's neck, then drove in the spurs, and swept on like a whirlwind.

Norah drew a deep sigh of relief, and thanked her lover with a look.

"Glad we had you, Maurice," said the Doctor, heartily, "that fellow did not seem to like the look of your pistol."

"Curious," replied Maurice, "The figure, and his seat on horseback, seem familiar. I 'm not so sure it was my pistol frightened him."

No other incident marked the progress of that pleasant drive, which, to Norah, seemed so short, and to Maurice so long.

At the porch of the little church, standing back from the neatly-kept churchyard, they found Father O'Carroll waiting for them, with Christy Culkin and Peggy Heffernan, fresh as a wild flower.

Impulsively Norah kissed her blooming bridesmaid, and called her friend.

"I have heard," she whispered, "how you saved them all. How brave you are. I should have died of fright. You know who told me," with a sudden half glance at Christy, who stood fumbling with his hat, the picture of awkward shyness.

But there was scant time for greeting or gossip. The Nuptial Mass had commenced, and the solemn words, more solemn from impending danger, went straight to their hearts.

Marriage, and all belonging to it, comes natural to a woman. Never was court damsel more deft or self-possessed in the discharge of a bridesmaid's function than the rustic beauty. She had the ceremony at her finger's ends, and the words of the solemn service by heart, ready to prompt the principal performers. Christy, on the other hand, was shy, and awkward as a schoolboy.

A sly whisper from Peggy at the beginning, "Cheer up, man alive; how will you ever go through it when your own turn comes?" completed his confusion.

The sacred pledge of eternal love and constancy was spoken at last. Norah's soft whisper went straight home to her bridegroom's heart, and made her father's eyes fill with sudden tears.

In a few quiet words the good priest commended to each other's care and love the newly-married man and woman, made one by solemn sacrament.

Norah Blake signed her new name in the old book, with hand that shook a little.

Maurice, in all the pride of a husband's ownership, kissed the tears from the eyes that looked into his own with meek, submissive love.

A sibilant sound from a dark corner of the vestry, followed by a muttered "Behave yourself, now do," seemed to tell that Christy's shyness had abated.

While the marriage was in progress another scene —trivial apparently, but curious—was enacted in the little graveyard outside the church. A few moments after the bridal party, a one-eyed weather-beaten beggar arrived, clad in the tattered livery of his trade. He must have been a tall and a strong man in his time, but now he appeared bent double with age. The sole covering of his head was a thick thatch of grey hair, which fell wildly across his face. His patched and tattered rags of all forms and colours were a mere caricature of clothes.

He lounged up to the iron gate of the churchyard, and through it, and leaning lazily down on one of the tombstones, basked in the May sunshine that made the still air pulsate with its warm glow. He was curious and restless this old beggarman, and the eye left him was evidently a keen one. It caught a metallic gleam in the bright sunshine on the top of a tall grey headstone that stood broadside close to the gravelled pathway leading to the church. With a quickness and lightness wonderful in so old a man the bent figure slipped down along the walk, then lifted itself suddenly over the tombstone.

There was a man behind, crouched close in the long grass and wild spring flowers, in which he had made himself a lair like a hare's, he had lain there so long. He was well dressed, young, and handsome. But his hat pulled close over his brows showed the lower part of his face.

His right hand, with something in it, was thrust hastily into his breast as the beggar accosted him.

"Help a poor, dark cripple, yer honour," he whimpered with the true mendicant's drawling whine. The single keen eye so quick a moment before was now turned almost round in its socket and presented a blanky, yellow bloodshot surface hideous to look at.

"The devil damn you, for a whining old imposter," growled the other fiercely. "I have half a mind to give you such alms as you little dream of."

But his anger was appeased when he looked into the other's blank sightless face. "Here," he said, still surly, "here is a guinea for you, and take yourself off from this place as quickly as your crooked legs can carry you, if you have any regard for that parchment bag of bones, your carcase."

The beggar, fumbling a little, seized the gold coin at last in the great coarse hand of a giant, and conveyed it to some receptacle in his rags. Then he burst forth into a torrent of fulsome prayers for his benefactor, praying that his shadow "might never be less," which, as it was nothing at all where he lay, was a safe enough supplication.

The person prayed for cut him short abruptly by striking him with his flat hand across the face and bidding him be gone. The beggar slouched rapidly down the walk, turned to the right, behind where his benefactor lay, and disappeared.

Five minutes passed — ten — fifteen. The place was filled solely with silence and sunshine. The low murmur of solemn voices from the church reached the strained ear of the solitary watcher. Then suddenly the thrill whistle of a thrush in a neighbouring grove clove the still air, and a goldfinch answered from a poplar tree that stood close at hand amongst the graves, tall and trembling with the trembling sunlight on it.

Did that peaceful scene soften him, or change Mark Blake's fell purpose? Not one jot.

Now the church door opens at last, and the sound of happy voices flows out on the mellow air. Norah, proudly leaning on her bridegroom's arm, trustfully gazing in his happy face, comes down the pathway from the church to where the phaeton waits.

Slowly, stealthily the crouching figure behind the high tombstone straightens itself. The bright metal glints again in the sunshine, as a pistol barrel slips softly over the rough edge of the stone. The eyes of the newly-married lovers are too absorbed in each other to notice it. They are scarcely twenty paces now from the spot where death lurks; moving on to it. The tip of the pistol barrel trembles a little, grating on its stone rest. Then it points straight to the heart of Maurice Blake. The finger steals stealthily on the hair trigger. A touch is death.

"They rolled over and over in the long grass."

But suddenly, in that awful instant, the crouching figure goes back swiftly, silently, prone on its back in the high grass behind the tombstone.

A giant's grasp is on the wrist of the right hand that still holds the pistol. A huge fist squeezes mouth and nostrils, even to suffocation, stifling all sound. The bridal party paces softly down the quiet sunlit walk, and wheels away as fast as swift-stepping horses can carry them, unconscious of the deadly peril escaped by a hair's breadth ; unconscious of the wild passion and death struggle they have left behind them in the lonely graveyard.

The first fierce and stealthy onset had taken Mark Blake completely by surprise. He lay for a few moments unresisting in the iron grasp of his captor. Then fury lent him sudden strength. He tore away the huge hand that pressed his mouth and nostrils, stifling him. He made a desperate effort to free his own right hand that still held the loaded pistol.

Freeny (for needless to say his sudden assailant was Freeny) resisted desperately. He knew that to release his captive's hand meant death to himself.

But he had to strain his great strength, even to the utmost, to hold him. The two men rolled over and over in the long grass like dogs in hold. No sound was heard on either side, but their quick, fierce panting and hoarse curses strangled between their teeth. Freeny's grey wig had fallen off, and his hair blazed red against the green ground. The face of Mark Blake was malignant as a devil's. The veins stood out on his forehead like a ship's cordage, and from his fierce eyes murder flamed. His whole strength was strained in the effort to turn the pistol's mouth towards his opponent's heart. He fought like a wild beast. Stooping down suddenly he buried his sharp teeth in his opponent's hand. With the keen spasm of pain Freeny's grasp on his wrist relaxed for a fatal instant. Mark wrenched his right hand free, flung himself on his opponent, turned the pistol at his face, and fired.

Even then the robber's quickness saved him. While his eyes glanced into the dark tube, scarce an inch off, his hand, flung up, instinctively struck the pistol barrel, almost as the flash came from it. The loud report so close to his head stunned him. He lay for a moment with quick beating heart, hardly knowing if he were alive or dead. He was conscious of a heavy weight on his chest. He pushed at it, and Mark Blake rolled limply off and turned on his back with a little jagged scorched hole through the centre of his forehead—quite dead. One glance was enough for Freeny. He leaped from the ground with the agility of a cat, and fled from the place as if death pursued him. Ten minutes later, he was on the back of his blood bay horse, thundering along the road, with such a look of wild terror as no man had ever seen before on his face.

Mark Blake lay where he had fallen—not a sound, not a stir—a ghastly object amongst the fresh spring flowers, with his blank, wide open eyes staring vacantly up at the sweet summer sky, that looked down on him in unconscious, unpitying beauty—

> " Cut off, even in the blossom of his sin—
> Unhousled, disappointed, unaneled—
> No reckoning made, but sent to his account
> With all his imperfections on his head."

Meanwhile, happily unconscious of his own escape from the very jaws of death, and of the terrible fate that had befallen his would-be assassin, Maurice drove with his fair young bride through deep hedge-rows, white with the May blossoms, and musical with the love melodies of the birds. The gentle breeze which their own swift motion made in the still air blew softly and sweetly in their faces. Happiness pervaded their souls as sunshine, the air, bright, warm, making every thought and hope radiant with its glory. For a time neither spoke. No words that were ever coined in human brain, or that melted in music from human lips, could tell their joy and love. They looked in each other's eyes and silently communed soul to soul. The rosy shyness with which Norah's love peeped out in the hours of court-ship had passed away; she was his wedded wife, all his own ; and he was hers for ever. Lightly she laid her hand upon his and kept it there, a symbol of possession. So they drove through the rich land and fair of kingly Kildare till they came to the proud seat of the Leinsters. On through the little town of Maynooth they swept, and passed the stately ruins of the tower and fortress of Silken Thomas, the first great rebel of the race of Geraldine. An amber-coloured trout stream, with fish glittering in its shallows, flowed past under a high-shouldered bridge, and plunged down through the wooded valleys of the wide Carton demesne. A little beyond they passed through the great gates of iron, wrought like old-world embroidery, into the broad demesne. Straight in front of the long vista, the stately pile of limestone faced them, with its regiments of windows shining in the sun, vast and beautiful. In outline so clear, it seemed not built, but carved. Behind, the immemorial trees stretched up in rolling hills of verdure, slope upon slope, even to the sky-line.

Lord Edward met them with hearty welcome at the stately portals. He led them straight to the spacious library, while he despatched half a dozen retainers here, there, and everywhere, in quest of Pamela.

His welcome was not half exhausted when Pamela entered with the baby in her arms. She was pale, for the blood had been stolen from the young mother's cheeks to feed the life dearer to her than her own, that nestled at her bosom. Proudly and tenderly she held to her heart the soft fluttering bundle of white lace and pale blue ribbons, from which peeped out a tiny face cut in delicate pink coral with blue turquoise eyes wide open in it. The wee hands, smooth, fragile as wild rose petals, moved restlessly in the soft white drapery, feeling their way in the new, strange world. With bright eyes and

Pamela.

quick step, still clasping to her heart the tender blossom of her happy love, Pamela came to where they sat.

"Maurice, my dearest friend, Pam," said the young husband, "You will love him for my sake."

"And for his own," she answered sweetly, with her pretty, foreign accent, putting her little hand frankly into his. "I know you well," she went on, with a winning look, impossible to resist. "Your portrait has been painted for me by my husband's praises. You will be my friend, won't you, as well as his?"

"Oh, Norah, Norah!" She burst out, with true French abandonment, stooping down to kiss the blushing face of the bride. "I'm so glad you will be as happy as I am—almost. You and I will be friends always, like our husbands, and—and you shall paint the boy's picture—there!"

With a gesture of infinite generosity, like one who bestows the crown of all the world, she put the little smiling atom of humanity into the arms of the bride.

Tenderly, very tenderly, Norah took the soft white bundle, and pressed it close to her bosom. The mysterious maternal instinct that is born with a woman, that makes the busy toddler scarce out of her cradle so tender with her dolly, thrilled the virgin heart of the newly-made wife. Her cheek glowed, and a tender mist of tears softened the love light in the depths of her clear eyes. Pamela drew her gently apart to the great window that looked out on the wooded lawn and wide-skirted meadows, and those two joined heart and soul in woman's blameless idolatry, baby-worship, with all the pretty lisping inarticulate nothings by which the deity is propitiated.

Smilingly, lovingly, the two men glanced after them, and then clasped hands again in mutual gratulation. Each read in the other's face his hopes and happiness.

"Thank God, it is as well with the old land as with us," said Lord Edward cheerily. "You have had your wish, Maurice. We have won without fighting."

"I trust so," said Maurice. "But I do not trust our rulers." For the first time there was a touch of sadness in his voice.

But Lord Edward laughed as light-heartedly as a boy. "I trust their fears, not their truth," he said. "Ireland is safe. They dare not refuse her freedom. Yet do you know, Maurice," he went on, "sometimes when the old wild spirit gets uppermost in me, I am half sorry we will not have to fight for it. You remember the vow we took long ago with clasped hands under the starlight, in the wild backwoods of free America, to be true to Ireland even to the death?"

"Our lives have seen many changes since, but in this we have not changed," said the other solemnly. "That vow holds still, and we are ready to redeem it. Not danger nor death, nor love itself is strong enough to hold us back if Ireland calls. I will never fail the old land in her need."

"Nor I," replied Lord Edward, with flushed cheek and flashing eyes. "Life has grown very pleasant to me of late. Never so pleasant as now. But now, as ever, I am ready, if God so wills it, to die for Ireland."

Something in the tones of the men's voices drew the women towards them.

As the ominous words "die for Ireland" fell upon her ear, Pamela clasped her baby tighter to her bosom, and nestled close to her husband's side.

"God forbid," she cried with piteous earnestness.

"God's will be done," cried Norah, firmly, though the sudden tears blinded her. "Your life is mine, Maurice. But when Ireland calls I would not stay you if I could."

Again Lord Edward laughed out cheerfully. "There is no danger of fighting or dying, you silly little Mother Hubbard," he said, patting his wife's cheek with playful tenderness. "We are all going to live happy for ever and ever, like the good folk in the nursery tales."

THE END.

PLYMOUTH
WILLIAM BRENDON AND SON
PRINTERS